The **Sponsored** Life

In the series

CULTURE AND THE MOVING IMAGE

edited by Robert Sklar

The
Sponsored
Life

ADS,

TV, AND

AMERICAN

CULTURE

Leslie Savan

Temple University Press

Philadelphia

Temple University Press, Philadelphia 19122
Copyright © 1994 by Leslie Savan
All rights reserved
Published 1994

⊗ The paper used in this publication meets the minimum requirements of
American National Standard for Information Sciences—Permanence of
Paper for Printed Library Materials, ANSI Z39.48–1984

Printed in the United States of America

Library of Congress Cataloging-in-Publication Data

Savan, Leslie.
    The sponsored life : ads, TV, and American culture / Leslie Savan.
        p.   cm.—(Culture and the moving image)
    Includes index.
    ISBN 1–56639–244–6 (hard). —ISBN 1–56639–245–4 (paper)
    1. Television advertising—Social aspects—United States.
    2. Television broadcasting—Social aspects—United States.
    I. Title.   II. Series.
    HF6146.T42S26   1995
    659.14′3—dc20   94–16530

For my mother

Contents

Acknowledgments   xi

The Bribed Soul   1

I. Too Cool for Words

This Typeface Is Changing
  Your Life   17

The Neo-Calvinists   23

Timekeeping Is Money   24

In Living B&W   25

Honest Engine   26

Avant-Hard Sell   27

Guess Again   29

The Lifestyle Lifestyle   31

On Background   32

The Fat Lady Sings   35

It's the Rote Thing To Do   38

Titular Head   40

Listless Is More   43

Local Anesthetic   46

Bookends, Pods,
  and Piggybacks   49

The Sound of Nine
  Ads Hyping   52

Sneakers and Nothingness   54

Heaven Can Bait   57

Burying Messages   61

2. Corporate Image Adjustment

Soldiers of Fortune   67
Born-Again Dow   68
Real Forced   69
Mr. Liberty   70
Hands Down   71
Touchy-Feely, Inc.   72
Defense Spending   73
Rock of Agents   77
Car-nal Knowledge   78
Big Apple   79
Mass Mascot   80
Takeover Makeover   83
Anxiety Calls   85
Bull   87
God's Little Agency   89
The Tie-Ins That Bind   91
The Brand with Two Brains   94
Whom Ma Bell Tolls   96
Beam Me Up   99
Let's Face It   103
Getting Carded   106
Gotta Hack It   111

3. Real Problems, Surreal Ads

Du Pontificates   117
Point of Purchase   119
Forget the Dead Babies   122
Uniform Standard   127
Where the Boycotts Are   130
30 Seconds
   Over Washington   133
A Piece of the Wall   136

Don't Leave Romania
   Without It   140
The Face of the People   143
Stay Hungary   146
Puff Piece   149
Toxic Moxie   152
Hawking War   155
Green Monsters   159
War Is Bell   161
Watts Nuke?   165
Ad-Free Ads   168
In the Red Again   171
The Off-Road to Rio   176

4. Our Bodies, Our Sells

At the End of a Sentence   183
The New, 1985 Crotch   184
The Sound of Sexism   186
A Hard Man Is Easy
   To Find   187
Wipe Out   189
Wild Thing, I Think
   I Smell You   191
Women Will Be Gals   193
Flow Jobs   196
The Trad Trade   198
Cockers   200
Ragtime   203
Getting Olayed   206
Leggo My Ego   209
Demagaga   212
Friend or Faux   216
Operation Miscue   219
Fear of Buying   223
Boys Under the Hood   228

5. Shock of the Hue

Down and Out
  on Mad Ave   233
Little White Lies   234
Constructive Engagement
  Ring   236
Cri de Coors   238
Gut Reaction   239
Cereal Rights   242
Rube Barbs   243
Addictions and
  the Drug War   246
Shock of the Hue   252
Be-Twixt
  & Be-Tween   256
Rubber Sold   259
Bash & Cash   262
Buy-It Riot   266
Logo-rrhea   269
Generation X-Force   272

6. The Sponsored Life

On the Rox   279
Rock Rolls Over   281
Jean Pool   289
Inner Tube   291
Desperately Selling Soda   294
The Afterschlock   299
Hip Hop   302
TV in Its Underwear   305
Lemon-Fresh Apocalypse   308
Miles To Go   311
Modern Times   314
Adblisters   316
TVTV   319
New Word Order   325
Everything Must Go   329
The Ad Mission   332
Pop Culture   338

Index   341

Acknowledgments

I'd like to thank the following people for their help in bringing this book to life: Susan Ramer; Janet Francendese; Sheenah Hankin; Jim Hoberman; Scott Pass; Stephen Kolozsvary; my creative pals Lisa Jones, Barbara O'Dair, Margaret Engle, Kathy Rich, Nancy Cardozo, Betsy Israel, and Darlene Van Der Hoop; my brother, Glenn; and my father, Sid, for exposing me to the underside of an ad, ad, ad world and for more than tolerating my attacks on it. I especially want to thank *The Village Voice*, where I've been free to write about even its advertisers; and the *Voice* staff, in particular Jessica Kerwin and the other interns who labored not even for peanuts, as well as Tom McGovern and Nakyung Han in photo. They guided me to the photographers who took the pictures for this book: Michael Ackerman (most of the photos are his), Sandra-Lee Phipps, Linda Rosier, and Alex Forman. And, of course, many thanks go to the editors I worked with over the years: Richard Goldstein (who dreamt up the idea of an ad column); Mim Udovitch; Lisa Kennedy; Ross Wetzsteon; Doug Simmons; Marty Gottlieb; the guy who currently, patiently edits Op Ad, Jeff Salamon; and, most of all, and for reasons even he doesn't know, my best friend and co-thinker, Dan Bischoff.

The Bribed Soul

Television-watching Americans—that is, just about *all* Americans—
see approximately 100 TV commercials a day. In that same 24 hours
they also see a host of print ads, billboard signs, and other corporate
messages slapped onto every available surface, from the fuselages of
NASA rockets right down to the bottom of golf holes and the inside
doors of restroom stalls. Studies estimate that, counting all the logos,
labels, and announcements, some 16,000 ads flicker across an individual's consciousness daily.

Advertising now infects just about every organ of society, and wherever advertising gains a foothold it tends to slowly take over, like a
vampire or a virus. When television broadcasting began about 50
years ago, the idea of a network that would air nothing but commercials was never seriously considered, not even when single-sponsor
shows were produced straight out of the sponsor's ad agency. But today, by the grace of cable, we have several such channels, including
MTV, stylistically the most advanced programming on the air, and
FYI, a proposed new channel that would run only ads—infomercials,
home-shopping shows, regular-length commercials, and, for a real
treat, programs of "classic" ads. Similarly, product placement in the
movies started small, with the occasional Tab showing up in a star's
hand, but now it's grown big enough to eat the whole thing. In its
1993 futuristic thriller *Demolition Man,* Warner Bros. not only scat-
tered the usual corporate logos throughout the sets but it also rewrote
the script so that the only fast-food chain to survive the "franchise

1

wars" of the 20th century was Taco Bell—which, in return, promoted the movie in all its outlets.

Even older, far statelier cultural institutions have had their original values hollowed out and replaced by ad values, leaving behind the merest fossil of their founders' purpose. Modernist masters enjoy art museum blockbusters only when they can be prominently underwritten by an oil company or a telecommunications giant; new magazines are conceived not on the basis of their editorial content but on their ability to identify potential advertisers and groom their copy to fit marketing needs. In the process, the function of sponsored institutions is almost comically betrayed. The exotic bug exhibit at the Smithsonian Museum's new O. Orkin Insect Zoo, for example, opens with the red diamond logo of Orkin Pest Control and displays various little beasties, ever so subtly planting the suggestion that if they were to escape their glass cages you'd know who to call. Though the Smithsonian would never be so crass as to actually recommend Orkin's services, it is crass enough to never once mention in its exhibits the dangers of pesticides.

As for all those television-watching Americans, hit on by those 16,000 paid (and tax-deductible) messages a day, they're even more vulnerable than their institutions. Most admakers understand that in order to sell to you they have to know your desires and dreams better than you may know them yourself, and they've tried to reduce that understanding to a science. Market research, in which psychologists, polling organizations, trends analysts, focus group leaders, "mall-intercept" interviewers, and the whole panoply of mass communications try to figure out what will make you buy, has become a $2.5 billion annual business growing at a healthy clip of about 4.2 percent a year (after adjustment for inflation). Yet even this sophisticated program for the study of the individual consumer is only a starter kit for the technological advances that will sweep through the advertising-industrial complex in the 1990s. Today, the most we can do when another TV commercial comes on—and we are repeatedly told that this is our great freedom—is to switch channels. But soon technology will take even that tiny tantrum of resistance and make it "interactive," providing advertisers with information on the exact moment we became bored—vital data that can be crunched, analyzed, and processed into the next set of ads, the better to zap-proof *them*.

Impressive as such research may be, the real masterwork of advertising is the way it uses the techniques of art to seduce the human soul. Virtually all of modern experience now has a sponsor, or at least a sponsored accessory, and there is no human emotion or concern—love, lust, war, childhood innocence, social rebellion, spiritual enlightenment, even disgust with advertising—that cannot be reworked into a sales pitch. The transcendent look in a bride's eyes the moment before she kisses her groom turns into a promo for Du Pont. The teeth-gnashing humiliation of an office rival becomes an inducement to switch to AT&T.

In short, we're living the sponsored life. From Huggies to Maalox, the necessities and little luxuries of an American's passage through this world are provided and promoted by one advertiser or another. The sponsored life is born when commercial culture sells our own experiences back to us. It grows as those experiences are then reconstituted inside us, mixing the most intimate processes of individual thought with commercial values, rhythms, and expectations. It has often been said by television's critics that TV doesn't deliver products to viewers but that viewers themselves are the *real* product, one that TV delivers to its advertisers. True, but the symbiotic relationship between advertising and audience goes deeper than that. The viewer who lives the sponsored life—and that is most of us to one degree or the other—is slowly re-created in the ad's image.

Inside each "consumer," advertising's all-you-can-eat, all-the-time, all-dessert buffet produces a build-up of mass-produced stimuli, all hissing and sputtering to get out. Sometimes they burst out as sponsored speech, as when we talk in the cadences of sitcom one-liners, imitate Letterman, laugh uproariously at lines like "I've fallen and I can't get up," or mouth the words of familiar commercials, like the entranced high school student I meet in a communications class who moved his lips with the voiceover of a Toyota spot. Sometimes they slip out as sponsored dress, as when white suburban kids don the baggy pants and backward baseball caps they see on MTV rappers. Sometimes they simply come out as sponsored equations, as when we attribute "purity" and "honesty" to clear products like Crystal Pepsi or Ban's clear deodorant.

To lead the sponsored life you don't really have to do anything. You don't need to have a corporate sponsor as the museums or the movies do. You don't even have to buy anything—though it helps, and you will. You just have to live in America and share with the nation, or at least with your mall-intercept cohorts, certain paid-for expectations and values, rhythms and reflexes.

Those expectations and how they unfold through advertising is the subject of this book. It's based on eight years of columns and articles I wrote about ads and other pop culture phenomena for *The Village Voice*. Despite advertising's enormous role in our lives, most of the media feel that, like hot dogs and military budgets, advertising goes down most easily when it's unexamined. They react this way, of course, because they're sponsored. Conveyors of commercial culture are free to question nearly all of modern life except their own life-support system. This conflict of interest means that unlike "official" cultural products—films, TV shows, books, paintings, and so on—advertising finds few regular critics in the mainstream press.

When the Center for the Study of Commercialism, a well-respected, Washington, D.C.-based nonprofit group, called a press conference in 1992 to announce the results of a study that showed the press repeatedly censoring itself under direct or anticipated advertiser pressure, not a single TV or radio reporter attended, and only a few papers even mentioned it. If journalism looks at ads at all, it usually settles for soft-shoe analysis, pieces that ask, essentially, "Does this ad work?" Most newspapers are pleased to do celebrity profiles of ad directors or agencies that have a few hits on their hands (possibly the agency will direct more ad dollars the paper's way, but more importantly over the long run, such stories prove that the publication offers a "positive environment" for advertisers). Ads are usually examined only when they make "news," through scandal, product failure, or superstar megadeals, like Madonna's or Michael Jackson's with Pepsi.

At the *Voice*, however, I could criticize ads in a fuller social and political context because, first of all, the paper is an alternative exception and does try to maintain a separation between advertising and editorial. And, as much to the point, I wasn't tearing into ads run by the futon shops, restaurants, and other local retailers that make up the bulk of *Voice* advertising.

That has allowed me to do the basic spadework of ad criticism— looking at the false claims ads occasionally make or the corporate misdeeds lurking behind the PR spin. But the real subject of my column, "Op Ad," has always been more *how* it works—how commercial values infiltrate our beliefs and desires, how we become more and more sponsored.

The chief expectation of the sponsored life is that there will and always should be regular blips of excitement and resolution, the frequency of which is determined by money. We begin to pulse to the beat, the one-two beat, that moves most ads: problem/solution, old/ new, Brand X/hero brand, desire/gratification. In order to dance to the rhythm, we adjust other expectations a little here, a little there: Our notions of what's desirable behavior, our lust for novelty, even our visions of the perfect love affair or thrilling adventure adapt to the mass consensus coaxed out by marketing. Cultural forms that don't fit these patterns tend to fade away, and eventually *everything* in commercial culture—not just the 30-second spot but the drama, news segment, stage performance, novel, magazine layout—comes to share the same insipid insistence on canned excitement and neat resolution.

What's all the excitement about? Anything and nothing. You know you've entered the commercial zone when the excitement building in you is oddly incommensurate with the content dangled before you: Does a sip of Diet Coke really warrant an expensive production number celebrating the rebel prowess of "ministers who surf," "insurance agents who speed," and "people who live their life as an exclamation not an explanation"?!? Of course not. Yet through the sympathetic magic of materialism we learn how to respond to excitement: It's less important that we purchase any particular product than that we come to expect resolution *in the form of* something buyable.

The way ads have of jacking up false excitement in the name of ultimately unsatisfying purchases has given Western societies a bad case of commercial blue balls. You're hit on, say, by yet another guy on TV hawking fabric whitener, but—wait a minute—he "can't be a man" because he packs a different brand of smokes. And maybe you moan, "I can't get no, no no no . . ."

Anyway, that's how the Rolling Stones put it in that seminal semiotic text "(I Can't Get No) Satisfaction" back in 1965. Commercials are the tinny jingles in our heads that remind us of all we've abandoned in exchange for our materially comfortable lives—real extended families, real human empathy, real rebel prowess. The result of stale promises endlessly repeated is massive frustration.

But Mick Jagger is younger than that now: Long after "Satisfaction" had dropped off the charts, the Rolling Stones became the first major band to tour for a corporate sponsor, Jovan perfumes, in 1981. By then Jagger had become a symbol of the most popular postmodern response to advertising's dominant role in our culture: the ironic reflex.

Irony has become a hallmark of the sponsored life because it provides a certain distance from the frustration inherent in commercial correctness. For some time now the people raised on television, the baby boomers and the "Generation Xers" that followed, have mentally adjusted the set, as it were, in order to convince themselves that watching is cool. They may be doing exactly what their parents do—but they do it *differently*. They take in TV with a Lettermanesque wink, and they like it when it winks back. In many cases (as Mark Crispin Miller has described so well in *Boxed In*), the winkers have enthusiastically embraced the artifice, even the manipulativeness, of advertising as an essential paradox of modern life, a paradox that is at the crux of their own identity.

The winkers believe that by rolling their collective eyes when they watch TV they can control *it*, rather than letting it control them. But unfortunately, as a defense against the power of advertising, irony is a leaky condom—in fact, it's the same old condom that advertising brings over every night. A lot of ads have learned that to break through to the all-important boomer and Xer markets they have to be as cool, hip, and ironic as the target audience likes to think of itself as being. That requires at least the pose of opposition to commercial values. The cool commercials—I'm thinking of Nike spots, some Reeboks, most 501s, certainly all MTV promos—flatter us by saying we're too cool to fall for commercial values, and therefore cool enough to want their product.

If irony is weak armor, how do we ward off the effect of billions of words and images from our sponsors? No perfect wolfsbane exists, but I can suggest some tactics to keep in mind:

When watching, watch out. Literally. Watch as an outsider, from as far a distance as you can muster (farther even than irony)—*especially* when watching ads that flatter you for being an outsider, as more and more are doing.

Big lie, little lie. All advertising tells lies, but there are little lies and there are big lies. Little lie: This beer tastes great. Big lie: This beer makes *you* great. Not all ads tell little lies—they're more likely to be legally actionable (while big lies by definition aren't). And many products do live up to their modest material claims: This car runs. But all ads *must* tell big lies: This car will attract babes and make others slobber in envy. Don't be shocked that ads lie—that's their job. But do try to distinguish between the two kinds of lies.

Read the box. Look not just at whether an ad's claims are false or exaggerated, but try to figure out what portion of an ad is about the culture as opposed to the product. Read the contents as you would a cereal box's: Instead of how much sugar to wheat, consider how much style to information. Not that a high ratio of sugar to wheat is necessarily more malevolent than the other way around. But it's a sure sign that they're fattening you up for the shill.

Assume no relationship between a brand and its image. Marlboro was originally sold as a woman's cigarette, and its image was elegant, if not downright prissy. It wasn't until 1955 that the Marlboro Man was invented to ride herd on all that. The arbitrary relationship between a product and its ads becomes even clearer when you realize how much advertising is created to overcome "brand parity"—a plague more troubling to marketers than bodily odors. Brand parity means that there's little or no difference between competing brands and that the best a brand can do is hire a more appealing image. When advertising works at all, it's because the public more or less believes that something serious is going on between a product and its image, as if the latter reveals intrinsic qualities of the former. Peel image off item, and you too can have more of the freedom that ads are always promising. Likewise . . .

We don't buy products, we buy the world that presents them. Over the long run, whether you actually buy a particular product is less important than that you buy the world that makes the product seem desirable. Not so long ago a BMW or Mercedes was required if you seriously bought the worldview that their ads conveyed. Still, buying an attitude doesn't automatically translate into product purchase. If your income precluded a BMW, you might have bought instead a Ralph Lauren polo shirt or even a Dove bar (which is how yuppie snack foods positioned themselves—as achievable class). Sure, GE wants you to buy its bulbs, but even more it wants you to buy the paternalistic, everything's-under-control world that GE seems to rule. Buying *that* will result, GE is betting, not only in more appliance sales but also in more credibility when spokesmen insist that defrauding the Pentagon is not *really* what GE's all about. That is to say . . .

The promotional is the political. Each world that commercials use to sell things comes packed with biases: Entire classes, races, and genders may be excluded for the coddling of the sponsored one. Lee Jeans's world (circa 1989) is a place where young people are hip, sexual, and wear jeans, while old people are square, nonsexual, and wear uniforms. The class and age politics here is more powerful than the Young Republicans'. There is politics in all advertising (and, more obviously, advertising in all politics). It makes sense that these two professions call what they do "campaigns."

Advertising shepherds herds of individuals. When Monty Python's mistaken messiah in *The Life of Brian* exhorts the crowd of devotees to "Don't follow me! Don't follow anyone! Think for yourselves! . . .

You are all individuals!" they reply in unison, "We are all individuals!" That is advertising in a nutshell.

Advertising's most basic paradox is to say: Join us and become unique. Advertisers learned long ago that individuality sells, like sex or patriotism. The urge toward individualism is a constant in America, with icons ranging from Thomas Jefferson's yeoman farmer to the kooky girl bouncing to the jingle "I like the Sprite in you!" Commercial nonconformity always operates in the service of . . . conformity. Our system of laws and our one-man-one-vote politics may be based on individualism, but successful marketing depends on the exact opposite: By identifying (through research) the ways we are alike, it hopes to convince the largest number of people that they need the exact same product. Furthermore, in modern pop culture, we construct our individuality by the unique combination of mass-produced goods and services we buy. I sip Evian, you slug Bud Light; I drive a Geo, you gun a Ford pickup; I kick sidewalk in cowboy boots, you bop in Reeboks. Individuality is a good angle for all advertising, but it's crucial for TV commercials. There you are sitting at home, not doing anything for hours on end, but then the very box you're staring at tells you that you are different, that you are vibrantly alive, that your quest for freedom—freedom of speech, freedom of movement, freedom to do whatever you damn well choose—will not be impeded! And you can do all that, says the box, without leaving your couch.

It's the real ad. The one question I'm most often asked is, Does advertising shape who we are and what we want, or does it merely reflect back to us our own emotions and desires? As with most nature-or-nurture questions, the answer is both. The real ad in any campaign is controlled neither by admakers nor adwatchers; it exists somewhere between the TV set and the viewer, like a huge hairball, collecting bits of material and meaning from both. The real ad isn't even activated until viewers hand it their frustrations from work, the mood of their love life, their idiosyncratic misinterpretations, and most of all, I think, their everyday politics. On which class rung do they see themselves teetering? Do they ever so subtly flinch when a different race comes on TV? In this way, we all coproduce the ads we see. Agency people are often aghast that anyone would find offensive meanings in their ads because "that's not what we intended." Intention has little to do with it. Whatever they meant, once an ad hits the air it becomes public property. That, I think, is where criticism should aim—at the fluctuating, multimeaning thing that floats over the country, reflecting us as we reflect it.

Follow the flattery. I use the word *flattery* a lot. When trying to understand what an ad's really up to, following the flattery is as useful as following the money. You'll find the ad's target market by asking who in any 30-second drama is being praised for qualities they probably don't possess. When a black teenager plays basketball with a white baby boomer for Canada Dry, it's not black youth that's being pandered to. It's white boomers—the flattery being that they're cool enough to be accepted by blacks. Ads don't even have to put people on stage to toady up to them. Ads can flatter by style alone, as do all the spots that turn on hyperquick cuts or obscure meanings, telling us—uh, *some* of us—that we're special enough to get it.

We participate in our own seduction. Once properly flattered, all that's left is to close the sale—and only we can do that. Not only do we coproduce ads, but we're our own best voiceover—that little inner voice that ultimately decides to buy or not. The best ads tell us we're cool *coolly*—in the other meaning of the word. McLuhan used to say that a cool medium, like television, involves us more by not giving us everything; the very spaces between TV's flickering dots are filled in by our central nervous system. He refers to "the involvement of the viewer with the completion or 'closing' of the TV image." This is seduction: We're stirred to a state so that not only do we close the image but, given the right image at the right time, we open our wallet. All television is erotically engaged in this way, but commercials are TV's G-spot. The smart ads always hold back a little to get us to lean forward a little. Some ads have become caricatures of this tease, withholding the product's name until the last second to keep you wondering who could possibly be sponsoring such intrigue. The seduction may continue right to the cash register, where one last image is completed: you and product together at last. It'd be nice to say that now that you've consumed, you've climaxed, and everyone can relax. But sponsorship is a lifetime proposition that must be renewed every day.

The themes singled out in this introduction run throughout the book, each chapter illustrating them with a different category of ad. If category's the right word. The chapters are loosely organized around various topics, and I chose columns that seemed to best illustrate the topic at hand—though commercials often invoke many issues and therefore occasionally overlap several chapters. But to a certain extent that's inevitable. Advertising daily, hourly, overlaps with everything else on TV, in the home, at the store, on the street.

The first chapter, "Too Cool for Words," deals the most directly with style, aesthetics, and technique in advertising. The last 10 years or so have seen a frantic scramble of all the visual, audial, and temporal elements in ads. Footage shakes, is chopped up, reverts to black and white, and—as if the image itself were in retreat—explodes into words. This chapter also includes the unbearably trendy ads: Maybe they ride a trendy slogan ("It's the right thing to do") or an emotional trend (nostalgia for "place" or hype over "lifestyle"). Because the ads in this section strain so hard to be "cutting edge," you'll find among them the arty (some sneaker spots, ads that use opera), the artsy-fartsy (Obsession, Infiniti), and the 100 percent ironic (Joe Isuzu, subliminal spoofs). The chapter starts with a piece not about advertising per se but about a typeface, Helvetica, that at the time permeated ad attitude.

Chapter 2, "Corporate Image Adjustment," is about the true star of the '80s (and the poster boy of the '90s): Big Business. Often there's a bad rep (Dow, Drexel Burnham, E. F. Hutton) or, almost worse, a stale rep (John Hancock, Miller beer, Coca-Cola) that a corporation must advertise its way out of. The past decade was full of businesses heavy into S&M: hostile takeovers, arbitrage, greenmail, corporate fraud. Growing out of the go-for-it, that's-*his*-problem, Reagan-endorsed ethos came the ulcer-producing anxiety sell (as in AT&T, Merrill Lynch, and Apple computer ads). But this is also the land of the corporate crocodile tear and the Vaseline-smeared lens, and all that fear and greed was more commonly transmogrified into visions of goodness and warmth—like the agency melodramas for Perrier, Chevrolet, and Hands Across America, to name a few. Sappy, however, is not always safe—it can tempt the muckraker in each of us—and so other companies simply produced the most unassailable version of themselves possible: funny animals or cartoony humans. That is, they let their mascots handle their PR, Joe Camel doing the most phallic, uh, facile job.

"Real Problems, Surreal Ads" looks at the spin fib-friendly corporations put out when they butt up against the real world. These columns recount how advertising tries to confront, evade, or capitalize on controversial national and international issues, among them: the fall of communism, the gulf war, defense contracts, environmentalism, business ethics, boycotts, and the geopolitical news closest to ad people's hearts, the recession.

"Our Bodies, Our Sells" focuses on advertising's portrayal of women. Women and advertising are ensnarled (though I hate the trendy word, it fits) co-dependently. After all, modern advertising and the modern woman's sense of identity grew hand in hand: Mass market consumerism was largely invented for lady customers by the great 19th-century department stores. Because women still do most of the nation's shopping, advertising still aims primarily at them. And since so many ads are built on a problem/solution structure, a structure that leads from the unenviable to the ideal, advertising is powerfully and frighteningly integrated into the formation of female identities. (And by advertising, I also mean women's magazines, where editorial unabashedly plugs advertisers. It's a phenomenon that promotes not only Calvin and Revlon, but dumbness and dependency—relying as it does on the assumption that we won't make the connection, and if we do, we won't care.) These columns aren't so much about the notorious stereotypes—the yellow, waxy build-up housewife or the babe draped over the car (an endangered species since women now make almost half of all new car purchases)—as about the newer stereotypes that evolved as a reaction to all that: the career dominatrix, the gals who find "empowerment" by stomping asphalt in Reeboks.

Chapter 5, "Shock of the Hue," is about how advertising presents "the Other"—and how some ads use the momentary shock of seeing someone who's "different" appear on the same tube that's usually so busy defining "normal." The Other is usually racially or ethnically different, but the Other may also be someone who has AIDS, is homeless, does drugs, or is simply square. Except when they're target-marketed for their "purchasing power," Others often function in advertising to make the mainstream look good: The square tells everyone else they're hip, African-Americans certify white soul, the Japanese are machine to American mensch. But the notion that difference is suspect doesn't jibe with what advertising *also* tells us: You are all individuals! Dare to be different! Some campaigns try to clip the contradiction by presenting models of *generic* individualism, like the cartoon character Fido Dido. But whenever advertising volunteers to fix problems like drugs or racism, the contradiction only winds tighter. Commercial infrastructure militates against it really fixing anything that has to do with addiction or prejudice, since commercialism must addict and prejudice us to products, to ways of reacting, and to itself. Advertising must create and maintain needs, as drugs do. It must also posit "others"—whether "Brand X" or other values countering the hero brand's—as basically inferior or even threatening, as racism does. So much of advertising is set up on those Manichean good/bad, problem/solution, threat/security structures that even when an Other person isn't on the scene, an otherness is.

The last chapter, "The Sponsored Life," harkens back to the beginning of this introduction. Advertising is always hitching rides onto other vehicles—tying its products in with movie and charity promotions or, as has been proposed, sticking its messages onto a mile-long satellite that from Earth would look like a moon-sized logo. Forward-thinking agencies have also extended the definition of an ad vehicle to include Hurricane Hugo, the San Francisco earthquake, and the coming millennium. Advertising's even buying its way into people's urge for a more spiritual life—until recently one of the few ways out of the sponsored life.

But the sponsored life is more than finding corporate sponsorship under every rock (musician). It's also revising our concept of what an ad is—and what an ad's consciousness of *itself* is. And so this chapter considers something like office design as an ad for a corporate approach to life, warns about PSAs that warn you not to watch so much TV, treats popular catchphrases as slogan spores, and takes on phenomena that mess with the relationship between consumer and commercial—such as the commercial-parodying Energizer Bunny, the ad-loving Jordache girl, and all the TV commercials that show people watching TV commercials.

Within each chapter, the columns and articles appear chronologically. (Which is why the chapters move from short to long pieces: Over the years, "Op Ad" grew.)

I have not added follow-ups of events that may have occurred after a column was published—corporate takeovers, layoffs, image overhauls, or new political developments. Rather, I assumed the reader would take into consideration the dates of the columns and know that they represent the issues of that time. In some cases, readers will know the subsequent event (like Drexel Burnham folding); sometimes the follow-up will be found elsewhere in the book (like the end of the GE boycott). But I feel I should end any suspense in a few areas: The Nestlé boycott continues, green marketing has turned rather yellow, some rankings of corporate misdeeds have changed since "Point of Purchase" was written in 1988, and *Rolling Stone*'s *Marketing Through Music* is no longer. I hope the columns' contemporary nature offers a little ad history (like that breakthrough moment when the word *period,* as in menstrual, was first uttered in a commercial). In surprisingly many instances, a company's image has remained fairly stable—in fact, some ads I wrote about in the '80s are still running.

I hope this book does two things: provides a sense of how specific ads, campaigns, and marketing trends got to be the way they are, and lends some cumulative insight into the symbiotic relationship between modern consciousness and advertising. Ads have been playing with our sensibilities for quite a while now. As long ago as 1902, William James, in *The Varieties of Religious Experience,* wrote that, with the universal acceptance of material comfort as the ultimate good, "We have lost the power even of imagining what the ancient idealization of poverty could have meant: the liberation from material attachments, the unbribed soul." How advertising spreads and deepens this uniquely American form of spiritual graft is the real subject of this book.

Chapter One

TOO COOL FOR WORDS

This Typeface

Is Changing Your Life

The quest for a clean public restroom is usually in vain. We assume a restroom to be dirty and disease-ridden, and settle for what we have to. Occasionally, though, I've found a restroom that, before I'd even entered, I've assumed with relief was not dirty but clean. I realize that it was a restroom sign, with its modern, Teflon-smooth letters spelling "women," that led me to expect a clean toilet. Although it was surely no different from any other toilet, I thought it had to be more sanitary. It was similar to the way an attractively packaged cleansing cream, like Helena Rubinstein's "Deep Cleanser," could convince me that what was inside was the best of all possible creams. It was those same clean, modern letters on the package.

These letters seem to be everywhere. They tell us "This is a dial tone first phone," this box is for "U.S. Mail," and to "Enjoy" Coke, "It's the real thing."

Along with NBC's well-publicized logo change, the lettering used on all NBC-produced programs and printed material is being converted to the exact same style.

This lettering style, or typeface, is graphically renovating or coordinating everything from newspapers (including *The Village Voice* logo) to "new towns" to multinational corporations.

The typeface is called Helvetica. From more than 9000 widely varying typefaces, a few "modern" ones have become designers' favorites.

But Helvetica is by far the most popular and biggest selling typeface in the last 10 years.

It comes in a variety of widths, weights, and spacing arrangements. The basic form is Helvetica Medium, and it seems "most itself" in lowercase letters.

The "signs of the times" can be found on the literal signs of the times. The use of Helvetica on so many of them expresses our need for security, for visual proof—if nothing else—that the world's machinery still runs. Subliminally, the perfect balance of push and pull in Helvetica characters reassures us that the problems threatening to spill over are being contained.

Helvetica was designed by a Swiss, Max Meidenger, and first produced by the Haas Typefoundry in 1957. Haas says it was designed specifically for the Swiss market ("Helvetica" means Swiss), and was intended to be a "perfectly neutral typeface without any overly individual forms and without personal idiosyncrasies."

Helvetica is a "sans serif," as it lacks the little extra strokes, called serifs, at the end of its letters' main strokes. Since serifs lead the eye from one letter to the next, they are supposedly more legible, particularly for small print. But the difference is minimal for most sign size letters, and many designers say they use Helvetica precisely because it's so easy to read. As Ed Benguiat, a leading typeface designer and the art director of Photo Lettering, Inc., says, "You don't read the word, you read power. . . . For that one or two-word display message, for buckeye and force, you use sans serif."

But why is Helvetica the most popular of the sans serifs? "It's beautiful," said Benguiat. "It's a pure letter."

Other designers describe Helvetica as "contemporary," "easy to read," "no-nonsense," "neutral," and even "cold." The first word that comes to their lips, though, is "clean."

It is not surprising, then, that when Walter Kacik redesigned New York City's garbage trucks in 1968 he used Helvetica. The trucks are all white except for one word, which is in black, lowercase Helvetica: "sanitation." Photographs of them were exhibited at the Louvre and at the Museum of Modern Art. Kacik chose Helvetica, he said, "because it was the best of the sans serifs and it didn't detract from the kind of purity we wanted." The result was that "people trusted these trucks."

Indeed, cleanliness implies trust. We've been brought up to associate the two ("I'm clean, officer.") and their opposites ("You dirty, rotten, two-timing dame!").

Cleaning up images is the main business of some marketing and design firms. Probably the most influential of them is Lippincott and Margulies (L&M). It is not an advertising agency; it bills itself as a "pioneer in the science of corporate identity."

Finding a corporation's identity almost always means redesigning its graphics. (Occasionally a name change itself is in order—L&M gave us such newspeak sounds as Amtrak, Pathmark, Cominco, and Uniroyal.)

In its own brochures (in Helvetica), L&M denies that it offers "face-lifts" or "standardized solutions." It claims to work from the inside out. Considering the expense to its clients ("Coca-Cola spent over a million dollars for the little squiggle," a former L&M executive said), its soundproof-room confidentiality, and its scientific bent, L&M might be regarded as a corporate shrink.

L&M's list of more than 500 identity-seeking clients includes: American Motors, General Motors, Chrysler, Exxon, Amtrak, Chase Manhattan, First National City Corporation, Bowery Savings Bank, Chemical Bank, American Express, U.S. Steel, ITT, the Internal Revenue Service, the New York Stock Exchange, RCA, NBC, MGM, J. C. Penney, Coca-Cola, and Con Ed.

Only a few of these companies, such as Amtrak or Con Ed, use Helvetica for the logo itself—a logo is almost obliged to be unique and most are specially designed. But as a supporting typeface (and, in most cases, *the* supporting typeface) on everything from annual reports to cardboard boxes, nearly every one of the companies listed above uses some form of Helvetica.

For instance, "Coca-Cola" is distinctive, but Helvetica says "It's the real thing." The new American Express logo is specially drawn, but everything else is in Helvetica. (And when non-Roman alphabets like Chinese cannot take direct Helvetica letters, they will be drawn as closely as possible to it.)

L&M vice-president in charge of design, Ray Poelvoorde, said Helvetica "already has sort of become an unofficial standard." Asked if using such a pervasive typeface wouldn't undermine the costly corporate identity, he said, "You're offering a very nice courtesy to the general public who is bombarded with many messages and symbols every day. And for a company not well-known, to ask the public to memorize more symbols . . . is fantasy."

But if he is right, then the companies that are remembered, that are finding their identities, are doing so by looking more and more alike—almost like one big corporation. A unilook for Unicorp.

Some designers do think Helvetica is overused. Some are even bored with it. But few believe that it is a mere fad. Most companies choose Helvetica in the first place because they expect it to remain contemporary for quite a while. And most companies cannot afford more than one identity change. This is especially true for New York's Metropolitan Transportation Authority.

Since 1967, the MTA has been gradually standardizing its graphics from about a dozen typefaces to a combination of Helvetica and Standard Medium. (The two are almost identical, but the latter was more available to the MTA.)

In contrast to the subway's filth and potential for violence, the cleanly and crisply lettered signs lend a sense of authority. They assure us that the train will come and diminish the chaos created by the graffiti-scrawled walls. (It's no accident that the designer of Norman Mailer's "The Faith of Graffiti" branded the book's covers with Helvetica.) The subway-sign renovation alone, less than a quarter complete, is conservatively estimated to cost from $500,000 to a million dollars.

This MTA graphic system was originated by Massimo Vignelli, who founded, and has since left, an appropriately named design firm, Unimark International, with Walter Kacik, the man who revamped the garbage trucks. Vignelli created Bloomingdale's logo and, more recently, the graphics, in Helvetica, for the Washington, D.C., Metro, still under construction. He thinks Helvetica is not merely a fad but that it can be used faddishly. "As good as it is when used properly, it becomes very bad looking when used badly," as, he suggested, in a wedding invitation.

What is its proper usage? "All kinds of signage are fine." In fact, a system of "symbol signs," with supporting Helvetica letters, intended to replace the numerous sign systems around the world, has been devised by Vignelli and other leading designers. (The design committee is headed by Thomas Geismar, whose firm, Chermayeff & Geismar, is L&M's chief competitor for the corporate identity market.)

Symbol signs are simple silhouetted pictures that act as signs: a knife and fork will mean restaurant; a question mark, an information booth. The symbols are scheduled to be tested at various terminals in New York, Boston, Philadelphia, Williamsburg, Virginia, and the state of Florida this summer. Helvetica is already used at airports such as Seattle, Dallas-Fort Worth, and Kennedy, but the symbol system might usher it into other transportation facilities.

The symbols will often need lettered support, but, in deference to varying cultural styles, the system's guideline manual does not recommend any one typeface. When other cultures shop around for a typeface, however, they will probably be influenced by the example used throughout the manual itself, one deemed "legible, aesthetic, and compatible" with the symbols: Helvetica.

The U.S. Department of Transportation, which commissioned the system, will ask other federal agencies and state governments to adopt it. Then, in order to become an official standard, the symbols will be submitted to two standardization organizations (the American National Standards Institute and the International Organization for Standardization), which certify and promote standards in everything from abbreviations to industrial parts. Helvetica, riding the back of a symbol, might pass through a well-guarded standards stronghold.

Meanwhile, it already headlines all publications of the Departments of Labor and Agriculture. It's also the only standard style for the U.S. Post Office. With an eagle it appears on the new mailbox stickers saying "U.S. Mail" and "Air Mail."

Governments and corporations rely on Helvetica partly because it makes them appear neutral and efficient, partly because its smoothness makes them seem human.

This chic, friendly aspect of the typeface bothers one designer. James Wines, co-director of SITE (Sculpture in the Environment) and a Pulitzer Prize winner for graphics (the category has since been discontinued), said about Helvetica, "It represents an update authority. Not old government, but new government." He goes further: "Helvetica is part of a psychological enslavement. It's a subconscious plot: getting people to do, think, say what you want them to. . . . It *assumes* you accept some system. It means it's predetermined that you're on their route, that it's not casually happening to you."

Helvetica signs ease us not only through building corridors, but through mental corridors. Ready for any mistaken move in a modern maze, a sign greets us at the point of decision, a mental bell rings in recognition, and down we go through the right chute! A slick-looking sign lubricates our grooves of thought and taste, making the product whose name it bears easier to accept. After transforming ugly garbage trucks into slick sanitation vehicles, Walter Kacik should know when he says, "Helvetica enhances things that normally wouldn't work."

It serves to tone down potentially offensive messages: "Littering is filthy and selfish so don't do it!" And Lenny Bruce's autobiography is packaged in Helvetica.

Helvetica skims across all categories of products and places to stamp them "sanitized," "neutralized," and "authorized." Cleanly trimmed of all excess until only an instant modern classic remains, its labels seem to say, "To look further is in vain." As Vignelli said, "What you see is different from what you perceive. You see Helvetica and you perceive order." With more unusual lettering, "you perceive fantasy."

Fantasy and a well-ordered society have always been at odds. And, as James Wines says, by designing fantasy out of our society, we are headed in a dangerous direction. "Our world is a designed extension of service," he said. "Other worlds are an aesthetic extension of spirit."

The writing's on the wall.

June 7, 1976

Obsession's odors

The Neo-Calvinists

On a set resembling a loft lit by De Chirico, four characters recall the same event: a woman leaving them. The Older Man sighs, "My angel." The Young Man hisses, "She was a fever from which I'll never recover." The Boy wonders, "Did I invent her?" And the Woman (!) sobs, "How could so much love do so much damage?" The object of their obsession is a will-o'-the-wisp Calvinette so flighty "a disturbance of the air could start an earthquake in her." Knowingly, she takes an object from each admirer, bringing it to her open mouth. Each ad ends with the breathy slogan: "Ah, the smell of it!"

Audiences may gag on the suggestiveness (NBC has axed the boy's spot, and will show the woman's only after 11 p.m.; the other networks haven't decided what to do). But the $17 million campaign—one of the most expensive for an upscale scent—should make Calvin Klein's Obsession move faster than the five other designer fragrances being introduced in '85. As directed by Richard Avedon, the four ads stoke a potent fantasy: you—innocent yet hot, sensitive but wild—can become the object of obsession to anyone: man or woman, young or old. Ah, the sell of it!

April 2, 1985

Timekeeping Is Money

Cool types pop in and out of cabs and phone booths, laden—no, light-ened—with Swatch bags, umbrellas, and shields (sunglasses to you). A guy in a car, wearing PJs and shaving cream, flashes three candy-bright razors. They echo the Swatch watches worn in twos and threes and the two hot women who knock hips, setting a horny man's *Herald Tribune* on fire. Two plaid Swatches knock their clocks.

With 35 shots in 30 seconds, Swatch is it—more bubbly than Coke (same ad agency, too). It's time, it's now: carbonated commercials burn through digital dominance, big hand and little hand meet at the epicenter of Pop. Yo Jordache and Jou-Jou, Yo Candies and Sasson! Swatch is fizz on the wrist.

Swiss watches nearly stopped running, thanks to silicon-chipped cheapies from Japan. Enter Swatch, the vid-id watch that's spinning off "Fungear" accessories and "Funwear" clothes. Swatch makes made-for-MTV ads, sponsors MTV awards, takes MTV's marketing honcho and makes her its own. Swatch ads gobble up groups: Fat Boys, Thompson Twins, Belouis Some. In two years, sales have ex-ploded from $3 million to a projected $125 million; marketing bud-get, too: $3.7 million to $14 mil in order "to show the lifestyle of Swatch."

Life's a round-the-clock kinda thing, but when Swatch time is shown, whether on watches or bags, it's almost always 10:10. Hands up! Arms raised! Happy people! 10 p.m. is dull, but minutes later . . . it's nighttime's edge, when fun fizzes, or, Swatchless, fizzles out. It's 10:10—do you know what your lifestyle is?

October 25, 1985

In Living B&W

What's black and white and sked all over? Some very striking TV commercials. If you want somebody's attention, as a perfume ad used to say, just whisper. B&W ads are visually whispering to us about—what else?—the past. The past as (1) warm and funny. By intercutting old *Dragnet* clips with current material, Tostitos gets munchier. (2) Classy and classic. They used to know how to make things, anything, back then.

Going for classic, Guess made an ad looking like a B&W movie; Ralph Lauren, like a B&W home movie. Each was dismayed to find their black and white blue jean ads chic to chic on the *Miami Vice* premiere. Guess's spot, bordered top and bottom in black to make you feel like you're at the movies, is an updated *Misfits*. A cowpoke—all tough boots, spurs, gloves, faded denim—gets out of a pickup truck in the desert to rope, brand, and wistfully let a horse go free. Only then do we see that the cowpoke's a cowgirl (this is the sex part). No squeamish Marilyn, Ms. Guess is up on women's as well as animals' rights.

For Lauren's dungarees, preppies try hard to seem dirt-farm authentic, frolicking in the rural brush, playing stickball with a rotten piece of wood. To look home-movie flat, the ad was made on videotape instead of film and transferred from color to B&W. "We wanted a nonslick, very work-clothes feeling," the Ralph person says, "a '40s or '50s feeling, when there weren't designer-style jeans."

As Oscar Wilde said, photography is an art because it tells lies. B&W is artier because it tells more lies. It can make trends seem timeless, silly characters seem archetypal. It's a kind of art to get people to pay designers for predesigner jeans.

November 5, 1985

One of these captions is lying.

Honest Engine

The most titillating ads on TV don't use sex or drugs or rock 'n' roll: They admit they tell bold-faced lies.

By now everyone's seen the Isuzu spots in which actor David Leasure, with lounge lizard insouciance, lies outrageously about the car. This round-eyed fop, standing on an assembly line, says in one ad: "Hi. I'm Joe Isuzu"—as the brazen admission, "He's lying," flashes on screen. The car, he tells us in various spots, "gets 94 miles per gallon, city," goes from Paris to Rome in two minutes, has built-in frozen yogurt machines. High on a Utah mesa, he claims in all sincerity: "Isuzu will accept marbles and seashells as payment." Dealers have "millions in stock," he promises, "and if you come in tomorrow you'll get a free house."

Hearing someone lie so openly in an ad and get caught is the emperor's new clothes for the TV generation. Advertising always has to counter consumer suspicion that none of it is true. The funnier ads dissipate doubt in a burst of laughter, but Isuzu goes further—stepping outside the conventions of advertising, reveling in hucksterism while mocking it. Though the ads seem mildly subversive, their net effect is a stronger sell. Suspicion disarmed, you're prepped to believe the corrective subtitles that say, no, the car actually gets 34 mpg city. You end up trusting Isuzu.

The only people to trust these days are those who obviously lie: with them, at least we know the truth lies elsewhere—we know their moral parameters. As the pathological liars on *Saturday Night Live* and David Byrne's upcoming movie, *True Stories,* reveal, lying is the underlying truth of the '80s. Really.

September 23, 1986

Avant-Hard Sell

It's only mildly surprising that Laurie Anderson has made a commercial. She scored the music for a spot in Reebok's first TV campaign, but there's nothing 8mm, slo-mo, or "avant-garde" about it. To her dodge-'em car sound effects, people walk as if they're driving—in quick, short steps, a group of black leather types skid on their "cycles"; a chauffeur-driven "limo" carries execs chatting on cellular phones. At the end, her familiar cool voice says, to standard voiceover rhythm: "Reebok walking shoes. Your mileage may vary."

The ad's friendly, bright, and toylike. But Anderson is usually busy refracting consumer culture, creating a sense of people ping-ponged between products, signs, and electronic transmissions. Ironic critique, accessible deconstruction—that's Laurie. But she handles this ad straight. What gives in avantland?

"I'm doing it mostly because I'm putting in a new studio—so my initial reason was the money," Anderson says. "But I also had fun playing with new equipment. The agency said, 'Do whatever you want.'

"Like most people, I have a fairly ambivalent attitude toward consumerism, a love/hate relationship, but I don't want to be so judgmental. There are plenty of ways to participate in the culture and plenty of ways to sell out. I use a state-of-the-art audio studio—that doesn't mean in my next concert I won't be as snide as I always am about technology."

Ambivalence has grown hand-in-hand with consumerism and American humor. Torn between resenting Mad Ave's attempt to manipulate us and loving the passive pleasures it provides, we devise attitudes to live with it: spoofing consumer culture, accepting it only ironically, enjoying it *because* of its contradictions, or swallowing it straight. Anderson's not Warhol—using products so wholeheartedly that he inverted our perception of them—but Warhol made it possible for Anderson to be an ironic accepter. Now, years of rock stars' unquestioning endorsements have made it possible to view Anderson as a straight accepter.

For the agency, Chiat/Day, N.Y., which first considered using her for a Sara Lee ad, Anderson was fresh. "We try to avoid *styles* of advertising," says creative director Bill Hamilton. (Other ads in the Reebok series are designed to push its athletic brands, broadening its image from yup-sneaker supplier.) "I'm not putting her on for her star value, but for her production value," says Hamilton, who'd like Anderson to direct future spots. "Most people outside New York don't even know who she is."

But as a star of the mainstream avant-garde—a growing group of well-heeled artists who are avant without the garde (as opposed to those breaking the borders of what polite society will accept)—Anderson, like David Byrne, is leading AV's latest dip into mass pop. Already, soundalikes of *O Superman* have turned up in ads for the cotton industry and Sterling cars (Anderson's agent is wondering about legal possibilities); big-suited Byrne-like dancers bop for Orangina.

"The bottom line is it's very hard to be an artist in the United States of America, and if you can find ways to help support yourself, go ahead," says Anderson. "It's very easy to say all advertising is bad.

That's very simpleminded. I don't have anything against the structure or even the politics of advertising as long as it isn't harmful."

But when I hear Anderson structuring a tag line like every tag on TV, it harms the idea that there's something the sponsored world won't touch.

September 8, 1987

Guess Again

Everyone seems either pissed or dazzled by the latest Guess jeans spot, in which paparazzi hound a celebrity couple in London 1967. She's blond, miniskirted, and frost-lipsticked; he's dark and Mafia-mean. As they rush off a plane, photogs flash, lenses zoom, and an ominous ticking builds—something between a panicked heartbeat and a time bomb. Appropriately, as "personalities" their careers aren't identified; they're Every-celebs. (Actually, the actress *is* a personality: model Mandy Smith, best remembered as the 14-year-old old lady of Rolling Stone Bill Wyman. "She's really been through all this shit," says director Roger Lunn.) The lovers are chased from limo to hotel to restaurant to theater; the ad, says Lunn, "is about the assassination of a young couple by photographers." Thus, the spooky beautiful music, a Polynesian war chant rescored. It's the music and the visuals (duping 16 mm film twice into 35 mm) that make the spot seem to strobe with stress—menacing counterprogramming to the assurance of most TV. It's the "plot" that makes it so annoying.

In one sequence, Smith wears a prison-stripe outfit; the play they see is *Mousetrap,* upping the sense of pursuit: Bad cats chase the frightened, famous mice through mazelike alleys. Finally, reaching what they expect will be the sanctity of their hotel room, Mandy and her man are trapped: a posse of paps pops bulbs, and only the ticking remains.

To wonder "what's it mean?" is, by current ad standards, real unhip. Guess is after effect, not meaning. But plenty of meaning forms when viewers and material meet. The mystery is, why play with feeling trapped? Does Guess think it's unfairly hounded by the press, which usually interprets its print ads as rapes of young women by lascivious men? "Oh, no," says Guess partner Paul Marciano. "The press has a right to say whatever they want." Do viewers who already feel trapped—in a job or marriage—identify with the celebrities? If so, it's a vulgar accident: "We don't think that deeply when we create a film," says Marciano. ("I don't like to call it a commercial. It's a small film.") "We go with what we feel is strong atmosphere, we go with our gut feeling." Is "Paparazzi," turning on '60s nostalgia and the latest '80s film look, a comment on change? No—decades are just set pieces. In '85, Guess made a '40s *Misfits* takeoff; next it was the '50s and *The Last Picture Show.* Both were laid-back. "This year," says Lunn, "we thought we'd really sock it to them." But, Marciano allows, the ad is about *something:* The celebs' fear prefigures today's real terrors— hijacking, AIDS, cholesterol—and somehow relates to them, he says.

Surely the ad rouses the same ambivalence we feel toward *Dynasty-* like portrayals of the rich as miserable—evoking both class envy and relief at one's lower-risk life. The hyperstimulating imagery but fractured meaning, the fear and the envy, can make you want to complete the excitement in an action: buy something a quasi-famous person has touched, the Guess jean. (The only time Guess appears in the ad is when Smith holds a pair in a boutique and her enforcer flags them down as if to say "Nah!" That's the "anti-ad" part, says Lunn. It's also the coolest part, but so fast you barely notice.)

There's something awful about such cool ads that makes them work. They're self-regarding and preening. The style itself tacitly disdains substance as "earnest." The message sent is that it's okay to self-indulge (otherwise, why keep buying more denim?). The effort to impress by acting distant and coyly mysterious makes this spot more about the right to narcissism than to privacy.

Not that jeans ads should be frank discussions of double stitching, but when ads stretch so far for effect, they encourage an association between vapidity and cool. The stylish effeteness in, say, a lot of performance art, or in some of our own jokes, are little amateur spots of Guess.

October 20, 1987

The Lifestyle Lifestyle

Another perfect '80s couple—this time exercised beyond couch pota-todom to be bedroom french fries—is almost watching TV. He—Nautilus-made abdominals, dark hair slicked back, eyeglasses worn to be passionately whipped off—is on the floor watching TV in silk pajama bottoms. She—mussed blond hair, silk teddy, feminine but sexually assertive—snakes across the bed to seduce him. The action is intercut with the somewhat sexy videos of Bill Medley and Jennifer Warnes's "Time of My Life" and Anita Baker's "Sweet Love." The woman—with surprising ease, despite interruptions from Hall and Oates—lures the man from the tube. "It's bound to happen," a throaty male voiceover explains. "Once in a while we lose a viewer or two. Even though our audience *loves* to watch their music—hit music—they have other things to attend to. We got exactly what you're looking for"—in the cold glow of the TV, the couple kisses (guy on top)—"even if you're not watching."

Yes, sex is better than TV, the ad says, and, sure, you have better things to do than watch it—*you* are not bored and lonely. But, face it, TV is still a *partner* to your lifestyle, even when you opt to be intimate. You baby boomers even have the set turned on when you're turned on. Afterwards, you can pick back up on the show—all the easier with videos, which do not require great attention to plot. TV rays no longer neutralize sex. Your sex life can merge in and out with the flickering screen: videos as the moving-picture equivalent of an overhead mirror. In fact, TV might get you into bed faster—look how well it worked for *them*.

This is VH-1's first ad campaign since it "refocused" about a year

The Lifestyle Lifestyle **31**

ago. Out with the Julio Iglesias and country crossovers that helped launch the cable channel three years ago; in with more Anita Baker, Kenny G, Billy Joel, Lionel Richie, and other "adult" rock.

"When the channel first started, we were much more broadbased, and, frankly, it wasn't that successful," says VH-1's VP of marketing and advertising, Leslye Schaefer. "You can't watch Julio Iglesias and turn around and watch a George Harrison clip."

The other reason for VH-1's "completely new personality" is to further distinguish it from sister cable channel MTV. VH-1 is targeting a 25- to 49-year-old market; MTV, 12 to 34. "We feel we're really on target with the graying of the whole entertainment business," says Schaefer. "It's in movies, in records, on TV." Like *thirtysomething, Moonlighting, Kate & Allie.* And last year, for the first time, adults bought more records than teens.

"We deliver programming that superserves a particular audience." Superserves? Narrowcasting like only cable can: not just playing the music that appeals to this audience—heavy on the soft rock, repackaged Elvis, and Beatles—but "specialty programs, like *Sunday Brunch,*" tuned to "a Sunday morning 'kick back and relax' lifestyle."

Lifestyle is at the crux of the new ads, as another spokeswoman explains: "The ads say, 'Look, you don't always have time to watch, but we understand your lifestyle.' "

"Lifestyle" is now a lifestyle. The Lifestyle lifestyle means entertainment-technology/body-technology, at your fingertips. Monitor, computer, remote control; sex and digital and rock 'n' roll.

March 22, 1988

On Background

Chances are good that when you see a product or person being sold, you're seeing it against a simple, textured canvas backdrop that says, in a word, "class." The backdrops usually come in tones of gray, sometimes beige; the canvas is crushed or is painted with cracks, swirls, scratches, and smudges that make it look vaguely like marble, smoke, clouds, or old walls. Some variation of the smudgy setup appears in TV spots for, among others: Kodak Coloredge Copiers, Epson Computers, Magnavox, Extra Strength Alka-Seltzer, NBC's and CNN's Olympic logos, Just For Men hair coloring, Hertz, Jennifer Convertibles, Certs, Vicks Percogesic, Fiber One, Tums E-X (a very heavy version of the look), Colgate, and Gorton's Fish Fillet. The smudge appears in print for: Winston cigarettes, Xerox, Sharp, Sony, Dewar's profiles, *Playboy,* Nationwide Insurance, Trident gum, Barneys Wall Street store, and the recent *New York Times Magazine* cover starring Cindy Lauper and Sony's Chairman Akio Morita. The last encapsulates its aesthetics: hip and rich.

"I don't know why we used it," says a spokesman for hip and rich Barneys. "I guess it looks natural. It sort of describes an old distressed wall." The last walls they used were real, but this time they needed studio control. And anyway, he says, "Half the people in the city have faux walls now."

The Smothers Brothers smudge for Magnavox.

Maybe half of Barneys customers do. But the rest of us merely gaze at the faux pauses everywhere. The style is called simply "textured" or "limbo," but the effect is mottled money. "It adds mystique and character to the person in front of it," says Charles Broderson of Broderson Backdrops, who paints backgrounds mainly for ads. "They're somewhere but you don't know where. It's like looking at an old painting—the background can mean a lot, but you don't realize it because it's subliminal."

Not surprisingly, the look isn't new. Portrait painters have used scumbled backgrounds like this since before the Renaissance and often with extra light emanating from the central figure—a technique used in ads today to create product halo. Textured backdrops have also been big in fashion photography. Irving Penn used them extensively; he'd even haul veiled Moroccan women in front of roughed-up canvas instead of Marrakech reality.

But advertising didn't really pick up on the style until about 1981, when Bloomingdale's used it for a men's store campaign shot by Lord Snowden and tied into *Chariots of Fire,* says Broderson, who did that backdrop. In the last couple years, it's replicated like a retrovirus, as all catchy design does.

"We wanted to do something different," says John Colquhoun, a Saatchi & Saatchi art director, who used the scratchy background for a Fiber One TV spot, where it practically growls, "Fiber!" "In doing so we did something overused. But that wasn't important. To get involved with setups—what kind of magnet to put on the refrigerator—didn't seem necessary. It might have even taken away from the message." Nowhere smokey marble avoids "keying you into demographics," he says.

But inevitably the style sends its own message and sparks its own autonomic nervous response among certain demographics. The look is postmod to the max, part of that gray/white/mauve attitude that tries to put across "commitment," but isn't overidentified with any place, any house even too up or downscale, so as not to cut into sales potential. The look alludes to the past but is scrubbed clean of all place and specifics. It says this person or product has been through a lot, but they're not going to burden you with it—just know that he/

she/it is the best possible result of a lot of stuff, like objects in a museum (which is where the "walls" seem to be lifted from). The product doesn't stand before you with warts and all; the walls have the warts—tastefully done. The cracks, smears, and asymmetry of it all only add "dignity," as wrinkles do to politicians like Lloyd Bentsen.

The rival of the mottled-money look is the commonplace all-white, seamless backdrop, the all-time favorite foil of the '60s. Lately, it's been used most strikingly in NYNEX's TV ads, which isolate objects, like the armchair that strips its upholstery a la Gypsy Rose Lee. The white void presents human beings as objects on a slide for your inspection. The smudged backdrop, on the other hand, dissolves some of that viewer superiority, to present the audience with a thing of taste and simplicity.

The depths and layers of the marble-like veins and swirls suggest both opacity (this product is solid) and ubiquity (slip it into any lifestyle from Nebraska to Amagansett). Scratchy flatness suggests nitty-gritty reality, but one so muted it can be ignored on demand. Tasteful, vague, seemingly beholden to no special interest, the classy void—come to think of it—is exactly what all TV pols aspire to.

October 18, 1988

The Fat Lady Sings

The latest rock 'n' roll to sell out to advertising is opera. Although opera was once the MTV of the 19th century—violence, sex, and high-concept visuals—for the latter half of the 20th, it has been typed as a screeching strangeness appreciated only by mobsters and ladies with blue hair. But since *Diva,* opera has been gaining an exotic note of surrealism (mobsters and blue hair seen through new eyes). At once "aristocratic" enough for the young fogies of the Republican generation and tabloid enough for TV—even spawning talk-show-sized superstars—opera can hit just the right balance between elite and accessible to close sales high and low. At least tolerably short *samplers* of opera can—a whole aria would be overkill. So the once truly popular musical theater for the masses may have found its most popular stage in the 30-second format.

This Christmas may seem to be bursting with opera ops, but the fat lady has been singing over the last few years for: Volvo and Cheer (both used Catalani's "La Wally," the hit of *Diva*); Bolla wine ("M'appri Tutti Amor" from the operetta *Martha,* in a great ad in which an old Italian gent, wine glass in hand, gives an appreciative, silent toast to a gorgeous young woman); British Airways ("Flower Duet" from *Lakmé* by Delibes, more recently "Va, Pensiero" from Verdi's *Nabucco*); Guess jeans (Puccini's *Madame Butterfly*); and Chanel's Coco (music "inspired" by Ponchielli's *La Gioconda*).

At the moment, Puccini has the most ads on the air. The composer was chosen for Tuscany, a men's cologne by Aramis, to evoke "Italy," partly because he's a Tuscan homeboy. They even give him a plug. "From the land of marble and masterpieces, Puccini, gelati . . ." and so on, with shots of each emblem set to 30 secs of *Madame Butterfly.* The heavy Italian pitch is the result of owning the name Tuscany but learning through research "how many people think it has something to do with elephant ears," says a Tuscany adman. "Only 4 per cent knew it was a northern section of Italy." But partly because of this campaign, which says the cologne is "created in Italy for Aramis," nearly as few know that Tuscany is actually made in the U.S. "Created" means "the package, the scent, the attitude, the name" were conceived there, he says. Tuscany was designed as Aramis's arm into the Italian market, where it is now number one. Made here and exported there, it is being sold here as a cologne that, with Puccini pitching, is all about there.

Nevertheless, the Tuscany man says about the Puccini ("O Mio Bambino Caro" from *Gianni Schicchi*) used for Tott's Champagne—a new product by Gallo—"I don't say it's subliminal, but it's really putting itself in a world where it doesn't belong—old-world and great." Gallo's other fabrication, Bartles & Jaymes, would go all redneck over Tott's ta-da opera ad: it's elegant and classy, but, like B&J, it doesn't mention Gallo. The less said the better, Gallo figures. A woman de-

capes, a car spans the Seine at dusk, and all we know is: "Tott's champagne. Tonight."

A new arrangement of Mozart's *The Marriage of Figaro* carries the class in an ad for Scorpio, a car made in Germany for Ford's Lincoln-Mercury. Mozart even pauses just as the car, likened to a sleek animal, maneuvers suddenly around a fallen boulder—the music resumes, our hearts resume their rhythm, and the ad touches both the animal and the aristocrat. (But like some other German products, this one can't help but spill out something that evokes 1933. Scorpio, the voiceover says, "learned to run in the Black Forest of Germany. But unlike others, it also learned to be nice to people.")

Rossini's *The Barber of Seville* manfully accompanies the hair-removing action in a spot for the German-made Braun shaver—not for the little joke so much as because "it's the kind of music you'd sing when shaving," says the adman. Either way, opera was the obvious way to go. "We are really trying to be classy, BMWish, Porschish, but at the same time accessible," he says. "We wanted an opera so accessible that Bugs Bunny would sing it and in fact did."

Classical music is occasionally used to lend products class also, but classical's not on opera's roll. Opera is sharper, pierces more cleanly through the thick materialness of commercials, the weight of the *things* pushed in your face (hocking you, hocking you to buy). Opera not only classes up the product but seems to lift the 30 seconds from the gross realm of selling to one of sensibility. Maybe that's why opera works best with products that go against the operatic grain—rock 'n' roll products like Guess jeans or Avia sneakers (in an old ad), or Reeboks and Nikes, both of which have ads with the barest operalike strains. The product gains by the contrast. It acts as ballast—good old familiar, buyable *thing*—to the etherealness of operatic emotions. Products play alto to what most Americans think of as a bunch of squeaking sopranos.

December 27, 1988

It's the Rote Thing To Do

In Quaker Oats ads, avuncular but firm Wilford Brimley ends each spot with the reminder about eating his brand of bran: "It's the right thing to do." That's what George Bush said about sending his son and grandson to view the wreckage of the Armenian earthquake: "I know it was the right thing to do." Brimley's been saying it longer than Bush, in some 30 commercials since September '87, which is when the primary campaigns were getting off and belief in a right thing became the sole shared article of faith of pols left and right. Jesse Jackson spoke the slogan the most ("When [Dukakis] and Mr. Bentsen reach out to the Reagan Democrats and seek to recall them," he said, defending his defense of the ticket, "I think it's the right thing to do."), and others, smelling Jackson Action, flew with it. In the GOP keynote address Governor Tom Kean said, of helping the less fortunate, that "morally it is the right thing to do." We even realize we can be duped by it. Bruce Springsteen on friends who went to Vietnam: "They went because the government told them it was the right thing to do."

It's difficult to tell who started it, Brimley or Jackson, as oat bran and the primaries began rolling about the same time. But on the set of Spike Lee's upcoming movie, *Do the Right Thing*, someone said he thought it's an old Italian saying. Whatever the genesis, it's a tagline for all reasons. As the stern offspring of Coca-Cola's "It's the Real Thing" and AT&T's "The Right Choice," "It's the Right Thing To Do" may be wordier, but listen to those words buzz: *It*—second only to *thing* as carry-all noun, *it* has mystique (The It Girl); *Right*—what we want to be; *Thing*—can't talk without it; *Do*—from yippie injunction "Do It!" to Nike slogan "Just Do It," the promise that we can *do* something about . . . about whatever is enough to make us do something like buy something.

Like Coke and AT&T, Quaker could pull off a superego mojo because, as Bruce Guidotti of Quaker's ad agency, Jordan McGrath Case Taylor, says, "Quaker owns the category [of hot cereals]. It gives us a little more permission to do it without sounding presumptive." And Wilford Brimley was the right choice. He was believable not just because he played a "crusty grandfather who tells it like it is" on *Our House,* but because "he's eaten oatmeal all his life," says Guidotti. Not to mention that, light-colored and wrinkled in a bulky kind of way, he looks like oatmeal. Of course, much of the campaign's success—Quaker Oats sales are up 20 per cent—is due to the craze for oat bran. (Among the many new products, Kellogg's Common Sense Oat Bran uses a softcore soundalike: "A sensible thing to do.") Lowering high cholesterol may be a healthy thing to do, but that alone doesn't explain why the phrase has become the "Go for it" of the late '80s.

"There's a renewed interest in moral and ethical decisions. Ethical choices in almost every arena have gotten a lot of publicity in the last four or five years," says Guidotti. The slogan also came out of a "recognition that there's a neoconservatism or neotraditionalism creeping back," he says, citing a 1987 survey pointing to renewed "traditional" values, a renewal George Bush, for one, has profited by.

It's true that regarding the ethics of medicine, sex, marriage, law, the environment, education, and economics there's a fear that we don't know what the fuck we're doing. We want moral certitude, an existential anchor, or at least the sense that there is a right thing. Many people may realize that anybody can merely claim something's right. Orrin Hatch says Reagan should pardon Oliver North, explaining, "It's the right thing to do." *Right* may be a matter of belief, but we are still likely to lend those who utter the phrase more moral weight, not because they're more right, but because as "neotraditionalists," they espouse the suddenly more attractive system of right and wrong in the first place.

Belief in such a system is the basis of all mass marketing, in advertisements for products or for oneself. The sense that there's a right and wrong product choice rests on a much deeper insecurity. Many people imagine that in *every* area of life there is a right way to do things, but that they invariably do it the wrong way. "I think I shave my *legs* the wrong way," says one woman. "If I cut my salad, I'm sure I should be tearing it." Such people don't crave an ethical construct so much as they assume one exists; its shape is everything they're not. I realize we're talking about the high ethics of dietary fiber and presidential pardons on the one hand, and the private rules people follow in order to be high-school popular on the other—it's the difference between the right thing and the cool thing. But ads inevitably conflate the two. When the masses internalize what they imagine is right-think and mix it with cool-feel—what a powerful marketing tool!

Don't get me wrong. Often there simply is a right thing to do. Every day. In fact, fear that I might be doing PR for moral glibness—clearly the wrong thing—made me say this. And a slogan can be a useful nudge to remember one's ethics. But advertising, *thriving* on social insecurities, is definitely the wrong place to push the right thing to do.

January 10, 1989

Titular Head

Who says TV is destroying Americans' ability to read? Why, three out of every 10 commercials, at least, contain a lot of written-out words. I'm not even talking about the usual tag lines at the end, but about names that ads introduce themselves with ("You Can Do It" for a McDonald's pitch, "Power Lunch" for Macintosh); or blurbs that enter later, in monklike silence, bestowing wisdom ("Jean Shy tries Dove instead of soap"); or words that percolate throughout to carry the narrative (Michelob Dry's "What Dry Is," Goodyear Auto Service's "Do You Feel Vibration?"). While some titles are superimposed, most do the classy white-type-on-black-background thing and resemble each other. For moments the screen is a clean slate, and we are to focus on its lovely simplicity: "Not Smart" (Cracklin' Oat Bran).

Match these titles or blurbs to their product:

1. "The Speech"   a. MCI
2. "Lover's Reunion"   b. Goodyear
3. "Petty Larceny"   c. Philadelphia Brand Cream Cheese
4. "Second Honeymoon"   d. Lee Jeans

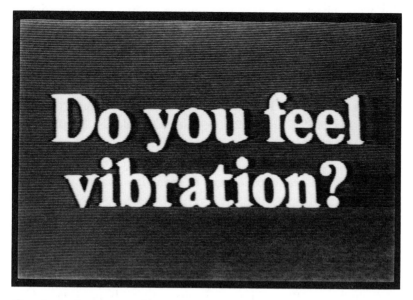

Do you feel vibration?

Goodyear hopes you do.

5. "The CEO"	e. Baby Boom
6. "Mutual Interests"	f. Macintosh
7. "Maternity Leave"	g. American Express
8. "Surprised?"	h. Vicks Formula 44
9. "The Surprise"	i. McDonald's

Titles tease the viewer to get involved: We want to know what happens next, but more importantly, we receive the small flattery that we're in on a process—the great river of television can be halted and parts of it named (a little thrill previously experienced only by TV and ad people). It's another way for ads to identify with art.

McDonald's has been titling its ads for eight years. If ads are not ads but short stories with beginnings, middles, and ends, then McDonald's is a storyteller and we can all gather 'round. American Express has been telling stories since 1987; its Shearson American affiliate ran spots a few years ago that were nothing but title cards. But in the last few years agencies have been getting almost totally titular.

They may be influenced again by music videos—every vid begins and ends with the titles of the band, song, and album. But titles are also a throwback to silent movies—giving ads the weight of "film." Like silent movies, titled ads seem to have a reliable overseer to the action, a force that can lend ads an organizing principle—and thereby seem to make your life more manageable, too.

Titles really got chugging with the life-management obsessed John Hancock "Real Life, Real Answers" campaign in which the protagonist's stats ("Salary: $32,000; Interest/Dividends: $200") were flashed in white typewriter script on black. "There was more time spent on titles than pictures," says Don Easdon, co-creator of the campaign. "It was a very antislick way of giving information. It's not in your face."

But now it's all over our face, picked up early on in Apple Macintosh's office-piranha campaign with hit-'em-hard names like "The War Room," "The Red Eye," "The Pitch." "The names immediately show a shared understanding with the business experience," says Robert Chandler of BBDO. Titles also solve "the problem of having an announcer try to squeeze too much information into 30 seconds."

"In the old days titles were used strictly to underline the selling idea," says John Ferrell, who conceived the frenzied Goodyear spots in which written-out questions flash on for less than a third of a second, "but gradually the thinking became that it might be more dramatic to focus on the type." For Goodyear, where the new ads have "raised awareness to an all-time high," the idea was to make the questions seem like they were being asked directly of the viewer. "This campaign requires that viewers get involved—if they don't, they won't get it."

Michelob Dry messes with the type itself. In the phrase "This Is What Dry Is" the consonants appear first, the vowels drop in rapidly, Hangman-style. The editor, Larry Bridges, says he was influenced by Russian constructivists. He has also intercut titles and pictures for Lee jeans. "When you cut to a title instead of a picture, it plays against expectations," he says. "Throwing them off the moment they think they know the secret increases interest. Denying them the satisfaction of the conclusion, you can then introduce things. You can convince and persuade by interruption. Titles become another thing to put in the way of expectations. It has a double purpose—to inform and to disinform."

Or, as an MTV ad, composed only of title cards, says: "[These words] will hang out for 15 seconds until it's time for another commercial/These are words that could be saying something/but they're not/they're just sitting there/LIKE YOU."

Answers: 1h, 2i, 3c, 4g, 5a, 6d, 7f, 8b, 9e

February 21, 1989

Listless Is More

"Cutting through the clutter"—that's the one idea, the one phrase that ad people say repeatedly—it *never* gets new and improved. They have to stand on their heads, they believe, to make their ads stand out from the other 20 to 30 spots per network hour. Clutter-cutters usually react to what went before as predictably as mini/midi. After the orgy of rockin', fast-cuttin', blip-till-you're-hip Nike, 501, and Michelob ads, the latest new spots have little or no action, music, or sound, just long lingering pans so slow that they're more like magazine ads where you have to turn the page to reach the climax. They may nod toward a '60s less-is-more ad style, but this is often listless is more.

Listless-is-more does more than gut clutter. It resonates, or is supposed to, with the latest, New Traditionalist soul trend: to cut to the basic thing, to go for no-frill thrills, to stay with one shot, steady guys, nonpromiscuous production values, and kill you with simplicity.

Like the Corona beer ads that are as laid-back and luscious as the tropical alcohol mood itself. The scene is two Corona bottles on a rocking boat: an empty bottle slowly rolls back and forth against an upright full bottle; the rhythmic knocking is the ad's music. And that's it—until, come punchline time, the empty hits the deck. In another spot, the camera focuses on a tropically lit stucco wall and, near the

Corona's still shot

windowsill, two Coronas. A tinny "Makin' Whoopee" is playing on the radio, a woman giggles, a man's hand reaches for a brewski, and a lizard on the wall moves.

Mexican Corona long ago replaced right-wing Coors as the cool brew from the West. Corona's trendiness (mocked in a Heineken spot) has turned on being a product not advertised but "discovered"—it could set you apart from the crowd. Disaster would fall if the brand's first TV campaign blew that word-of-mouth mystique. "The goal was to break away from all the beer commercials that use quick-cut action, titles, and beautiful people, to cut through all that BS," says Terry Barich, a creative director at Campbell Mithun Esty Advertising. "How do you become hip? Maybe it's what you don't say. Creating involvement by the *lack* of stimulus, the ads mimic the word-of-mouth way the beer started."

Now to the desert (the nothin'-doin' look shines brightest in hot climes). The camera slowly ambles up the denimed legs and white-

T-shirted chest of a gorgeous dude standing alone on the highway. A red Ferrari speeds past—and suddenly scoots back. Though he hasn't lifted a thumb, the driving dame, apparently stunned by his bod, looks like she's going to ask *him* to hitchhike. Instead, she asks, "Excuse me, are those Bugle Boy jeans you're wearing?" "Why, yes, they are Bugle Boy jeans," he answers, bending down to her window. She zooms off, leaving him baffled, bent, and suddenly looking more like Gomer Pyle than James Dean.

The Bugle boys just want to pow you with their plainness. "Even the fact that there's no music is virtually pattern-breaking," boasts its maker, adman Larry Postaer. And simplicity sells. "It's been the most effective commercial I've ever been involved with." Since the campaign began, brand awareness rose from 30 to 76 percent, he says.

The less shown the purer the thing. For its priciest model, the Z car, Nissan smacks a piece of white paper so close to your eyeballs that you see its hills and valleys. Some force types the letter "Z" as the take-no-prisoners voiceover cuts through the clutter left by God: "This is where we started—a clean sheet of paper, no boundaries, no rules, no preconceived ideas—just a desire to build the best sports car in the world."

The ads for Kellogg's Corn Flakes talk a lot, but they're aiming for the Z state. No kitchens or sun-speckled porches here—their cereal-tasters pose in a room so barren that police could use it to rough up perps. (Actually, says Kellogg's, it's supposed to be "a mall-intercept room," that inner sanctum of American spirituality where companies often conduct market research.) Wearing the emblem of basicness—white shirts—Kellogg's young boomers babble until they trip into Corn Flakes's simplicity and then, at last, shut up. "I mean, a cereal today is supposed to be fun—wild shapes, jellybeans. . . . You got anything like that? These are just—flakes. . . . Unless you're going for a retro thing, right? [Chomp, chomp, chew, chew.] Yeah, it's simple and basic—I like that."

Of course they're going for a retro thing, and it's cringe-making, seeing these commercial creations pretending to be unpretentious. Like post-MTV types who get their first apartment, they're saying,

"Yeah, I used to like novelty and kookball stuff, but now I desire the simple life." It's more grown up to play the parent feeding themselves.

Ads of or about simplicity may be even more prone to advertising's habit of cresting on cuteness. They gotta wrap it up, gotta pull it off, gotta make their punch 'cause they haven't made any points yet but the sensual ones. They've got to underline their own understatement. Even the best ones, like Corona's, which end with: "What you see is what you get." "We didn't want to use a tag line originally," says Barich. "But we did want to sign off with something so that it feels like it's a commercial. Otherwise, it would be like thumbing your nose at the viewer."

Even though such ads try to cut through clutter, they stretch but don't break commercial form. Their few awkward seconds of silence are the TV version of the gap between Alfred E. Neuman's teeth.

May 30, 1989

Local Anesthetic

Now that mass marketing has made regional identification as vestigial as the snail darter, it's using a pining for roots to sell us more things marketed worldwide. To replace the extremely popular 501 Blues campaign, Levi's has tapped what is becoming the latest lucrative emotion: a yearning for place.

The campaign, 501 U.S.A., looks like 501 Blues, with the same nubby textured photography and chockablock editing (by the same director, Leslie Dektor), but snippets of disjointed teen dialogue replace the music. Actually, *that* makes these spots look like some by Jordache, Lee, Keds, Nike for kids—i.e., commercials that imitated 501 in the first place. The difference is that the coolest thing here isn't supposed to be the sound of the kids' attitude, but their hometowns.

Panting with anticipation, each of the eight ads opens in black-and-white with the name of a town—Antelope Valley, California; Dubuque, Iowa—followed a beat later not by a year, like you might expect, but by the digits *501*. Then we get groups of mostly real kids (only a handful of actors) talkin' their unscripted lines, cuttin' up, and strikin' odd poses that look like something between dancing and t'ai chi done by ostriches. (Such postures are cropping up in a lot of ads lately. Here they accent the "kookie," I-gotta-move-my-body tone that jeans must evince.)

"Nowhere else but Texas," one boy says in the Houston ad. Amid shots of gleaming skyscrapers, a girl feeding a boy watermelon, and some ostrich moves, one guy in a tie says: "Money makes the world go around. Let's not forget that." Another dude wonders, "There's something about a girl's—it's like their shape or something, it's . . . I don't know" (16- to 20-year-old boys are 501's target market). Finally an off-camera guy: "*We* make the world go around." To which a blond boy manly admits: "I love my mom."

In "Cape Ann, Massachusetts," a city boy observes: "It's like water, sand, and sky. What is there to do? You're doing it." And that's right by him. "Dubuque—Dubuque is a car thing. You know, everybody does a car." One black and five white guys conclude about Lake Charles, Louisiana, "I don't believe there's another place in the country that's like this. It's got everything I want."

There was nothing wrong with the blues campaign. Sales doubled after it began in 1984 and are still going strong. It's just that the company "wanted to stay cutting-edge," says Levi's marketing manager Dan Chew. So they took a lead from their research. Levi's interviews a few thousand teenagers quarterly; in the last two years, they noticed a changing heart. "Kids are becoming incredibly loyal to where they live," says Chew. "There's still some people who aspire to move away, but there was a real pride in where they live, in both big cities and rural areas. What eventually led us to our emphasis on this was the level of emotion about it."

Nostalgia doesn't have to be only for the past. Contemporary nostalgia isn't temporal but spatial. McDonald's also slaps the name of a place and a number onto ads: "Rupert, Georgia, 5:42 a.m." Surf detergent shows off real-life families in their real, demographically balanced hometowns. Visa ads try to find places somehow too "authentic" to accept American Express.

Pride of place is both tipped by the media and is real. It has provoked the return, even, of the Midwest, spotted by a *Newsweek* article called "The Heartland Is Hot." Maybe some of this home-front boosterism was stirred by the flag-waving that began with the presidential primaries, encouraging angry, put-upon adults to hide in the bathroom, spiritually speaking. Fear makes you draw in your horizons: I don't want to go out in the world. I'm OK, my place is great. A feeling of belonging can be a kind of prejudice. Maybe some of the rummaging for roots stems from a fear that life is too much a global village. Fear of mega-sameness created by mergers, the Japanese, and, most of all, TV, can lead to the sense that even countries don't matter anymore (in 1992, Europe goes blob)—so mass marketers lurch for the local. You can go back in time, as so many ads do, or you can go home again.

Now, these kids may have to buy the same 501s at identical-looking strip shopping centers all across the country, but commercials help them rediscover the unique consumer qualities of their towns—at least the ones that have survived the malls. In these spots kids are never shown in a mall. And they're rarely shown solo. Friendship is 501 U.S.A.'s subtheme. "All the friends I have are really good friends," says Dubuque, while Boston is, naturally, more discriminating: "I've been lucky. I have two friends." Location is destiny: his buddies are an artist and a ballerina.

"Our research is showing youth today are under more pressure on many different fronts," says Chew. "So we wanted to focus on the things that don't change: friendship, the importance of where you live, the pleasures of where you live."

Creating nostalgia for where we live is another way to make us feel better than the crowd: We come from unique and intense backgrounds. We keep hearing hype about how consumers are getting more control of their media—we can switch channels! watch VCRs! the networks lick out boots! Eventually, we are told, we will even "control" the ads we see; we can *choose* to call them up on our PCs!

Well, yeah, the content is more varied, but, bottom line (a phrase implanted by the media), we're still staring at TV and computer monitors. While we're all having the same experience at once, lolling in our leisure before the flickering screen, it becomes even more crucial for advertising, in order to sell us identical products, to tell us that we're all quirky individuals, carrying with us the cool of our very special place.

Until recently, I thought that deep down people hated wherever they were because it wasn't New York. But, of course, that snobbism is in me. When I was growing up in St. Louis, I believed that my part of town, University City, was the best, that I was going to the best junior high in U. City (even if we had a football team castratingly called the Acorns). I was almost in with the best kids at the best school in the best place in the country. Till I was 16, and wanted nothing more than to get as far away from St. Louis as possible.

August 1, 1989

Bookends, Pods, and Piggybacks

In 1953, a cartoon show called *Winky Dink and You* became the first instance of interactive TV, albeit in a low-tech kind of way. *Dink* host Jack Barry told kids to put a special piece of cellophane—which they could get along with a special crayon by ordering the Winky Dink Kit—right onto the television screen. Then the kids would trace and connect special dots off the monitor—and presto!—they'd receive a secret message! Today, with a technique somewhat less ingenious but as simple and transparent as the cellophane, some ad campaigns are getting adults to connect not the dots but the spots.

A pretty woman makes the usual complaint about "a headache this big" and confides that she took two Excedrins. But instead of the ad resolving itself, she merely moans. A few unrelated commercials follow, and just before the show returns, she's back, with exactly the exhausted but surprised look of awareness that a pain has passed. "No more headache," she glows, actually kissing the bottle of Excedrin.

"To make sure that your family is safe, go test your smoke detector right now," William Conrad orders us. "I'll be right back." After a slew of other spots, Bill's back on your case: "You didn't test your smoke detector because it was too inconvenient, right? Well, with the new Light Test smoke detector from First Alert, you wave a flashlight on the golden button to know if it's working." He demonstrates, the gizmo works, and so does the ad.

Tandem ads, which have also been used for Kellogg's Crispix, Banquet Microwave Hot Bites, and Miller Lite, are known as "bookends"—two 15-second spots that wrap around other commercials, the first establishing "conflict," the second "resolving" it. But because they spice up and reshape the familiar "commercial pod" that floats between programming, these two-piece ads might better be called bikinis.

While *Winky Dink* broke the barrier of the screen and used "real space" to interact with kids, these spots, interactive advertising for adults, use "real time." Snuffing out a headache, being remiss in checking your smoke detector—the ads are supposed to mark the actual passage of time required for small, everyday acts. It's another way the medium tries to tell people that behind the electron curtain there hovers an intimate presence, a friend, a down-home *baba* who recognizes your needs, your worries, even how long it takes your butt to go numb.

But bookends are also the result of the proliferation of 15-second ads. Rare until a few years ago, 15s now account for 38 percent of all ads, according to the Television Bureau of Advertising. Going at half the price of the more common 30-second spots, 15s were tempting for advertisers to buy, but the challenge was to keep them from blending into the Seurat background. Manipulating the fresh element of real time could keep viewers awake. But if you're going to juggle time, it helps to keep content steady. So the emphasis is on narrative, not style as in music video spots. And narrative is far less culturally threatening than the jump-cutting, jaggedness, and discontinuity that are the stock-in-trade of new wave advertising.

Bookends mess with the steady drip drip of the commercial break—that alone would make some people like them. But given the TV industry's overcautious sensibilities, even that could seem rad: CBS wouldn't sell time to First Alert, one of the earliest bookends, because Conrad asked viewers to *walk away from the TV set*—they might miss important messages from other sponsors. "They wanted us to buy the 45 seconds or so of advertising in between," says a spokesperson at First Alert's agency, DMB&B.

The one-two punch of even a nonbookend pair of 15s can outwallop a flabby 30. (Though 15s cost 50 percent of a 30, they're 65 to 80 percent as effective, various studies have found.) Many more products—Doritos, Clorets, Ziploc, Dairy Barn, Lea & Perrins Worcestershire—use "split 30s" than use bookends. Split 30s are two 15s for one product in a pod; they're not conflict/resolution duets like bookends, but are merely as thematically related as any two spots in any campaign. Often they're piggybacked, one after the other. That way "you get more bang for your buck," people at two different agencies told me. "Most ads need three or four exposures before they really register," says an account executive at Della Femina, McNamee. "The first exposure is just to capture attention. The second time, you might get brand recall. Piggybacking 15s is a catalyst to make that happen sooner."

But winky-dinky 15s are under attack. Some networks, though they initially offered 15s when they were more desperate to sell time, are suddenly worried about "TV clutter," an obvious tautology. ABC recently announced that it would reduce the number of 15-second spots by 20 percent, charge a premium for them on some high-rated shows, and charge an additional 5 percent for bookends.

Regulating the frequency and rhythm of commercial pacing is like regulating someone's alpha waves when they're asleep. Does the frequency itself send out a secret message? Like, "Help, my pants are stuck to the couch!"

August 8, 1989

Bookends, Pods, and Piggybacks **51**

The Sound of Nine Ads Hyping

The Shinto chic of the ads for Infiniti, Nissan's new luxury car division, wants to whop you with its tranquillity in the highest-concept way. Its focus on a single, stylized nature scene—raindrops striking the surface of a pond, or a flock of geese against an autumn sky—stands out from the hubba-hubba of most auto ads. By never showing the product and talking only about its transcendental qualities, these nine "pre-launch" ads also entice viewers to project a regality onto a car they won't see until mid-October (in the actual "launch" campaign). But as classy as the imagery is, the copy, like a tourist on a Kyoto weekend, keeps jabbering about "philosophy," finds Japanese minimalism in $40,000 sedans, and even evokes "the Walrus." The come-on is more American high cute than haiku.

To peaceful footage of trees blowing in the wind, a voiceover in a flat Northeast-corridor accent explains, "The car is connected to an engine, a suspension system. The car fits in the road, which fits in a landscape." He says it with studied stumbling, carving footholds for American minds to scale the slick inscrutability of it all. "And when all of this—the will of the driver, the ability of the car, the feel of the road—when all of that is one thing, together, then you get a sense, a true idea of luxury. Infiniti." (The vainglorious name is even more precious for its third "i.")

In yet another instance of everything coming together, the copywriter, Bill Heater, is reading his own stuff. Heater headed up the influential but lugubrious John Hancock "Real Life, Real Solutions" campaign—which lured upscale types with the same pretentious authenticity. Infiniti, virtually tailor-made for this group, is supposed to be a new category of car: "functional luxury," somewhere between luxo-luxury European models and the just nice functionalism of mid-priced imports. Honda's Acura led the Japanese into this market; Nissan's Infiniti and Toyota's Lexus now follow. Infiniti expects 65 percent of its sales to come from "intercepts," says its marketing director, Peter Bossis. "We want to intercept Japanese-car owners as they head up the price ladder, rather than go after BMW owners."

It's a class grab through the ever-revolving psychographic side door. The target market, according to Infiniti's extensive research, not only has household incomes of $50,000 plus, but they are "inner-driven people who are less concerned with driving status symbols." "They're neotraditionalists," Bossis says outright. "Money is still the root of power, but these people are more judicious with how they spend it. They're more concerned with intrinsic kinds of values."

About four years ago, using similar VALS (Value and Lifestyle) research, Lincoln-Mercury mined the same shaft with a revival of luxminor cars and advertised with VALS-conducted '60s rock 'n' roll. Later, Nissan materialized the much-loathed, loft-dwelling "engineers," who feigned excitement over designing cars "for the human race." Even Nissan's corrected, less sickening yups traipsing Brazil give off a faint, wet-wool odor of smuggitude. Infiniti differs primarily in its higher price—$20,000 to $40,000 per metal chunk—and thus uses two upscale wedges to pry "new traditionalists" from their wads: "art" and "philosophy."

Artwise, this is Hiroshiga Meets Michael Steadman. The new affluent, as opposed to the nouveau riche, know that ostentatious wealth is spiritual poverty—so they're flattered by ads that *presume* their appreciation of simplicity.

"Everything you do you do for the driver," Heater reads in another spot. "That is the simple philosophy" behind Infiniti. Have you noticed how "philosophy" has lately become divorced from thick books and unemployable postgrads, and instead gilds phrases like "his philosophy of chopping garlic"? Infiniti's "Total Ownership Experience is more than just a slogan," one ad says; it's "a working philosophy." Schopenhauer might insist they're just selling cars.

Actually, one idea here isn't phony: the notion of driving prowess, of "man and machine unity," as Infiniti calls it. Of course, many carmakers claim the same; the lower-priced Mazda is positively cyborgian with its hype of "Kansei engineering"—"the sensation when all five senses come into harmony," Mazda says. "Somewhere between your head and your heart exists the perfect luxury car." To illustrate that feeling, advertising usually uses images of sex and power—

slipping into a tight fit, controlling the road. But more appropriate for the cocooning, safe-sex generation is the promise of satori.

It's unlikely that even two years ago ads would have gone so ga-ga over anything Japanese. The cramped and regimented factory that looks like an archipelago from space was a touchstone of fear. But these spots allude, safely, to "ancient" Japanese values, the humble little country where people spend all day raking rocks. Anyway, all the campaign's faux-losophy is an excuse to boost the not particularly Japanese—but very young upwardly mobile American—idea of "luxury." A leaner, cleaner luxury is Infiniti's selling point, even to the point of absurdity. Raindrops hit a pretty pond, stimulating in our narrator the raging query, "You wonder whatever happened to luxury cars. They rise and fall on the promise of status and prestige," he goes on. "But, you know, they leave room for the next generation, a new vision, more idealistic. The time has come, the walrus says, the time has come."

Unless Nissan's engineer is John Lennon, the Walrus isn't a very swift choice to represent idealism or even philosophy. As Tweedledee tells it in *Alice in Wonderland,* the Walrus beseeched the friendly, fat oysters to listen up. " 'The time has come,' the Walrus said, 'To talk of many things: Of shoes—and ships—and sealing wax—Of cabbages—and kings—And why the sea is boiling hot—And whether pigs have wings.' " After entrancing the oysters with such lovely nonsense, the Walrus and the Carpenter ate them.

October 10, 1989

Sneakers and Nothingness

Nike, Reebok, BKs, Cons, Keds, ASICS, Etonic, even L.A.-softened Gear—like the basic sex words, sneaker names punch their presence into the world with a lot of guttural, aggressive K sounds. (And look how "sneakers" kicked the soft ass of "tennis shoes," which so many of us non-East Coast types grew up calling them.) Sneaker identities hoist themselves into being out of nothingness, meaning embossed like logos on leather. The same goes for sneaker ads, which try to convince us that there's an innate relationship between a brand and an attitude. It's a relationship that goes poof in the night with each new ad agency a company hires (are Reebok buyers Bungee murderers, whimsical U.B.U. surrealists, or powerful Pumpin' real guys?). And yet out of this nothingness, out of a market that barely existed two decades ago, arises a $5.5 billion industry; an urgency that, yes, some kids have killed for; and second homes for college coaches who convince their players to model product. (The last, of course, is one reason for the small hole in March Madness—the Knight Commission investigation into, and the Bill Moyers special on, college sports and big money.)

As today's aspiring white Negroes—Mailer's late '50s label for the white hipsters who "absorbed the existential synapses of the Negro"—strive to imitate black male athletes (Nike says 87 percent of its domestic athletic shoes are sold to whites), sneakers tease all men with the possibility of making hipness out of nothingness. Sometimes women get to play too, as Nike helps us become us in an eight-page spread that ends "Because you know it's never too late to have a life. And never too late to change one. Just do it." That the most existential tag line in history comes from a sneaker company is pretty fuckin' K itself.

For both companies and consumers, sneakers are about defining yourself, becoming yourself through slogan, logo, and look. For now, number-one Nike, with 28 percent of the sneaker market, defines what defining yourself is. How does a manly shoe compete?

Out-cooling Nike is an obvious answer and many have tried, but lately the strategy has been to become more aggressively K. Attacks on Nike—by Reebok, BK, ASICS, and L.A. Gear—have created a confusing shoe-off. First ASICS, a Japanese company that is number three in the world but only 10th in the U.S., came out with an ad that said, compared to its GEL-Spotlytes, "Everything else is just hot air." (A superimposed slogan rubbed it in: "Do It Better.") The networks asked ASICS to tone it down to "Anything more is a lot of hot air." Still, ABC refused to run the spot—even while running L.A. Gear's ad in which hoops star Karl Malone slow-growls, "Everything else is just hot air."

"Money talks," explains a spokeswoman at ASICS, which spends $5 million a year in advertising while L.A. Gear wields $70 million. ASICS is asking for compensation from ABC and is considering legal action against L.A. Gear. But that's not all. Gear's agency, BBDO, quit in disgust over Gear's meddling into ad-making, including its insistence on "hot air," which the agency thought was cheesy. Pivoting, BBDO eyed Reebok, which was frustrated with its agency, HHCC. Reebok had already farmed out its Pump ads to another suitor, George ("I Want My MTV!") Lois. (Finally last week, Reebok gave the remainder of its business to its former agency, U.B.U. creator Chiat/Day/Mojo.) Pump tries to slam-dunk Nike with the tag line "Pump Up and Air Out."

It may seem odd, but besides manhood, sneaker companies are also hauling mothers into their ads: David Robinson's for Nike, Isiah Thomas's for ASICS, and "your mother" for British Knights. Moms anchor a guy, illustrate his heart, and yet serve to provide higher contrast between his toughness and the softer female world. The Nike and ASICS spots are lovable portraits, but BK took up the playground challenge and just blurted it: "Your mother wears Nike."

The new slogan doesn't make Nike equal to army boots (that would be only too fine nowadays); instead it equates Nike with a bunch of middle-aged suburban ladies chatting about plastic surgery and "top restaurants" while they play tennis in their Nikes. The poor ladies are crucified in order to define BK by what it isn't. The tack is similar to the savvy savagery that the same agency, Deutsch, lobbed at the Japanese in its Pontiac dealer ads ("If you're still thinking about a Japanese car," threatens a grizzly voiceover, ". . . maybe you should move to Tokyo") and at real, mainly Jewish salespeople and working-class furniture movers in IKEA furniture spots ("Do you even need these guys?" the narrator asks dismissively).

Deutsch is a pro at toppling buying resistance with a dash of stereotype, but it sees its BK campaign as "authentic rebellion." "Nike is authentic sports," an agency man there told me. "They've preempted it. It's tough for any competitor to break through that. So we went for authentic rebellion."

Authentic is where the arc is pointed. Converse just announced "the largest and most comprehensive ad campaign in its 84-year history," featuring the slogan "It's what's inside that counts." After eight months of research, Converse came up with "six key adjectives" to describe its "brand personality": "confident, genuine, hardworking, tough, unselfish, and passionate." And so the measure of one's authenticity is not brash bravado, but the kind of realness gnawing through Converse's new print ad: "You can always spot a guy who wears Cons. Not by what's on his feet"—that would be too easy—"but, rather, by what's in his soul. *He eats pain.*"

Like Converse endorser Bernard King, who came back from major knee surgery to his best season ever, and who said, at least for a Converse press release: "It's the voice inside that makes the difference in your life. Whether it's the kind of things you hear from your parents when you're growing up or what the doctors tell you after knee surgery. You're the one that has to decide to make it work and work well." The language is true and good, and even turns on an existential moment—until he finishes the thought in the dialect of the sponsored life: "The new Converse campaign says it perfectly for all aspects of life: It's what's inside that counts."

April 2, 1991

Heaven Can Bait

One night during the gulf war, I saw three ads in a row that featured as their main come-on fields of wheat. One after the other, endless horizons of sunstruck wheat shivered in the wind for Honda Accord, the Big Red Boat cruise line, and Infiniti. As spiritual image food, wheat is neat, thanks especially to *Field of Dreams* (that was a corn field, but corn doesn't cut it like amber waves of grain). If the desert is the traipsing ground of the Bible (and the background of many a car commercial), wheat fields are its heartland cousin.

But since last fall, tall-grass ads have been overshadowed by sky-and-cloud spots. These aren't merely ads that hang up sky for pretty background, nor airline ads that are always afluff with the stuff, but rather ads for cars, watches, and fast food that in essence make *you* the airplane, floating through intensely blue skies and cotton puff clouds, ads that take you to heaven's gate.

Basically, when advertising wants a powerful nature visual, it chooses from one of four swatches, each related to the archetypal elements: sky and clouds (air); oceans and pools (water); wheat fields and forest (earth); and for fire, well, let's make fire the desert or brilliant blinding light.

I admit that as a class, heaven ads are my favorite, and they have nothing to do with product content. It's just that they unroll some glorious, soothing scene from a dream and play it over and over — viewable blips from all our fantasies of flying and floating and free-

Swatch: swimming to utopia

dom. The ads sing what TV is always stuttering: "Get onto my cloud." Heaven ads in the sky or field—wheat fields being heaven on earth—hold out the deepest of promises: that we will prevail, that we are good. During the war—and even now—they also said that our ultimate mission rose as high above the earthly muck as those fighter pilots rose in their undetectable Stealths. Check it out:

- You're gliding through the sky, clouds are spilling over you right and left. Cut to a dashboard, then to an Acura Legend zooming down a mountain road, so high that it's at the cloudline. Like many a sky-and-cloud ad, this one was filmed at heaven's recruiting station, Mt. Haleakala in Maui, Hawaii, where, at about 10,000 feet, producers are guaranteed in-the-clouds drama.
- A man drives into a dank indoor pool. But when he looks at his Swatch watch, the water lightens up. "Just imagine," the voiceover suggests. As the man breaks the surface of the water he's as surprised as a dreamer to find himself in the sky, now swimming through Magritte-like clouds toward a floating island. (My favorite, because swimming is the closest we come to our fantasy of flying.)
- Pieces of fried chicken are tossed slo-mo through the sky. A lot of earthbound stuff happens in the ads for KFC's Lite and Crispy—mimes, dancing, etc.—but several times in each spot, skin-free chicken floats cloudward as if it had wings. ("Oh, no, you're not going to write about subliminal seduction," an ad guy moaned when I asked about the sky. He meant the largely debunked idea that art directors sketch penises and breasts into ice cubes and cloud formations. I wasn't going to suggest it.) Sky is obviously used here to make the chicken seem as light as the company's now preferred nomenclature, KFC—hold the "Fried." But that's the promise of the sky: This chicken ungrounds you from the weight of your body, up, up, and away.

There are more, for Honda, Infiniti's M30 convertible, and a cellular phone company called IKI. They all owe something to the classic "Share the Fantasy" Chanel spot in which a woman lies poolside under a brilliant sky as an airplane's shadow passes over, and she says: "I am made of blue sky and golden light and I will feel this way forever."

But the one ad to pull it all together is for the Big Red Boat, a Premier cruise line tied into Disney World. As a little girl clutching her Mickey Mouse doll stares out at the Kansas field of wheat before her, the roiling sky overhead turns into an ocean, and on that ocean comes sailing the Big Red Boat, and bursting out of the boat is an explosion of blinding light, and out of the light appears the castle from Disney's Fantasyland, and suddenly the girl and her parents are afloat on the boat, a sort of Noah's ark for families that otherwise never dine together.

If ads like these lend the ultimate halo effect, there may be a reason that transcends the mercantile. Patricia Malkin, the creative director at Saatchi & Saatchi who made the Swatch watch spot, had Magritte in mind for more than surreal imagery. "I'm always amazed that your fantasy life can survive in the corporate world," she says. "And I've always held Magritte up as a model of that. He was a banker in real life." That is, the heavenly thrust of ads may come from ad folks' own yearnings. "I notice it in the people in the business, in the people who've survived the [massive layoffs] of the '80s. I think the people who lived through it and are still around feel that they better be thinking about the true meaning of life. They realize that nothing they can buy in this lifetime is going to make them together and whole and happy." It was because of ideas like this that she helped position Swatch less as a gizmo than as a spiritual bauble—"a nonstatus status symbol."

And therein lies the lie of heaven ads. While there's no more universal symbol of eternity than the sky, by the 19th century, artists began to regard it as bourgeois. Which is what Magritte had in mind by painting a sky raining down bankers in bowler hats. Or what Steve Martin had in mind with his mobster-in-suburbia movie *My Blue Heaven*, in which the title cards are framed in pictures of blue sky and white clouds. The sky begins to stand for the suburbs of the spirit.

But blue sky has power beyond its human uses. In *On Being Blue*, William Gass writes, "Because blue contracts, retreats, it is the color of transcendence, leading us away in pursuit of the infinite."

Or, to quote the animated cloud who explains to a passenger on an airplane that he's a salesman for White Cloud toilet tissue, "It's more than a job, it's a family business."

April 30, 1991

Burying Messages

For most of the George Bush constituency, Newspeak still works; the rest of us can be better persuaded by Winkthink. Almost simultaneously, various Sons of Joe Isuzu have decided to moon our sensibilities with ads that spoof subliminal advertising, and, as commanded *super-liminally* (manipulation made obvious in the service of manipulation), we're laughing on cue.

These ads—for Seagram's Extra Dry Gin, Toyota Paseo, and others—flash quick but perfectly discernible messages in order to make fun of the juicy idea that ads are ripe with hidden signals that make us buy buy buy. Advertising has long been accused of doing just that—but this crew of camouflage cuties is spoofing proof that any sin can be turned into a virtue if you own up with irony.

Maybe it was the popularity of the Isuzu campaign or *Saturday Night Live's* "Subliminal Man" (recycled in a spot for Miller Lite); or maybe it was the end of the Red Scare that allowed us to finally laugh the decades-old Ad Scare off the stage. Like the fear that we were being controlled by commie agents, the big Ad Scare was a creature of the '50s, when, in 1957, a market researcher drew negative press for flashing imperceptible messages at a New Jersey movie audience. Some subliminals—such as audio messages in stores warning customers not to shoplift—were real enough, but they also spawned a conspiracy theory of everyday consumerism. Journalism professor Wilson Bryan Key sighted subliminal embeds like so many second Oswalds. In books starting with 1973's *Subliminal Seduction,* he found ads crawling with crudely drawn penises, scary faces, and the words *SEX, FUCK,* and—most terribly—*U BUY.* Sometimes he

Toyota's liminal subliminal

makes a persuasive case, sometimes he's ridiculous. The practice, presumably more insidious than the easy-to-read penises popping out of Camel ads, is widely denied by art directors, and some academic studies have dismissed it. But rather than produce evidence one way or the other, the Irony Age has instead produced spoofs.

Toyota's Paseo spot starts with a simple shot of a red car parked in front of a motel called the WindJammer, with the voiceover proclaiming, "We think you'll like the new 1992 Toyota Paseo so much, we don't have to use cheap advertising tricks to play on your emotions." Then the word *EXCITING* flashes. "So you won't see any young models in bikinis"—the word **S***EXY* explodes. "So there's no pressure"—*ACT NOW*.

It's quite funny and apt for Paseo's purpose, which is to convey practical yet sexy. "It's a double message," says Jon Bucci, a Toyota national ad manager. "It's targeted at mostly young males who have a conflict over buying their first car. They want something they can impress the parking valet with, but they need something they can afford." This "right brain/left brain" approach, he says, signals that they can have both.

But it's a pretty tame right brain by subliminal standards. The difference between flashing *SEX* and *SEXY* is the difference, in America, between dirty thoughts and wholesome fun. But then I watched the spot with a friend, who espied under the WindJammer sign an arrow sticking between two fleshy poles and reminded me what "jam her" refers to. In a second spot, the car is filmed in a gym labeled *GYM*. In the spirit of the ad, I began to wonder, Is this code for *GYN?* More plausibly and ominously, sitting in the middle of another of the ad's overt subliminals—a shot of a black man and white woman dancing near a swimming pool—is a lawn sign reading *KEEP OFF*.

It is possible that was an unintended oversight, and in the realm of the subliminal senses it's easy to get carried away. But *KEEP OFF* resonates quite neatly with recent findings by New York's Department of Consumer Affairs that blacks account for only 3 percent of the models in national magazine ads—subliminals by omission.

A subliminal spoof can operate as a clever decoy to divert you from its first cousins—the usual symbols and social cues that are the meat and potatoes of advertising. For Seagram to make joke subliminal ads, as it has done for the last year, *seems* brave; like most liquor companies, it's been accused of sticking penises and worse in ice cubes for years. "Everybody believes advertisers do subliminals," says John Gruen, an Ogilvy & Mather creative director who works on the campaign. "We said, 'If that's the case, OK, you win, here it is.'" And now the shadows of the cubes for Seagram's Extra Dry Gin kick in with some easy-to-find images, such as a tiny man and woman on a swing, under headlines about finding "The Hidden Pleasure in Refreshing Seagram's Gin."

Like most ad folks, he doesn't believe true subliminals exist. "It would be a big waste of time. It's difficult enough to be obvious." But a study that Seagram commissioned before launching this campaign found that nearly 62 percent of the public believe that subliminal ads exist, and 56 percent believe subliminals can get them to buy things they don't want. But, happily, the study found that 54 percent "liked the idea of subliminal spoof" ads! Whether those *SEX*es are viewers' projections or advertisers' implants, Rorschachs or Whore Shacks, doesn't really matter—either way it doesn't hurt sales. And whether real subliminals work or not, apparently the parodies do: "Sales have increased," says Gruen, "and in the liquor business that's not easy to do these days."

That's no surprise: these superliminal ads' many winks and blinks convey their own unspoken messages. The company flatters you that **you**'re sophisticated because you know about subliminals and know they're baloney—and *you* wouldn't be influenced by them anyway. The viewer can also feel kinship with the company, because they're both on the same side against overanalytical naysayers. Making fun of subliminal-seekers as squares reinforces the commercial world's biggest campaign ever, subliminal or otherwise: that we're all in this party together.

August 13, 1991

Chapter
Two

CORPORATE

IMAGE

ADJUSTMENT

Soldiers of Fortune

Biz is hell. In the war of deals, TV ads tell us, today's businessman's got the guts of a general. A World War I officer orders the cannons fired. Through the smoke, a confounding shape approaches, something he's never seen before—by God, a tank! As the horses' nostrils flare in slo-mo, the scene takes on the predeath silence of movie war. Then a baritone voiceover: "Data General asks, in tomorrow's business battle will you be buying yesterday's technology?" Data General sells computers.

World War II P-51 fighter planes race over Death Valley. "Competition is what makes American business excel." Again a sonorous voice. "Competition is what drives Hilton to be America's business address." Hilton, an account exec explains, is aiming at those who can say, " 'Yes, I'm in business and I'm competitive and I'm not ashamed of it.' We're telling them, we share your values."

So does American Airlines. Striding through an airport corridor out of *2001*, an exec who looks like the Equalizer and thinks like Ayn Rand tells his assistant: "There's no sense in rehashing. They have to improve the deal." His secretary hands him a ticket; he walks on, without a glance. She knows the strong must act that way and wishes him luck. "Luck?" he harrumphs. "Luck is for rabbits."

Having sent its bull to pasture, Merrill Lynch now presents the stockbroker as secret agent. Its new spots throb with anxious dialogue: "We got to crack this thing!" "Everything's on the line here!" These may be desk-bound Marlboro men, but with primal, testosterone-enhanced fantasies about their mission, they are the psychofinancial shock troops of Reagan's America. The bull is dead, long live the bull.

November 26, 1985

Born-Again Dow

The more hawkish a company's record, the more mawkish its self-portrait. In its first national TV ads, Dow Chemical is "repositioning." Like napalm and Agent Orange victims, Dow says it got burned during Vietnam and claims to have hightailed it away from the weapons business (though Greenpeace, for one, calls Dow among the country's worst polluters). Meanwhile, Dow has acquired companies that make cleansers and lozenges, and so wants to get closer to the consumer. To introduce born-again Dow, one ad has a mop-o'-curls college kid writing: "Just got back from my Dow interview. Sounds like my kind of research. Finding new ways to grow more food, ways to help sick people. I'm going to go for it, Dad." (Cut to Dad reading the letter, gulping hard.) "I'm going to try to make you proud." In another spot, graduating "Cindy" confides: "I never understood when Mom made me clean my plate because there were places where kids were starving. Now I'm about to walk into a Dow laboratory to work on new ways to grow more and better grain . . . I can't wait!"

Who better to absolve Dow than its old nemesis, college students? How better to tell students it's okay to go for the bread than by insisting they're going for the grain? Kids forgive Dow, Dow forgives kids, Mom and Dad trust Dow. And we're all sanctioned not to worry. This is Dow repositioned as family counselor and Peace Corps. Scandal-ridden E. F. Hutton, airing its own feel-good ads, ought to be consoled. Like Dow's new theme says: "Dow lets you do great things."

December 3, 1985

Real Forced

In expanding from insurance company to purveyor of financial services, John Hancock must persuade people that it's smart enough to
handle their dough—and that they have enough dough to invest. Each
spot in the gritty new "Real Life, Real Answers" campaign starts by
flashing the subject's vital stats in black-and-white print. At the bottom of the middle-class heap there's "Michael Mark" (a never-grow-
up SWM name if ever there was). "Single. Age: 26." Cut to Mike's
older brother, solid-jawed Dave: "So . . . how much you making now?
Thirty? Tell me—yes or no—are you making 30?" The ledger tattle-
tales: "Salary: $30,000." Dave: "You got any investments, any stuff?"
Mike beams: "Got the car!" Dave: "That's not an investment. You
got an IRA, life insurance?" Dave smells blood: "You're making 30
and you don't have anything like that? What d'ya think, you're 18
years old or something?" The final shot reads: "Answers: John Hancock IRAs, Variable Life, Mutual Funds."

Financial fuck-ups everywhere will swallow "Answers" just to stifle
demeaning Dave. All the new spots—a $44,000 couple (the stats re-
veal she's a stay-at-home) buying their first house; a $65,000, one-
child couple planning their own business—are based on this problem/
solution structure in which money-made angst is juxtaposed against
hard, *Dragnet*-style facts. Naked numbers, whether in a Dewar's profile or a personals ad, make irresistible reading. By squeezing life into
quickie categories, the Hancock spots carry the promise that problems
can be solved as neatly.

An agency spokesman says Hancock's campaign will span the lifestyle spectrum. An unwed mother here, a divorced dad with custody
there? Whatever your TV-movie problem, financial psychoservices are
the answer.

February 18, 1986

Mr. Liberty

Lee Iacocca has been riding high since the Statue of Liberty hoopla, and now he's cashing in his commemorative mint chips. In an ad to introduce the America (what else?) series of Omni and Horizon cars, Lee strolls through a Chrysler plant telling it like it is: "The small-car buyer delivered his challenge to the American carmaker loud and clear. 'Give me a better car at a better price and I'll stop buying imports.' I say, fair enough. The monkey's on our back."

Unfazed by his confused reference to drug addiction, a crew of workers gathers 'round. A foreman nods his head, a welder gives thumbs-up to Lee's spiel: "That's why Chrysler put together the America Project: Workers, engineers, suppliers, all working together." Now some 50 folks are following the Chairman—hardhats, suits, women, blacks, and finally white-coated engineers, who get to stand closest to him. The whole Chrysler team has decided to take $710 off the sticker price, making their cars competitive with the Yugo and Hyundai: "Maybe that puts the monkey on *their* back," Lee bloops again.

The spot will run only three weeks. "We never run Iacocca ads long. He'd lose his effectiveness," says Chrysler's agency man. "We use him only for big issues," like "this new philosophy of pitching in." But Lee's workers seem less entranced with cooperation than with the celebrity boss man—while Lee looks at us, they look at him; they nod in recognition, as if they'd use the same words if they could. Up yours, Republican kingmakers! the ad says—Lee's the People's Choice.

Not quite. A UAW spokesman in Detroit says that while the union is "behind the America cars as import-fighters, we're not impressed by his display of patriotism. Chrysler is probably the worst of the carmakers in its fervor for scouring the Far East for foreign parts." But as Iconacoccagraphy, the ad's sum is greater than the parts.

May 6, 1986

Let them drink Coke.

Hands Down

In a tastefully austere rec room of the future, a granddad and his young grandson are watching some home video on a giant screen. It's that historic day in 1986, Gramps explains, when Hands Across America raised "enough money so people wouldn't be hungry or homeless anymore." "People were hungry once?" the child asks. With a faraway look in his eyes, Gramps replies, "Once."

The pair walks off, but two cans of Coke, old and new, remain on a table, their blood-red color and the sugar that burbles beneath the only signs of life in this well-fed but sterile future. In 30 seconds, this Hands co-sponsor zaps the futuristic Pepsi spots joshing that Coke won't last to 2010.

Coke knows we don't mind their plugging themselves for charity; in fact, we *want* them to. Corporate logos, like the faces of Cosby or Kenny Rogers, are the imprimaturs that make '80s "protest" permissible. In return, we make it safe for corps to sell.

Hands's other co-sponsor, Citibank, advertises the event with your basic warm, reach-out cliché: a mother's hand shows her daughter's hand how to play the piano, a basketball team slaps five. Citibank—which won't unhand its South African investments and wanted to exclude people with small checking accounts from using human tellers—comes off as the people-who-need-people bank.

In these one-shot, big shot charity events, the only villain is fate. Even Reagan, taker of school lunches from children, is asked to join hands. It's nice to refurbish the Statue of Liberty and raise money for the hungry. What's nauseating is the happy hum of machinery. Our mega-charities rebuke Iran: We are not the great Satan, our marketing geniuses assure us. We'd just like to buy the world a Coke.

May 27, 1986

Touchy-Feely, Inc.

"Fears & Fantasies of the American Consumer," a major study by ad agency D'Arcy Masius Benton & Bowles, has turned up the sort of unearthshaking statistoids that newspaper lifestyle sections crave: "50 percent of Americans admit their lives are more stressful than five years ago, but they also feel their lives are more satisfying." (Another finding suggests the kind of contentedness: "Watching TV is the #1 source of pleasure and satisfaction.")

But the section on how advertisers can use the findings is juicy indeed. The study discovered, for instance, that more than money, sex, or careers, people care about people. F & F waxes on about emotional ties and, proving that ad people are almost people too, recommends: "Sensitive portrayal of this potent emotional force in people's lives offers virtually unlimited opportunity for campaign and strategy development." People "aren't simply out for themselves"; one in three has daydreamed about finding a cure for cancer. So: "Show characters in ads helping each other." Sex ads may become dinosaurs. "There is far more promise of empathy with couples who are sharing experiences, being friends." As for how to reach the single male, apparently the most miserable of cohorts, F & F suggests showing "situations that are closer to the insecure, stressful reality."

Whatever the dream, wherever it leads the heart, show "the product helping to bring people closer together." If this study carries clout, we'll be seeing more ads urging us to Reach Out and Touch Someone. As *SCTV* says, "It's better than living with them."

July 15, 1986

Defense Spending

How Advertising Deals With Death by Product

Our relationship to brand names is an intimate one. They give us a sense of continuity, a synthetic tradition. When the brands that are supposed to be the best thing about living in America are threatened, or worse, when they threaten us, we feel the absurdist whack of modern life. The chance of being murdered by the pain-reliever you swear by strikes with a terror that goes beyond the objective odds.

Odds are you'll never encounter a contaminated Polar B'ar, cyanide-laced Jell-O, Accent, or Slice—or even an exploding bottle of Slice, caused by fermentation of the *real* fruit juice. But tampering, terrorism, and, that old reliable, corporate chicanery are now so prevalent that they've spawned a whole new breed of TV commercial—the defense ad. The mission: to counter negative impressions left by those sourpusses on the nightly news. From Madison Avenue's point of view, the news is just advertising by the other side. Success in overcoming bad press depends largely on whether the product crisis has legs: Financial scandals have a broadcast half-life of about two days; terrorism is a hit soap opera.

E. F. Hutton's is probably the most sophisticated of the new defense ads. The investment house, which pleaded guilty last year to 2000 counts of fraud stemming from a check-kiting scheme, hired Bill Cosby to clean up its image. The pitchman for Coke, Jell-O, Ford, star of the top TV show, author of the bestselling book, blesses Hutton (for a reported $3 million) not only with his media cachet, but with copy he helped create that turns a corrupt image to advantage: this is one aggressive company.

"Here's E. F. Hutton's annual report," Cosby coos. "Now don't worry—I'm not going to read it cover to cover. I just want to point out *one* phrase, a phrase that comes up time and time again: '*Serving* [pause] the needs of the client.' " If you ever suspected that behind the all-around great guy's twinkly eyes lay a hint of threat, just watch Cos bully you softly: "I challenge you to find a better investment firm. E. F. Hutton—because [pause, raises eyebrows, looks cute] it's my *money*."

When E. F. Hutton talks now, if people really listen, they'll hear: Yes, we did something wrong, but we did it for our clients, for *you* (Wall Street's version of "Hey, I took da heat for you, I went up da river"). "Because it's my *money*" could be the tagline for the '80s.

Ad admissions really got going in 1978 when Jimmy Stewart came on TV to clean up after Firestone, whose tires kept blowing up and killing people. The fatherly icon chatted on about how he swung on a Firestone tire as a boy, about what a good fellow Harvey Firestone was. But no one bought it—the company still refused to recall the killer radials. (Only an eventual recall and a new high-tech ad campaign restored company honor.) A scandal-hungry press, stronger regulatory agencies (which largely didn't exist before the early '70s), and plenty of product problems have combined to make the defense ad a staple of TV's daily drama. Times have changed—but product-angst transcends even the current pro-business atmosphere.

In a way, all advertising is defense advertising: Usually its songs and dances are excruciatingly fine-tuned so as not to bore, offend, or provoke us to ridicule. Ads designed specifically to restore confidence should do all that, but, with a lot of help from market research, they must also decide whether to stonewall hard or stonewall soft. The first post-crisis step for every product is to suspend advertising. On return, companies play one of the following defense gambits.

Divert and Launch: Only 30 percent of consumers remembered the Contac capsule tamperings (compared to the 80 percent who recalled the Tylenol murders). So when Contac returns to the tube, with an ad budget up from $12 million to $20 million, they'll treat the more tamper-resistant caplet as a "new product launch," rather than as a Tylenol-style solution to a problem. (Excedrin, whose cyanide-laced capsules did result in deaths, is resuming ads this week—for its tablets.)

To avoid associations with terrorism, the Italian government will also use a happy-time technique when it advertises for tourists for the first time since 1972. Ads will emphasize the "little-known, the undiscovered Italy," i.e., not the Rome airport. "Yes, we're thinking let's not push Rome, let's not rub their noses in it," says Italy's U.S. account executive. He believes the strategy will work: "The American memory is short."

Let's Talk About It: But if memories linger, you could be forced to frankness. After TWA Flight 847 was hijacked from Athens, the well-known "Come Home to Greece" campaign was born. "Unaided awareness" of the country as a destination spot rose from zero to 22 percent, says Simos Dimas of the Greek National Tourist Organization. But then in April, four people were blown out of a TWA plane over Greece. The flight originated in Rome, but in the American mind, it might as well have taken off from the Acropolis. It was time to talk. In a new spot, E. G. Marshall spoke the taboo word—"The recent *terrorist* act . . . was not a Greek incident"—as the copy scrolled over the screen. (TV defense ads use the written word to lend authority. But seriousness is risky business, and a scroll looks like a civil defense emergency—the Dalkon shield IUD scrolled only when it was ordered to publicize the deadline for filing injury claims.)

Many ad people consider Greece's terrorism spot "a debacle," only reminding people of the reason for fear. But Dimas counters, "We don't accept this advertising garbage. It's repugnant to say that because something is irrational we'll deal with it irrationally." And what's more rational than free air time? "The spot resulted in $10 to $15 million worth of free advertising on *Nightline* and other programs," he says. "The ad's sole purpose was to get exposure and refute the arguments."

Tylenol, of course, has become the model of open crisis talk and smart marketing. It was Gerber's bad luck that complaints about glass in its baby food started pouring in shortly after Tylenol's tampering troubles. Gerber wouldn't pull its product and resisted advertising. But flagging sales and daily phone surveys showing "high consumer awareness" of the problem finally convinced Gerber to shift from hard stonewall to modified Let's Talk. The company president appeared in an ad (Gerber considered scrolling but decided a fearful message should be "personalized" with a talking head). He didn't say "glass" or even "problem," only "concern," but he appeared. And in the context of advertising, that was tantamount to modeling a hair shirt. Sales have been slowly increasing.

Catching Flights with Honey *and* Vinegar: Pan Am, which had just opened seven new routes to the Terror Continent, couldn't afford to wait for either of the above strategies to work. So it tried both. The airlines brought on *its* president to introduce the "ALERT program" of extra security precautions. Research found that people would appreciate the security more than they'd be turned off by its mention. Pan Am simultaneously hit with "incentive advertising" (go to Europe now, get a free trip for a friend later). Bookings are improving. But not as rapidly as British Airways', which was badly hurt after Maggie Thatcher backed our bombing of Libya. Pouring honey only, BA simply threw money at people in contest giveaways: 5200 free flights, the use of an entire Concorde for a day, a five-year lease on a London townhouse, and so on. "To emphasize security is very dangerous," a BA spokesman says, "because the next day something could happen."

The Glowing Report: You can stonewall with concrete only when you're enormous, multifaceted, and no one cares about the problem (GE ads can utterly ignore the corporation's defense contract scams), or when no one remembers the problem (only 15 years later could ads baptize DOW "Agent Orange" Chemical as a Peace Corps for concerned college kids). Also, if someone else is in trouble but his product is similar to yours, you can push spurious distinctions. After Chernobyl, the U.S. Committee for Energy Awareness ran full-page ads saying, essentially, "our nukes are better than their nukes." The claims had been deemed credible in "nearly 200 mall interviews." And the copy had advertising's reassuring rhythms: "Safe, reliable operations. Achieved because of a built-in protective system. . . ."

No one strategy works in every crisis. There are too many variables—the news play, the marketplace, public sympathy or antipathy, whether the company cleans house as well as image (as the SEC is requiring E. F. Hutton to do). Reality still counts. But simple honesty—"We got a problem and we're doing X, Y, and Z about it"—is inevitably the tack of last resort. Rather, most defense ads do what America does best—sell deodorant.

July 22, 1986

Rock of Agents

The theological trend is away from born-again fervor and toward secular fiscalism: capitalism as an expression of inner spiritual growth. These faithful don't have their own cable channel yet, but they receive dozens of short broadcast messages daily in the form of financial services ads. Mastercard's slogan, "Master the Possibilities," is apparently est-inspired. Merrill Lynch's new "Your World Should Know No Boundaries" campaign takes us to God's country, complete with a resurrected divine bovine. ("The bull is back!") But of all the campaigns, Shearson Lehman Brothers's "Minds Over Money" most clearly sets forth the new religious dogma.

The latest spot shows a large rock meeting a massive slab of steel. "We believe that between a rock and hard place," says a gravelly voiceover, "is a solution searching to be found." Suddenly a crack appears, a tunnel of light through which the camera flies, skimming the heavens, where financial options reside. "Seeking what others don't seek is capitalism at its best, and why you'll never look at a hard decision quite the same again."

About the time it became safe to say Praise the Lord, it also became okay to say "capitalism" in a TV commercial. "You couldn't have said it in the '60s, the '70s, or even the early '80s," says Bruce Nelson of Madris, Nelson & Colleagues, creator of the campaign. Now you can even be a capitalist about the word: "Whoever stakes the claim, owns it. We wanted to be spokespeople for this idea."

Shearson is targeting both "the *serious* investor" and its own brokers, who'd best shape up to keep up in a vastly more complex financial environment. "Five years ago, before deregulation, financial services meant mostly stocks and bonds," says co-creator Ira Madris. "Today, Shearson offers 200 products. The client/broker relationship is key: working in tandem for your money life. As a client, what's most important after my health? My money." And upon this rock ye shall build a portfolio.

November 25, 1986

Car-nal Knowledge

There's a second generation of patriotic ads more seductive and less obvious than the Miller/Bud/Chrysler blitz. These new spots—the Night Belongs to Michelob, Coke Classic, 501 jeans—are more like patriotic sex. The hook, as in Chevy's Heartbeat of America campaign, is the connection between personal and national passion.

Paced to some good rock (but backed by a macabre "heartbeat" thumping stethoscopically), Chevrolet's ads feature folks looking a little weary—until a Chevy zooms by, like a mysterious woman. Imagining themselves at the wheel, their blood suddenly boils. "Every ad creates tension and then release from the encounter with the car," explains a spokesman for the agency, Campbell-Ewald. Cars are carnal: One ad's beaming time-lapsed street lights, he suggests, are "the bloodstream of the country," while the red traffic lights are "the blood corpuscles." Whenever a convertible top goes up or down, like clothes, a sexual encounter is likely around the bend. Our Bodies, Our Cars.

And Our Cars, Our Country. It's the intimacy of these spots that distinguishes them from the Miller/Chrysler crowd—woozy with sunshine, those ads felt Republican. But in the Michelob/Chevy Springsteenian offspring, America meets Attitude: sexual heat, fast cities, overcast afternoons and ominous nights. One Heartbeat spot includes, as Iacocca never would, a Las Vegas sign announcing "Boy lesque." These Chevy folks could well be Reagan people, but they inhabit the realm of the senses: Heartbeat is an intimate way of saying Heartland (and an oblique dig at the "heartless" Japanese).

But these ads also touch a place in memory—when the family car was a Chevy, when equating Chevrolet with America was a reflex. This is nostalgia made fresh: "It's a more contemporary version of 'See the USA in your Chevrolet,' " the agency spokesman admits. "If you're going to say Heartbeat of America, you'd better be pretty hip or you're going to be laughed at." Some of us laugh, but not most. Research is turning up the desired response: "I would consider buying a Chevy whereas I wouldn't have before."

January 20, 1987

Big Apple

Like the rest of the world, Apple is moving toward the money, seemingly a grim process for the former happy-face computer company. In the somber, hyper-"real" tone of the John Hancock insurance ads (made by the same director, Joe Pykta), Apple's new business spots all feature two white male executives: one hasn't been initiated into the miracles of Macintosh, the other initiates. On a late-night plane in first class, two strangers bemoan the fact that, even now, they're hard at work. "You'd think when you get to this point, things would get easier," says one, a ringer for Felix Rohatyn. The other, a dumpy, older exec is nearly apoplectic that the snazzy graphics in Felix's report were done in-house on a Mac. "If we farmed them out," Felix says knowingly, "I couldn't afford to ride up here."

Apple's earlier spots—extravaganzas like "1984" and "Lemmings"—were about rebelling against the IBM monolith, and they were done with humor. The stomach-clenching tension is still there, but the company heroes have changed from bright eccentrics bold enough to break ranks to a couple of guys worrying about deadlines. And they're guys. Apple used to seem the humanistic computer company, welcoming to all—especially women. Now you see women and blacks only in another group of Apple spots aimed at teachers, parents, and students.

Caging the company image behind pinstripes coincides with the departure of former Apple chairman Steven Jobs and with the company's change of agencies from Chiat/Day to BBDO. "We see even more of a shift to business in the future," says an Apple spokeswoman. "As I've heard John Sculley [Apple chairman and CEO] say, 'Business is where the money is.' " And giving businessmen heartburn over the odds that a competitor will edge them out unless they buy your product is, as always, where the business is.

February 3, 1987

Mass Mascot

Every season or so, a new animal, animated character, or other anthropomorphic concoction comes along in an ad, and grownups go gaga, humming the jingle, buying the T-shirts, and invoking the character in daily conversation. The latest mass mascot is Mac Tonight, devised to up dinner "traffic" for McDonald's in So-Cal. When he hit last winter, Mac won cult status—the answer to a *Jeopardy!* question, star of a possible TV show.

Now he's going national, crooning *Mack the Knife*, reconstituted with burger lyrics. (The Brecht/Weill tune was used with permission, as it was for a '64 Schlitz ad.) The spots are finger-snappers, as Mac— quarter-moon head, jazzy body—floats on a cloud over a fantastical city playing a baby grand or zooms through a surrealistic carnival. It looks animated, but it's a real man in the moon, and the props are a lifesize theatrical set. So visually unusual, Mac at first doesn't seem to fit the ad mold.

But Mac Tonight packages several familiar media trends: (1) '30s and '50s nostalgia; (2) cabaret culture, which implies all sorts of license, but is Republican precious; (3) the Bill Murray lounge-lizard goof on that; (4) the Bruce Willis nuance on *that*—L.A. smoothie as good ol' boy; (5) the emerging middle-American acceptance of urban

Mac Tonight: up past Ronald's bedtime.

nightlife. The night may belong to Michelob, but now it's mellow enough for McDonald's.

Spuds is another commercial coolster whose renown grows; the latest Video Storyboard Tests, which measure ad recall, found: "For the first time in 10 years, the Miller Lite campaign has been outperformed by another light beer campaign—Spuds MacKenzie for Bud Light." But not everyone knows and loves Spuds: one seven-year-old girl thinks it's sick that a pit bull rides a surfboard in a poster. That's the rumor plaguing Bud—quick to note that he's an English bull terrier, a gentle breed.

The mass mascot is older than Speedy Alka-Seltzer. But lately they seem to hurl through the tube: dancing raisins, Joy's talking lemon, Max Headroom, Spuds, and Stroh's earlier canine guzzler, Alex. Alex, Max, Mac, MacKenzie—these smacky sounds must draw unconscious friendliness from our souls. The popularity of animals among the mascots can be explained by pet mania, especially when admen clothe them. Also, studies show the mere presence of animals make humans seem more trustworthy. Spuds's fame is particularly in tune with our blonde obsessions: he's a Donna Rice party animal, very Florida, while his blandness amid the hullabaloo is redolent of the Vanna White vacuum at the center of celebrity.

Nonanimal mascots are equally ripe for our projection. While the dancing raisins were clearly black, they could flaunt more "soul" than any TV human. Since Mac Tonight must be moonwhite, he's played grayer: some perceive him as black (like Louis Armstrong, who first popularized *Mack*); probably more think he's white, i.e., Bobby Darin. Without a black *person*, only blacklike characters, whites can more easily enjoy stereotypes they're supposed to suppress.

Whether animal or vegetable, ad mascots appeal because they don't harbor the greed we expect of their corporate owners. When actors do ads, one often wonders, how much did they get paid to spout this drivel? But as creatures of agency Frankensteins, mascots are companies' unassailable version of themselves. Curiously, this run of cute corporate characters has increased since we elected one for president.

September 22, 1987

Takeover Makeover

Vidalia, Louisiana. A ramshackle town whose unemployed inhabitants are video versions of the sharecroppers Walker Evans photographed in the Depression-era South. To haunting music, men sit on old tires in front of empty stores; a mother and her daughter stare into space, catatonically. In 1983, unemployment was 16 percent, a voiceover tells us. Hopes for a hydroelectric plant were dashed: "Most investment bankers never heard of the town of Vidalia, much less wanted to invest in it." But suddenly the music goes upbeat; a man, his son, and a dog hike up a sunny road; and we're told that three years later, thanks to high-yield (junk) bonds from Drexel Burnham, plant construction began, helping to reduce unemployment by 20 percent (i.e., 12 percent were jobless).

We *like* this Vidalia. We're pleased that a '30s-style myth really exists. But a funny thing—this sorry town of photogenic po' folk isn't Vidalia. The ad was filmed outside Ft. Smith, Arkansas. "The people are mad," says Vidalia mayor Sam Randazzo. "We have a progressive little town. We have modern buildings. The picture is very distorted—I don't know why they did it." Vidalia's high unemployment, he adds, was due mainly to a statewide recession in oil; by '86, when oil picked up, so did jobs.

One reason Drexel's agency, Chiat/Day, chose Arkansas for its Tobacco Road location was because the state has a right-to-work law. Drexel, the most controversial investment bank on Wall Street, needed some down-in-the-dirt-with-the-people grit. Its first TV campaign ever comes as the feds, reportedly after a yearlong investigation of Drexel, are expected to file charges within the next few months. The probe is expected to focus on Drexel's in-house genius, Michael Milken, who pioneered the use of junk bonds (high-interest, high-risk financing). Mike "Milk 'em Dry" is the messianic moneymaker who almost single-handedly produced the takeover and merger mania. (Michael Douglas's rap in *Wall Street*, inciting stockholders to smash management, could have been Milken's own.) His junk financing helped create raiders like Carl Ichan and Ron Perelman. One reason U.S.

Is it the Depression, or is it Drexel?

Attorney Rudolph Guiliani cut that sweet deal with Ivan Boesky was because he was after Drexel's main man.

But a second spot would also have us believe that Drexel's dollars go for the helpless: A sad little girl sings as the camera pans an empty playground, swings still moving. After Drexel comes to the rescue, financing the prohibitively high cost of liability insurance, real kids fill the yard, romping and laughing. Does Drexel have a do-good social program? Not at all. Poor people and playgroundless kids were chosen as "examples of innovative financing through junk bonds," says a Chiat spokeswoman.

Whatever Drexel's virtues, they're dwarfed by the damage the firm has done to thousands of employees who've been laid off because of mergers, management "restructuring" to fend off takeovers, and liquidations of raided companies. There's still debate on the role junk bonds played in the market crash by unnaturally jacking up stock prices. Worse, Drexel has been known to chomp on troubled companies that ask its help; according to *Newsweek*, it's now digesting Western Union.

Drexel says the old fat cats need slimming down, that its junk bonds have capitalized many medium-size companies that establishment financiers would have cut off. Largely true. But unlike companies that have developed community ties over decades—no matter how greedy their management may also be—nouveau fat cats don't even have to try to appear socially responsible. Drexel, so used to spinning gold out of straw, is now trying to lull us by telling grim fairy tales.

December 15, 1987

Anxiety Calls

If you're not a go-getter, you're an asshole, probably a fired one. "What you're telling me is I gotta scrap four data networks and start over—is that what you're telling me?" a boss humiliates an underling at a black-tie dinner. "I can't pull new customers out of a hat!" a businessman defends himself to his partner. "Ben," the partner scolds, "that's your job!" The ads end with music that sounds like prison doors slamming. But on the last few notes, you can hear a little upbeat ring-a-ling: there is light at the end of the tunnel—*if* you make the right choice.

AT&T's 10 ball-stomping ads (and more on the way) are aimed at employees who buy office equipment and the folks empowered to make them twist slowly in the wind for making the wrong choice. Fear has been used to sell to women for years: did she leave spots on the dishes, rings on the collar? AT&T's middle-level managers are the housewives of business. Will his teleconference connection please him? Did he hear that sales can't network with marketing?

Men have always been humiliated at the office; they just didn't want to come home after a day of quiet desperation and watch it again on TV. Ads once used power to sell to men. Years ago, a guy might have put his feet on his spacious desk and crowed, "Ya know, I used to have problems getting calls transferred from sales, but I got me some

Young Turk kills aging hack for AT&T.

AT&T, and now—Whoa! Gotta run, I have a golf game"—he winks—"with the new district manager."

In AT&T's world, there are basically two kinds of middle-level types: the young Turk for whom the job is a stopover on his way up, and the institutional hack. In the most devastating spot, the Turk, with rolled-up shirt-sleeves, heatedly informs the hack (a middle-aged man who looks like he'd rather be telling dirty jokes) that IBM PCs are has-been. "You're still blowing your budget on stand-alones!" "Listen," the older guy hackily tries to cajole, "you sound like a commercial." To which the Turk, in one angry swath, removes the hack's dick, stands tall for AT&T, and validates the ad industry: "*You* listen! These are facts!!" The hack is the Turk's warning sign; the Turk is the hack's nightmare—he'll move up and I'll be here forever. A product can't cure that fear—but if these spots leave you believing that, that's okay.

"We're not trying to scare the shit out of you," maintains John Doig, creative director at Ogilvy & Mather, who helped design this campaign as well as AT&T's previous one with the frantic hand-held camerawork. "We're trying to strike a familiar chord. For years, AT&T has put their arm around you, and encouraged you to reach out and touch somebody. But the way we in advertising have portrayed business has been fake. The business atmosphere is usually charged with passion rather than friendliness. By showing that AT&T understands the problems of business, we can show that we're able to offer solutions."

In an MCI counterad, a woman boasts that her boss told her not to change phone systems, it's been sounding so good lately. But she changed it six months ago to MCI, she says, smiling so contentedly she might have just scored a detergent victory.

Whatever AT&T's claims to superior quality, I've got to be skeptical. I have a simple AT&T home phone, less than a year old. If it's nudged in a certain way, the button that regulates ring loudness will shift itself from "high" to "off." Also, it's been designed so that the hang-up button is located right near the ear, so that if, say, I laugh too hard, the phone goes dead. But AT&T has another ad, from yet another division, that tells me in so many words, I ought to be grateful—other companies sell shoddy merchandise.

April 19, 1988

Bull

Even though Merrill Lynch's new slogan is "A Tradition of Trust," Larry Speakes didn't *have* to resign his job as ML communications director under a cloud. His happy-quote habit as Reagan's spokesman works with, not against, the happy history that Merrill is showing us right now in its ads. By odd coincidence, both Reagan's former employer, GE, and Speakes's are running airbrushed re-creations of their humble beginnings, when little guys worked their way up in a sepia-toned world.

Merrill's old-time ads take us away from scandals and crashes to focus on the gung-ho heart of Charles Merrill, circa 1915. In the mail room, a wire-rimmed bespectacled employee is eagerly reading "Mr. Merrill's" reports as a know-nothing colleague jibes him: "Hey, what do *you* know, Mr. Big Shot? Our job is to mail 'em, not to read 'em." The nearsighted go-getter parrots company philosophy: "Well, Tim, if I don't read 'em, I'll never get out of the mail room." "Charlie Merrill," says the voiceover, "believed in doing his homework." In another ad, we're told, "Charlie Merrill said, 'Find the best people and train them well.'"

Maybe those were Charlie's own words and not a copywriter's, but ads like this are the small-screen version of the made-up quote. Rather than cover for an utterance that wasn't made, the corp-quote usually paints an America that didn't exist. Benevolent patriarchs at the helm, worker-manager harmony, team spirit: you don't need to make up quotes—gestures, glances, adorable eyeglasses will do. These "Heritage" ads are extra useful after the crash, which taught us that the Big Boys make Wall Street unsafe for the little people. Companies like Merrill must function like politicians: Merrill, which began with a multitude of small investors, is now one of world's largest investment firms. But, like George Bush at the wheel of a Mack truck, it's still claiming to represent the common man.

Likewise, GE hauls us back to the past—before nuclear weapons, toxic wastes, and other stuff they'd rather you not be reminded of—in a couple of major productions from the Norman Rockwell Learn-To-Draw a Corporate Identity Catalogue. A bunch of guys in suspenders are playing baseball to a Joplinesque beat. "On a summer's evening in 1924, perhaps the most significant game in the history of baseball was played." Unlikely, but, "On that night a band of GE engineers ushered in the era of night baseball." A mousey guy, also wearing wire-rimmed glasses (the yellow ties of yesterday's yuppies), throws the switches—let there be light!

But don't let it shine in the shadows. The EPA has labeled GE as "potentially responsible" for contributing to numerous toxic dumps. According to INFACT, the group that led the Nestlé boycott and is now boycotting GE, nuclear weapons-related work makes up nearly

12 percent of GE's annual sales; and during the Reagan administration—which has included GE officials past and present—the company's prime weapon contracts increased threefold.

Nor was corruption a new GE product of 1985, when it pled guilty to 108 counts of filing false claims to the DOD. GE was cutting corners even before the significant baseball game, even when Reagan was hawking its electrics. According to a petition filed with the FCC opposing GE's purchase of RCA, GE had been involved in civil or criminal violations in 1911, 1932, 1936, 1937, 1941, 1944, 1947, 1948, 1949, 1952, 1953, and 1954. "INFACT has made many erroneous allegations about GE," says a GE spokesman. "We certainly have no intention of rebutting or debating on an allegation by allegation basis."

Had Reagan known that Speakes helped him save face with Gorbachev, the former GE pitchman probably would have told the Merrill man, "That's swell!" It's a tradition.

May 3, 1988

God's Little Agency

God is the creative director of heaven's ad agency; His clients include Perrier, NutraSweet, Smucker's, Gallo, and a few other big sellers. Amid frolicking animals, beaches at sunset, and quite a number of Catholic schoolgirls, these products appear on earth to spread the Word, imagewise.

True, Perrier's ads are positively divine, but whenever they come on I feel like smacking the smugness off its beatific face. "What if an ancient wind had blown north instead of south?" a deep voice resounds to the classy toot of a flute. "Suppose Jupiter had never aligned with Mars? There may never have been a place called Vergeze, or a spring called Perrier. But luckily, everything happened just right. It's perfect. It's Perrier." Yes, the images are perfect and lusciously shot:

11 ideal French men in berets, nine smiling schoolgirls, several stone houses you'd kill for, three red-cheeked peasant women, three country dogs, one cat, young lovers, and more carbonated bubbles than the Republican Convention had balloons.

Lucky I mentioned Republicans. The Creator of Perrier's spots—as well as the tonally similar Gallo Christmas and wedding spots—is Hal Riney, who was also the brain behind Reagan's "Morning in America" ad. Riney also serves as the voiceover of these spots—his deep gruff voice, pocketed by deep, halting pauses, makes him the stand-in for the voice of God. Riney's not involved in George Bush's ads or in his convention video, but the Republicans and other brand names have learned from him the art of the pastoral pitch.

Smucker's also uses the everything-is-right-as-it-is approach for its jellies; a muesli cereal (I've seen it a dozen times but the brand name's lost amid majestic hills) uses it to hype its whole grains. But after Perrier, NutraSweet is the most unabashedly Panglossian. In a series of ads designed to convince us that its artificial sweetener is more natural than mother's milk, they pull out all the symbols to evoke a time before things like artificial sweeteners were ever dreamt of: Girls riding horses in the sunset, a one-pump gas station, an angelic little girl drinking a glass a milk, an Amish family and their horse-drawn carriage! Skipping Catholic schoolgirls followed by a laughing nun!

The conceit, as the voiceover says, is that NutraSweet "wasn't supposed to start a revolution, but it did. . . . It let people enjoy life just a little more."

That's the trick in the hill-and-dale hype: A grandiose claim—NutraSweet's revolution, Perrier's perfection—is revealed in all humility. The ads are merely photo ops for God's gifts.

But these ads actually goose our most anthropocentric reflexes. Perrier especially jibes with the popular scientific theory that if earth were just one percent closer to or farther from the sun, we would've ended up a hot dead planet like Venus or a cold dead one like Mars. Imagine. Or, if it took events of such import as Jupiter aligning with Mars (utter fancy, perhaps derived from "Aquarius") to create Perrier, this must be the best of all possible worlds and waters—the only mortal act required is boutiquing it. It flatters man as well as Perrier. We're just perfect, and you can't make the world better than it is.

The past-perfect come-on is especially useful for Perrier, teetering on the precipice of white-wine-and-brie caricature. Now we know that Perrier harkens *much* farther back from Yupdom.

NutraSweet finds the right-leaning rub-off beneficial for other reasons. The company says extensive studies have never been able to substantiate the hundreds of complaints people have made about adverse health effects following the consumption of NutraSweet. But the ads say, don't even wonder if it's OK to soak your innards in a chemical— you are doing the right thing, the thing human beings *would* have done since time immemorial.

The pastoral pitch, of course, is Bush's pitch—America is peachy as is. Ads like this, regardless of the producer's politics, are naturally conservative. It's not just that they glorify the past but that they define perfection by nature's cycles and fecundity. God preaches the status quo.

September 20, 1988

The Tie-Ins That Bind

The Olympic Games are advertising's chance to tie Corporate America with Team America with Family America and You the Achiever into one big irresistible package. These Olympics, says *Ad Age,* are "the biggest event in the history of TV advertising"—$550 million to buy 30 hours of commercials in a 180-hour telecast, not counting the constant product placement of warm-up suits, sneakers, and the flash of Omega's logo every millisecond a winning swimmer smashes into the end of the pool.

And among these 3500 or so spots are many "tie-ins"—ads that pair unrelated products in a special promotion, or less formally, ads that tie a product to the event, either in an official sponsorship (costing

Olympic advertisers an estimated $338 million this year) or by hitching a free ride. But what tie-ins really tie together is not product to product or product to event, but *you* to product/event. The heart-hurtling Olympic emotion of individual achievement—as opposed to the grind-'em-to-slurry ethos of, say, the Superbowl—oozes like ectoplasm for 16 days, just waiting for ad alchemy to turn it into something you can wear, hold, or swallow.

This year's largest Olympic promotion is McDonald's and Coca-Cola's (a nearly inseparable duo), which ties each to the Games and then back to consumers in a loop of lovable lucre. It's called "When the U.S. Wins, You Win." If the inside of your two-liter Coke or Sprite bottle cap says "200-meter freestyle," for instance, and if the U.S. wins a gold in that event, you win a Big Mac (fries for a silver, a Coke for a bronze). To purchase is to pledge allegiance.

McCoke predicts that more than 65 million consumers—nearly one in four Americans—will win food prizes. When America wins, McDonald's and Coke win. But in a joint press release the companies insist the promo is just good-guyism, created "to give a maximum number of consumers a personal stake in the U.S. athletes' victories in Seoul." By the by, after their similar promo in '84, "Many winning athletes later told us that fans thanked them for the free Big Mac they won."

Seagram's Coolers brings you the most *Family Tie*-ins. Seagram's originally wanted to be the official cooler sponsor, but while allowing beer sponsors, the Olympic Committee put a cork on the cooler category. So Seagram's bypassed officialdom and splurged to "Send the Families"—paying the way for one family member of each U.S. Team athlete to Seoul. The sending part costs more than $2.5 million, says the Seagram's v.p. of marketing, while advertising and promoting this largesse runs about $7 million. The promo includes sending "the world's largest bon voyage card" and getting senators, congressmen, and mayors to hawk it (Mayor Koch led the "unveiling ceremonies"). Some 50,000 probably non-wino Americans signed it.

The ad announcing the number-one cooler's generosity follows a young track star and his dad, who rises at dawn to help him train in a bleak industrial city. *Rocky*esque shots of the boy hurdling over trash heaps are intercut with flashes of him winning in Seoul—the "before" shots in black-and-white, the imaginary victory clips in color. Why'd Seagram's do it? "To raise a mighty cheer for the honor of our country, for the glory of sport, and to show the world an American dream come true," the voiceover declares. Not for Seagram's coffers. The marketing v.p. would allow only that they'll do follow-up research to see if "it engenders more brand loyalty." The idea is for us to slug-a-lug dreamy thoughts of Family along with each "Let's party!" cooler rush.

American Express did not send the families, but it lets you think they sent the family retainers. An AmEx spot shows us the crusty old trainer who can't afford to follow his young equestrian, "Cath," to Seoul. Cath's very wealthy parents ask AmEx to reserve him a plane seat. Big deal. But there's such gushing about it, everything happens so fast, and the father and AmEx clerk look so much alike, that it seems as if AmEx pays to keep the eternal home flame burning. Visa, AmEx's arch rival in the Olympic marketing game, is not only an official sponsor (entitling them to warn in their ads that "the Olympics don't take American Express"), but is laying it on the local help in a "Mystery Shopper" campaign at 25,000 Korean stores. "Clerks who ask the mystery shoppers 'Do you have Visa' or 'I'd prefer Visa,'" says *Ad Age,* "will get cash prizes of up to $415."

We Americans—heck, even Koreans—are tied in by cash, credit card, and consumption to the indomitable will of stadium studs. Today, the Greek ideal of individualism has been pretty much reduced to choosing between Pepsi and Coke. If we don't run and dive with our heroes, we can at least drink and eat with them. Send the families, feel the heartbeat of America, add your two cents to history. It's just that this process makes family, heroism, and history taste like they come in Styrofoam containers.

October 4, 1988

The Brand with Two Brains

During the recent hubbub about whether departing Surgeon General Everett Koop would endorse mandatory restrictions on beer and wine advertising (he didn't, but he did ask that advertisers voluntarily restrain youth-oriented marketing), one ad honcho sighed with relief and said, "It would be false to suggest that the truthful advertising of alcohol is harmful." Wha?

The truthful advertising of alcohol (or of most products)—what would *that* be? It would be truthful to say that beer can get you bombed, but instead ads say it gets you babes. Yet there are other truths in advertising, and they're all about morality and mood. Right now, one company is confusing the nation with two totally opposite beer truths, each the distilled essence of its breed. Miller High Life says sacrifice for a fellow human being is the highest good, while Miller Lite says pro-wrestler-level weaseling is where it's at. These new campaigns are the two poles of beery advertising fundamentalism, suds rosa versions of Billy Graham and Jimmy Swaggart. And each comes with a long fundamentalist pedigree, evoking an agrarian America where carnivals toured the countryside and stalwart farmers, like the ones for Miller High Life, paid to watch seminaked wrestlers, like the ones for Miller Lite, act out their own fantasies of outraged honor avenged.

"I just passed Hassie McGuire's," Jim, a flat-accented farmer, tells his pals. "The corn hasn't been touched since Hank died. What do you say we help her out?" A jingle—plaintive and painful, it's been winding through my days—starts up: *What do you say to a man who never turns his back on a friend?* "Ed, we could use your combine. Thomas, we could use your truck." But the guys hem and haw. "I got 180 acres of my own," one whines. Jim stands up and stalks out: "Yeah, I guess good help *is* hard to find these days."

What do you say to a man who walks face into the wind? So don't you know it? As Jim *walks* to the widow McGuire's (rural Americans rarely walk anywhere, but maybe they do if it's into the wind), Ed drives by in his combine. "Need a lift? Goin' as far as McGuire's."

Turns out he's leading a whole darn convoy! After they've harvested her fields and toasted Jim with a Miller—*What do you sa-aay? What do you do-oo? Buy that man a Miller!*—the fortyish Hassie McGuire wipes her hands on her apron and looks Jim in the eye: "Hank would've been real proud of you, Jim." "Not as proud as he was of you, Hassie." My eyes watered—until a friend asked, "So who gets to sleep with the farmer's wife?"

As in a companion spot (a race-car pit-crew member saves a competitor's ass by pointing out that his rear wing is busted), the drama is resolved in a tableau formed beneath the bottle's label—through the golden sheen of the beer, the group reunites in silhouette as if in Heaven.

"Buy that man a Miller" seems to pour from the same beery sentimental/patriotic genre keg as Budweiser's or High Life's own, mid-'80s "Made the American Way" campaign. But these new ads, so bold in their story detail, tug the heart much harder. And unlike their Reagan-era predecessors, the moment of truth comes not through savoring work well done, but through personal sacrifice. A thousand pints of lite.

This is New Traditionalism, and the Miller PR department even repeats the New Trad slogan, à la Quaker Oats ads and George Bush's rhetoric: "These ads," the PR folks say, "are a celebration of the right thing to do."

But whether rewarded for success or for sacrifice, the prize is the same: *Buy that man a Miller!* The best we can do is *buy* something. This little refrain doesn't merely reinforce that American reflex, it also makes a virtue out of the *inability* to say or do anything else. It's not quite manly to put feelings into words. Better, you slide him one down the counter, nod, and walk off into the sunset.

But while high-principled High Life guys get beers bought for them, low-life Miller Lite dudes grab six-packs off the shelf and chug it before they've even screeched out of 7-Eleven's parking lot. At least, that's the truth in Lite's latest campaign, which has found its apotheosis in a World Wrestling Federation tie-in dubbed Lite-A-Mania, based on the gimmick that Jesse "The Body" Ventura can't guess the identity of "The Masked Marauder" (Bob Uecker). This campaign, the biggest promotion in the brand's history, is *so* Miller Lite—the glitzy chaos, the drop-in stars (Robert Goulet, Don Pardo)—that it's virtually invisible. *What do you say to a brand that never turns its back on a trend? What do you say to a brand that talks like it is breaking wind?* (Most men say, buy it! A survey in *Adweek* reports that men's all time favorite ad campaign is . . . Miller Lite! Bud Light, Budweiser, and Coors ads also made the testosterone top 10. Women liked Bud Light, but also Huggies and Kibbles 'n Bits.)

These campaigns, aimed at different beer-drinking markets, may seem schizoid, but only if you believe that products really possess personalities. They don't. They only possess ad campaigns, lick 'n' stick decals that can be applied or peeled off at will. Before being protested off campuses, a spring-break campaign for Miller's newest brand, Genuine Draft, was running print ads about how dudes could "scam babes," advising them to "use simple lines like . . . 'wanna get naked?' " What would Hassie and Jim say to that?

June 20, 1989

Whom Ma Bell Tolls

Between AT&T's barrage of cluster-headache commercials and U S Sprint's answer ads that giggle, "AT&T, lighten up," the viewer can reach out and call up a host of social anxieties. The financial stakes are high, and so the psychocorpodrama—all about fear of the new and dread of being made into a fool—is low.

The latest round of phone fun began on the road to Fiji. A young exec go-getter tries to call Phoenix from a phone booth, but instead gets Fiji—as illustrated by the big native who answers the phone at a tourist spot. Fiji! It's not only far away, but somehow its funny, foreign little name makes the error even worse. The go-getter is teed *off!* Well, at least he'll get credit for the wrong number, like AT&T always gives him. The operator, however, refuses, saying, "You aren't dealing with AT&T." But he wields the power of the dollar and the shorter quip: "I am *now!*"

It's the revenge of the big guy who's been mistaken—oh God!—for a little guy.

Sometimes "Fiji" arrives as part of a two-minute commercial package that includes more vignettes demonstrating how *other* phone companies are trying to put one over on you. There are real problems with some long-distance carriers, particularly when it comes to telemarketing hard sells, but AT&T throws them all in doubt. A good-looking gal representing baby-boomer enlightenment has just come home out of the rain. "The phone's ringing, I think it's him, but it's them—you know, those people who call you up and say switch from AT&T, we've got better quality. Like you try to pin them down to something and get some real numbers going. Well, I say, 'Look, just put it in writing.' Dead silence. And it just goes to show you," she says, with the hint of a nasty squint in her eyes and a nah-nah-nah in her voice— "it's still not AT&T."

Lines from other AT&T ads twist a most subtle class knife: "Was I absent the day they gave out the big savings?" "Bottom line is, I'm not buying it." "Yaddy yaddy yaddy all day long." It's not that the actors are playing elites—they are pointedly middle-class and "regular." It's that they spray business-spawned phrases as if they were mace. AT&T's heroes are amicable people who know when to access their don't-fuck-with-me data bank. They intimidate the viewer, with a soft snobbery, into not being intimidated by the hard sellers. The overall impression—enhanced by AT&T's nonstop airing of these spots—is that the whole world is against Sprint, MCI, and other low-class trash, and if you're not, you're a dupe!

Sprint's response is succinct: A woman appears in the dark and as the lights fade in says, "AT&T has left a lot of people in the dark. . . . Sprint has real operators, our fiber optics make your calls sound better than AT&T's, plus Sprint still offers better overall savings than AT&T. And we *will* put it in writing." She glances floorward, as if she's playing with fire: "AT&T, lighten up."

The ad plays on the urge many people have to tell AT&T, "Shut up already!" Its lightness undercuts Ma Bell's message to its zillions of progeny that it is very dangerous to go out and play. And while flout-ing AT&T's hegemony, Sprint's tagline—"It's a new world"—gets ad-ditional spin off the emerging "new world order" in Eastern Europe and the Soviet Union. Sprint—the very name says swift and nimble—is posing as nerve to AT&T's muscle. Clearly that's why they chose a pretty blond woman who speaks so, so softly and makes her eyes twin-kle. But why is she also so coquettish, her eyelids practically aflutter?

What's really going on on the tube is a kind of litigation lite. Unlike the "cola wars" (which often just boost Coke's and Pepsi's sales while squeezing smaller brands off the shelves), the phone wars aren't phony. In fact, it was an antitrust suit by MCI against AT&T that helped result in the divestiture of Ma Bell in 1984. Since then, AT&T's share of the $55 billion long-distance market has steadily declined, from the 100 to about 67 percent. MCI has about 13 percent and Sprint 9. (To maintain dominance, AT&T spends more than $1 mil-lion a day on advertising for all its products and services, including long-distance, making its ad budget larger than any other brand's, in-cluding McDonald's.) AT&T and Sprint have both won complaints against the other's ad claims with the Better Business Bureau. The ac-tion is hotter between MCI and AT&T. Last year, MCI sued AT&T for false and deceptive advertising (one AT&T ad, according to MCI, said that MCI serviced only 75 percent of the globe, which is true, but it showed a globe with Europe missing, wrongly implying that MCI doesn't go there). In January, AT&T countersued, saying that MCI's telemarketers, like the jerks referred to in the "Put It in Writing" cam-paign, will say anything to sign you up. An AT&T spokesman says, "They'll tell people that AT&T is going out of business, or that AT&T and MCI have merged—outlandish claims." An MCI spokeswoman says that's "baloney." So far MCI has not responded as Sprint has with an answer ad. A trial date is not yet set.

As to the actual price claims of the big three's ads, David Wagen-hauser, director of the Telecommunications Research and Action Cen-ter, a public interest group, says, "Overall—and there are exceptions to everything—AT&T is somewhat higher than the others. But in terms of advertising, I don't think any of the companies have clean hands. They all sling mud and they're all coated with it. The ads in general do little but confuse consumers, and the confusion can lead to the conclusion that 'I'm not going to look into this, I'm just going to stay with what I have,' and that may be a mistake." That's how confusion, and social angst, give AT&T the house advantage.

September 18, 1990

Beam Me Up

Desperate times call for gorgeously desperate ads. The unrelenting need for admakers to "cut through the clutter" of other commercials to make theirs stand out has recently produced two grab-ya-by-the-right-brain pratfalls by Volvo. First there was the car-crunching spot that turned out to be faked. On the other end of the Godzilla/Bambi spectrum is the sonogram of a fetus that appears to be waving its hand to hail a Volvo. In their hyperenthusiasm, each spot created its own set of PR problems. But like most all advertising, each ad is just doin' what an ad's gotta do: tell the Big Lie (if not also the smaller, fact-based ones)—namely, that the unsponsored life isn't worth living.

In the demolition spot, a monster truck called Bear Foot rolls over a row of cars, flattening them all—except the Volvo 240. As the blood-thirsty crowd in Austin, Texas, screams its disapproval, the voiceover snootily comments: "Apparently, not everyone appreciates the strength of a Volvo." The Texas attorney general filed a lawsuit when some of the 400 extras hired to play arena rednecks tipped him off that the cars were fixed. Under the first rollover, the Volvo was crushed, so crew members reinforced a second car with two-by-fours. Not good enough. So they added steel beams—*and* weakened the roofs of rival cars.

Volvo, saying it had no idea that the cars had been altered, pulled the spot, ran newspaper ads to apologize, and paid Texas $316,250 to avoid a suit over deceptive advertising. Then Volvo's ad agency of 23 years resigned the account. But Volvo insists the idea for the ad is valid, based on the car's success in a similar 1988 contest in Vermont. (The relocation is noteworthy: If, after proving the car's safety, the ad's other goal is to reinforce the car's upscale rep by sniping at low-lifes, the dream milieu would be, according to stereotypes, yahoo Texas over yup Vermont. Austin, however, is the Vermont of Texas and the one town where you're likely to find Volvo lovers.)

If only the ad had been labeled a "dramatization," says a Volvo spokesperson, there wouldn't have been a problem. "We can demonstrate that Volvos have extremely high mechanical strength." The Vermont performance—and recent contests that tried to crunch Volvos for the postscandal thrill—substantiate it, he claims. Propping up a product for repeated takes in a long day of shooting is necessary, he says. But the Volvo flunked the test during the ad's filming, and a "dramatization" tag doesn't bridge the gap. When news shows began to use reenactments just like "reality-based" TV, reality merged more with what we want reality to be—a fudging that was a tenet of advertising long before the birth of *A Current Affair*.

Volvo, the womb on wheels

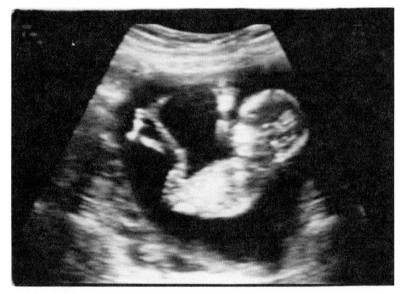

From Bear Foot to Itsy Bitsy Hand. In the sonogram ad, all that happens is that a fetus wiggles and eventually moves its hand, as if it were waving. "Is something inside telling you to buy a Volvo?" the voiceover asks.

It's implausible that Volvo was trying to make a prolife statement—if few politicians will brave that, why would a carmaker? Volvo's fetus is really working the same safety beat as Bear Foot. "An extremely high number of families with children buy Volvos," says the Volvo spokesperson. But why go beyond babies into the womb? "Motherhood and the womb are very logical extensions of the safety message," he says. The cautious Volvo has always been positioned as something of a womb-on-wheels anyway: If a product was ever going to tap the uterus as a logo (at least in the imagination), Volvo/vulva was it. And if a fetus were a value-free symbol, its use would be no more of a rip-off than any symbol is when appropriated for the market.

But, of course, a fetus isn't value-free. When you first see the ad, you might think it's a prolife spot, or a promo for *The Silent Scream,* the fetus-starring antiabortion film from a few years ago. Of the 46 phone calls and letters that Volvo has so far received (not an unusually high number, the company says), 37 protested it for being an antiabortion message, one person calling it "emotional blackmail." Some prolife postcard writers slammed it for using an "unborn child" to endorse a car. Which raises an interesting question: If prolifers don't mind using babies to pitch products, why mind a fetus? "They don't even want to consider it as a person, but as an angel," says Renee Schwalberg of the Committee To Defend Reproductive Rights. She and others criticize the ad for "attributing autonomous emotions to a fetus."

Volvo says it takes no position on abortion. They went through "hundreds of sonograms" to find this particularly lively one (*not* retouched, they add), and despite the mild fuss, they've no intention of pulling it. The ad's just doin' what an ad's gotta do, says the spokesperson: "We wanted an ad to break through the clutter."

The difference between the steel beams and the fetal hand is the difference between symptomatic lies—the sort that play with the facts—and systemic lies—the exaggerations, illusions, and fantasies that form the very language of selling. Symptomatic lies that were caught in the act litter ad history: When GM ran out of its heavily promoted Oldsmobile "Rocket Engines" in the late '70s, it substituted inferior Chevy engines. McDonald's advertised its then beef-fat-enhanced Chicken McNuggets as "100 percent chicken." Until recently, Sara Lee sold a "light" cheesecake that had more fat and as many calories as its regular version.

Rather than make specific product claims, systemic lies take the safer road of associating a brand with sex, class, or godlike reassurance. Or to use what the Better Business Bureau calls "permissible hyperbole"—that is, using obvious exaggeration to goof-proof a claim. If you're going to tell a lie, tell a big one—McDonald's will "save the universe," Bo knows diddly, or a fetus is telling you to buy a Volvo.

The reason that state attorney generals, like Texas's in the Volvo case, are poking at deceptive commercials in the first place is because the Federal Trade Commission, which is supposed to monitor advertising, was told to take the decade off by the Reagan administration— which had its own interest in the larger system of magical thinking and dramatized reality. As Reagan proved repeatedly, we *do* like to be lied to—as long as the lie comes in a pleasing guise. It's like having a wish come true.

Volvo's lies, both hard (steel beams) and soft (car beams up fetus) are not so uncommon, though they're uncommonly whammo. It's typical that the hard-fact lie gets crushed while the big emotional one drives away.

November 27, 1990

Let's Face It

Why do penis faces keep rising up out of Helms country? Camel's "Smooth Character" cartoon dromedary has been poking his phallic face around for a while now. Everyone knows what he really looks like, tee hee hee, or they do when it's pointed out. But like most mass-cult sexual icons, he eventually receded into the big billboard in the sky—until Camel really put the face in your face by having not one but five penis-face poster boys, now playing in a blues band called "The Hard Pack."

The two-month-old campaign is intended "to increase awareness" that Camels are available in boxes—which they always were, nothing new there. Each dude has a name (there's Floyd on the sax, Eddie on drums, and so on) and will eventually represent one of the hard-pack styles (lights, ultra lights, etc.). A West Coast campaign introducing Camel Ninety Nines actually pumps the Hard Pack with the slogan "Long on Smooth." Can they really, knowingly, be doing this—this industry stroked into profitability by the cover-your-genitals senator from North Carolina?

Well, it helps sales. Since R.J. Reynolds introduced the Smooth Character in late 1987, the brand has increased market share—one of the few filtered, big-name brands to do so in recent years. The idea was to go after young men, a demo that Philip Morris's Marlboro has a lock on. With 26 percent of the market, Marlboro is No. 1; with 4.3 percent, Camel ranks sixth, according to securities analyst John Maxwell. (The power of advertising: Originally, Marlboro was considered a woman's cigarette; it wasn't until 1955 that the Marlboro man was invented to change all that.) Marlboro may be macho, but Camel has *cojones*—it's as plain as the nose on its face.

Not that sex in ads is necessarily objectionable: no, better liminal than subliminal seduction. But as with Levi's Cockers, uh, Dockers ads that focused on crotches and buttocks, the Camel ads are defended by their flacks, who deny the phallic connection up and down.

"It never fails to absolutely floor me," says Maura Payne, a spokes-person for R.J. Reynolds. "People who project such lunacy onto the

The non-penis-based Joe Camel

ad—it is absolutely without merit. It would be crazy of us to include that in Old Joe's design. He is as God designed him. He is a camel, he has always been a camel. That's what camels look like." And to prove it, she sent me a photo of a camel head-on. The photo was made to muzzle sick nuisance callers like me.

But with these fleshy smooth characters popping out from every subway stop and convenience-store checkout counter, such denial—the explicit corporate sort as well as the implicit cartoony innocence of a product mascot—places the campaign in a surreal zone. We might make dumb dick jokes all the time, but when we think we notice a major corporation—one of the world's largest advertisers—doing the same, it's like catching a teacher fondling his students.

The double message—it's a dick; nope, it's a camel—can be far more potent than explicit sex or explicit wholesomeness. In fact, when I closed my eyes recently, I saw the man I was with as a life-size, flesh cigarette in blue jeans.

I did find one person—let's call him Deep Emphysema—involved with the project (though not an RJR employee) who doesn't entirely take the blame-the-camel defense. "We weren't consciously trying to develop a phallic symbol. That's not the way to attract smokers—men are the prime smokers anyway of Camels," he says, closing his eyes to the obvious. But the campaign's creators weren't unaware of what it looked like. "There were comments made and there was a resemblance, but the overall program tested so well we felt that would overshadow any negative publicity."

The Smooth Character came to this country via France. He was a fun-loving caricature of the classic camel on the cigarette packages (whose body, as you may have heard, has long been accused of embedding a sketch of a man with at least one penis; RJR denies it). It was up to Camel's North Carolina agency, Trone, to update Smooth for the brand's 75th birthday in 1987. Until then, Camel had been stuck with an image frozen somewhere between World War II and '50s greasers. They didn't want to alienate that customer, but they did want younger ones—and so drew the French camel doing younger-man activities, like fish flying and drag racing.

But the Hard Pack is under attack not just for being penile, but for being cartoony. As his first act as New York City consumer affairs commissioner, Mark Green slammed Camel ads for violating the tobacco industry's own code against advertising directed at children. A petition filed with the FTC is still pending.

And a group called STAT (Stop Teenage Addiction to Tobacco) has called for a boycott of RJR Nabisco products, focusing on Oreos. STAT is running a "That's Not a Camel" contest—the best ad spoof wins $100. "We're not demanding that they stop advertising and promoting cigarettes," says STAT's Joe Tye, "just that they stop the egregious methods of influencing children."

Meanwhile, ads that make fun of the whole notion of subliminal advertising are suddenly the rage. A magazine spread for Seagram's Extra Dry Gin placed an easy-to-spot swimsuit-clad lady reclining in an inner tube in a glass of gin ("Can you find the hidden pleasure in refreshing Seagram's gin?" the copy teases). Absolut Vodka shadows its name into some ice cubes with the headline "Absolut Subliminal." A pizza store owner in San Francisco embedded a photo of his face onto a piece of pepperoni for an ad. And, of course, many sincere people have found the face of Jesus in the spaghetti on a Pizza Hut billboard in Atlanta.

But Camel's penis face is perfectly obvious. It attracts with funny, forbidden thoughts, and tests how sophomoric we can really be. Like, why am I writing this? To do my share to halt pushing cigarettes on children? Sure. To say out loud, under the guise of respectability, penis, penis, penis? Yes!

June 11, 1991

Getting Carded

Just in time for an improved $mas season—and almost as if to prove there really is a "Clinton recovery"—one miserable company wished upon a card and, like magic, got better. Remarkably, the company is GM. Not the carmaker itself—which just announced nine more plant closings and 18,000 jobs lost—but its new credit card division. The GM MasterCard was introduced only September 9 and already it has over 2.5 million accounts.

"That's unprecedented in such a short time," says James Daly, editor of *Credit Card News*. GM's ad manager for the card, Ron Muratore, brags, "AT&T, now the fifth largest credit card issuer, held the previous record, but it took 78 days to reach 1 million accounts. We reached that after 28 days." GM, the card, is even talking about how "we're helping to get the economy going again."

Though they've already spent an estimated $70 million on advertising and sent out 50 million pieces of direct mail, what's making the card work isn't the ads, but the deal that the ads only somewhat misleadingly present: They tell you that every time you use the card "GM will credit 5 percent of your purchase toward any new" GM car or truck. "That could mean hundreds, even thousands of dollars in savings." (More on the potholes in the plan later.)

In almost the same twinkle of an eye, GE, another giant of industry, came out with its own piece of plastic paradise, the GE Rewards credit card. It's less clear how this card, whose rewards also come only through increased, almost constant, consumption, is doing, because the more secretive GE won't talk. But it is curious that the two Generals, which couldn't be more different—one a corporate disaster, the other a corporate superman (when GM was looking for a new chairman, one rumor had them wooing GE chair "Neutron Jack" Welch)—made essentially the same marketing move at the same time.

GM desperately needs to sell more cars, and its card's gimmicks were created toward that end. But it's unlikely that GE's shiny new badge was invented to attack *its* prime corporate problem: PR b.o. The conglomerate's defense division, with its devastating record as a nuclear-weapons maker and nuclear polluter, made GE the best-known boycott target in America. But just two weeks ago, GE announced the amazing: It's selling off all its nuke works, including the infamous Knolls Atomic Power Lab featured in the Oscar-winning documentary *Deadly Deception*. INFACT, the group that led the six-year boycott, declared victory and will probably end the boycott—even though GE will hold $1 billion in convertible preferred stock in Martin Marietta, the defense contractor to which GE is selling the goods. GE insists that removing itself directly from the defense business "has absolutely nothing to do with the boycott. It was purely a business decision." But at a time when GE is trying to launch a consumer credit card—meant to inspire more "involvement" with the company along with more profits—it does help to get rid of any bad odors.

The charge of the charge cards probably has more to do with the ever-slippery notion of consumer confidence. Both the GE and GM cards were in development during a time when we lost confidence in our leader, our government, our economy—maybe corporations *were* the last bastion of competence, à la Commander-in-CEO Ross Perot. Inspired by the success of the AT&T Universal card and to a lesser extent the "affinity" cards of the '80s, many of which fed a few pennies to charity each time you charged a purchase, the GM and GE cards have made it look like they have a fresh new way for the consumer to make money. Though dreamt up during the Bush administration, the cards are being tossed across sales counters under president-elect Clinton and his promise to "focus like a laser beam on the economy"—so now they seem like your own personal pocket phasers.

Because at bottom today's credit cards, intent on tying you into something much larger than yourself through a variety of incentives, are magic cards, participate-in-America cards, vaguely alluding to democracy and equal opportunity, malls-for-all-and-all-for-malls cards. Not because they allow you to endlessly consume—they do that, but if that's all they did, they'd be pathetically old-tread '80s. No, the new-wave '90s cards reach even higher than the high interest they charge for your unpaid monthly balance—they reach for your spiritual interest, for *universality*, *affinity*, and heavenly *rewards*.

In fact, these latest cards take on an almost Clintonesque, "communitarian" sheen: With each purchase, you can tell yourself, you are not merely borrowing and consuming, but "reinvesting" in your own future. The companies make money by making millions of Americans come together in some grand emotion—linking savings to being saved, reviving the old idea that corporations stand for something familial or religious. The other family and church members here remain just an idea, but they are conjured through the act of purchase and the act of watching the ads.

Both the GM and GE ads play to the glory of this venture, but GM, as usual, is unafraid to be schmaltzy, while GE, as is usual in most ads created and narrated by Hal Riney, is pretentiously understated.

"Dave Baldwin doesn't spend a whole lot of time thinking about a yacht," Hal intones as middle-aged David looks perfectly content, thank you, to play the sax on the front porch with his young daughter by his side. "And, once again, the Reeds won't be skiing in Switzerland this year. But like you, they'll make sure the kids have the latest sneakers, the dog gets all his shots, and the car gets new tires when it needs it. These are the basics. There's not a lot of glory in providing them. But at least now you can get something back by the way that you pay for them." A brief explanation of the rebates and coupons that you get with the card follows—all the time hinting at the luxuries the savings could buy. In other words, this was a card made for the spiritually correct '90s—you cringe from greed, love to think of yourself as being basically basic, but if a financial angel *were* to drop a ski trip on you, well, it's probably your earthly reward.

GM goes for the more dramatic dream. The ad starts with nostalgia—kids chasing a '50s fender, gas station greasers hailing some dude's new wheels—to remind you of America's "love affair with the automobile." It switches to the '90s with shots of new cars, saying you can turn "buying power into horsepower. Plastic into steel"—by using the GM card, you can pile up enough rebates to buy a new car. Set to a yearning, grandiose music, the spot features a blond teenage girl who looks wistful and lonely until her father delivers—can it be?—a brand new car wrapped in a big white ribbon. Her face, our hearts, the economy lift.

"GE is out for a mainstream American feel," as GM's Muratore analyzes it. "Ours is the little boy or girl in every one of us that yearns for that shiny car and those warm memories we grew up with [not to be had, he needn't add, with a Japanese car]. We found a way to make that dream come true along with value. There *is* that pot of gold at the end of the rainbow."

The emotion's that simple. But the financial formula that leads to the pot is not. "Every time you use it, GM will credit 5 percent of your purchase toward any new car or truck," the TV spot says. But not *every* time. There's an annual $500 rebate cap. (And you'd have to charge $10,000 a year to get that.) You can build to, max, $3,500 over seven years. Not enough to buy the whole gift-wrapped car as the ad implies. However, you can add to your rebate account, without caps, by buying from GM's "partners" in this deal—MCI, Avis, and Marriott Hotels.

GM will profit from the 16.4 percent interest charged for unpaid balances, though it will share those profits with Household Credit Services, which actually issues the card. But the real gravy for GM is in the sale of more cars.

If, say, over time 500,000 out of an eventual 10 million GM card-holders end up buying a GM car who wouldn't have otherwise, that would be quite a significant increase for a company that annually sells 4 million to 5 million (down from about 7 million in the late '70s). This kind of synergistic planning between a product and an incentive to buy it is the kind that most of GM seems incapable of—other than with its very successful Saturn (the only GM product you *can't* get with the rebate). If only GM put this kind of creativity into meeting— rather than fighting—CAFE standards.

GE won't talk about how well or poorly its card is doing, but reading between the lines suggests not-so-great: "It's a niche product," a spokesman for the card explains. "The GE Rewards card is not the same kind of card as some of the other cards out there."

Its workings are more complex: For every $500 you charge, you get a $10 "reward check." Every three months, regardless of card usage, you get $10 coupons from 24 participating merchants (including Macy's, K mart, Northwest Airlines, and Sprint). Also, every three months you get a magazine in which those sponsors detail their own promotions. And if you do have the time to shop 'round the clock like this deal demands, you will probably go into revolving debt and have to pay GE's high 18.4 percent interest rates (in addition to a $25 annual fee).

You have to look beyond the gimmicks and focus on the interest rates on unpaid balances to see if either card means any savings at all. (About 75 percent of all cardholders do carry a balance, an average of $2500—total U.S. credit card debt is a record $248 billion.) Bankcard Holders of America, a consumer group, compared the GE 18.4 percent and the GM 16.4 percent cards to a low-rate card of 12 percent. "In order to offset the higher cost with GE saving certificates . . . you would have to spend at least $4000 annually," they found. "If you spent $1000 on the GM card, you would earn a $50 rebate toward a GM car. If you used that rebate, you would offset the higher cost of the card. If you did not, a low-rate card would be the better deal." (For a list of perfectly legit, low-rate credit cards, call BHA at 703-481-1110. The list is $4.)

Meanwhile, Jerry Seinfeld is doing an ad for American Express. With a goldfish at his side (this is not one of his funniest shticks), he says that between the national debt and cards that charge up to 19 percent interest we're drowning in debt. The fiscally responsible answer, he implies, is AmEx, because you must pay it in full each month. He presents this as if it were some bright new idea, another magical way to save. But what use is this to people who, following television's dictate to spend beyond their means, cannot pay in full each month? For them, AmEx created Optima, another revolving credit card. The detail-minded Seinfeld is mum on that.

December 15, 1992

Gotta Hack It

The way sodas insinuate themselves into your life! My life anyway. I don't even drink the stuff, but here I am writing about sugar water, carbonated chemicals, canned nothing, bottles of burp for the 200th time.

Coke and Pepsi have always used reports of their fictional warfare to hook you into their PR cosmos (though the only real bloodshed comes from them squeezing smaller brands off the shelves). But today, rumors of war come from a far deeper front—if you are to believe the ad community, the latest life-and-death struggle strikes at the molecular level of cultural consciousness itself.

What could this be? It's a turf war between Madison Avenue and a Hollywood talent agency for control of Coke's ad business. In 1991, the best-known brand in the world turned away from its agency of 38 years, McCann-Erickson, after Creative Artists Agency head Michael Ovitz convinced them he had the celebrity clout to deliver a whole new approach to advertising—the magic key to outhipping Pepsi (the equation Pepsi=young, Coke=old has haunted Coke since Pepsi's "New Generation").

CAA has made 24 of the 26 new Coke spots that will be rolling out over the next year. Some are fresh, many are stale, but no matter: The ad industry is terrified. While McCann made only two of the ads and

New ads in old Coke bottles

contributed the unifying idea—the tagline "Always Coca-Cola" (a sublimation for "Always McCann"?)—CAA pushed the newish strategy of customizing ads to specific TV show audiences. One spot, "Digging Dog," for instance, is reportedly handcrafted for *The Simpsons,* while a supercool music vid ad, "Ice Pick," is made for MTV. Though Ovitz fanned the fame, no celebrities appear in this round of spots; CAA contacts are more evident among the Hollywood "creatives" (Rob Reiner, Josh Brand) who made some of the ads. In fact, farming out production to freelancers is one strategy CAA promised would undercut the costs—and the cultural sluggishness—of bureaucracy-laden ad agencies.

In keeping with the Kemp-Clintonian times, Coke calls its approach "the new paradigm" of advertising. It's true that Coke is rethinking something structurally; it's just that the something—which group of overpaid people gets which piece of the pie—is as meaningless as the product itself.

Nevertheless, Coke bottlers are raving over the ads, some big heads at McCann rolled, and there is talk that CAA will colonize the gut of other advertisers, such as GM and Nike. Coming at a troubled time for agencies—recessionary loss of revenue, clients' agency-hopping—the CAA/Coke deal has led to talk of an adapt-or-die revolution. What the threat of health-care reform is to the medical establishment, the CAA coup is to the advertising establishment.

Nearly as revealing as the sheer quantity of CAA stories in the trade press was an *Adweek* panel of agency titans, who treated Coke's new campaign as if it were the supercollider of ad physics: "Is CAA's work advertising as we know it, as the world knows it, or is this a category where the client doesn't seem to need advertising?" asked Richard Costello, whose clients include Absolut vodka and Evian. Identity politics never gets more serious than this: "Pepsi is youth, it's as simple as that," said a J. Walter Thompson strategist. "To own youth is a powerful motivator. But what then is Coke?" Another agency president had the answer: "Coke is that which is best about America."

As to the new ads themselves, most were scornful: A "creative gangbang." "The emperor's new clothes." "There are nice pieces," said Joanne Davis of Martin Davis & OMON, "but the brilliance of what's been done is the publicity on it."

Agreed. The ads have a looser overall structure and are more playful than Coke has been lately. There's some sci-fi here, a few cute animals there, and a lot of straining, sometimes successful, to pull out all the cool stops—but what else is new? Mainly, it's the animated and tech-tweaked spots that stand out. "Timeline," drawn chalk-on-slate fashion, brags that all history was fire and rocks, fire and rocks, until 1886, when Coke came along and peace and tranquillity broke out. (Bosnia, quit whining.) But even some of the cooler ads seem somehow familiar. The much hailed spot featuring animated polar bears who gather at the top of the world to watch the aurora borealis and pop open Cokes one by one reads like a Klondike redux.

A set of four spots is called "Real People," but features the same old pretty actors, who merely simulate real by talking in run-ons. "This guy must be a swimmer," a female voiceover rattles on over a handsome beach man baring his bod, "—one of those lean, 100 percent fat-free, low-cholesterol types with eyes that focused so intently I just knew he got it. And it made me even more interested—and really thirsty—so I had a Coke."

Actually, through the variety of styles, the ads *do* have a look in common: They're post*something*. Don't ask post what, they just have that supposedly fresh *post* feeling: self-conscious, artifice-friendly, full of contradictions—which is okay because they always come out looking cute.

And one other element remains nearly as constant as the "Always Coke" tagline on the retro bottlecap logo: Coke's lovely, old-fashioned, glass bottle pops up everywhere—and will soon be available across the country in newfangled, *plastic* form.

The gods must be desperate. For what are the big-product wars all about but religion? Outgoing Coca-Cola Co. president Donald Keough perhaps best revealed Coke as the true Buddha when he said at the press conference introducing the ads, "Coca-Cola must be reinterpreted anew for each succeeding generation . . . because Coke itself must remain timeless and yet new at the same time." And when you slurp those exploding chemicals, you're doing nothing less than riding the survivor bubbles of the apocalypse: "If some force destroyed all the physical assets of the global Coca-Cola system overnight," Keough said, "all the bricks and mortar, all the route trucks and bank reserves, all the office buildings and bottling lines, then we could quickly rebuild that entire system if we had only two things: our trademark and the formula. The world banks would, in a matter of days, give us the resources to rebuild."

Love falters, diets fail, populations are destroyed, God is dead, even celebrities fade, but there's always soda.

March 23, 1993

Chapter **Three**

REAL

PROBLEMS,

SURREAL

ADS

Du Pontificates

By now you know that Bill Demby will make that basket and that Du Pont will get the credit. But the tearjerking ad is designed so skillfully you *just don't care* who profits. On a graffitied basketball court, Bill, a black Vietnam vet who "lost both legs to a Vietcong rocket," strips to his basketball shorts, revealing his plastic legs. A guy on the bench staring at Bill with that familiar mix of shock and fascination is our first proxy: He allows the able-bodied audience to react as if they were there, but also provides the distance so they can almost *enjoy* his queasiness because they don't really have to experience it.

As Bill joins in the game, awkwardly lunging at first, Du Pont joins in, too. "Researchers discovered that a Du Pont plastic could help make truly lifelike artificial limbs." Bill shoots for a basket (the basket's torn, like him), it bounces off, and he falls to the ground. Two guys look at each other: You're not sure if they're thinking, we shouldn't have let a gimp play, but the audience can identify with their self-consciousness. Refusing a helping hand, Bill resumes play and, to the voiceover's words "Thanks to these efforts, Bill Demby is back," he makes a hoop! Bill and a buddy exchange a look of triumph—we can breathe easier!—and Du Pont throws its big arms around everyone: "Better things for better living."

Bill is a real guy who works in a disability awareness program in Maryland. "We conceived the ad and then went out to find a person whose real story would fit it," a Du Pont spokesman explains. They chose Bill at an amputee's game because "he exuded the most presence"; the other players were found on New York courts. The telling glances that move this spot recently won the director, Rick Levine, a best ad director award from the Directors Guild. They've won Bill various awards and talk-show appearances. "If you're talking about things the public thinks is important, you're pretty much going to have their attention when an ad comes on," says the spokesman.

Du Pont's self-satisfaction in turning a timely issue into an ad is made clearer in another spot. As a man's rushed to the hospital, the chemical maker trumpets: "Du Pont worked to create a highly accurate method to help protect our blood supply from the deadly AIDS virus. Their system enables us to have more confidence that the blood we need to live won't be hazardous to our health." A subtle schism between "us" and "them" hovers throughout.

Lately, Du Pont's been getting good PR for no longer doing dangerous things. Du Pont recently announced it would stop making plutonium and tritium for nuclear weapons. As the world's largest producer of ozone-destroying chlorofluorocarbons, Du Pont finally agreed to phase out 95 percent of its CFCs around the year 2000. "We have

The chemical maker's on your team.

mixed feelings about Du Pont's decision," says Paul J. Allen of the Natural Resources Defense Council, which first proposed a ban. "They've come grudgingly to their current position." Meanwhile, he says, an earlier U.S. agreement to cut CFC production in half by 1998 will allow Du Pont, as demand and price soar, to reap windfall profits. Du Pont opposes a Senate proposal that would impose windfall taxes or fees. With "the perception about Du Pont" pretty cheery of late, Allen says, "some of the steam behind the bill may be evaporating."

Down the line, Du Pont can always transform these developments into an ad, maybe about how its efforts saved a young girl from skin cancer. A spokeswoman would only say, "There are no plans at this time."

April 26, 1988

Point of Purchase

Advertising bears little or no relationship to products and even less to the companies that make them. GE, running ads that sing "we are the good things," makes bad things, like parts to nuclear weapons. Procter & Gamble, which has some progressive employee programs, like flex-time and daycare, still airs some ads that make it seem like a repressive little old lady. If there's little difference between brand-name products, there's plenty between their companies—all pointed out in a new con-sumer guide, *Shopping for a Better World*. It rates 138 companies (from good to poor) and their 1300 brand-name, supermarket prod-ucts on 10 social issues: advancement of women and minorities, involvement in South Africa, concern for the environment, charitable giving, community outreach, animal testing, nuclear power, military contracts, and the companies' willingness to disclose all this. Published by the Council on Economic Priorities, a nonprofit public interest re-search group, the booklet is based on CEP's more detailed *Rating America's Corporate Conscience*. The new pocket-sized guide is designed for quick reference at the supermarket, right at (as marketers say) "the point of purchase."

"Of course, we still take such matters as price, quality, and nutrition into account," says CEP's Alice Tepper Marlin. But those things being equal, the guide can serve as "a meaningful alternative to the slick advertising that creates product distinctions which are trivial, artificial, or just plain meaningless." (Products by "responsible" corporations, she says, usually turned out to be less expensive than those by the "irresponsible" ones.)

The companies that pulled in top ratings in at least eight of the 10 categories were Procter & Gamble (Cheer, Bounty, Ivory Soap, Folgers), Campbell Soup, Quaker Oats, General Mills, Clorox, Scott Paper, Polaroid, Eastman Kodak, Ben & Jerry's, and Newman's Own (100 percent of the latter's pretax earnings go to charity).

Companies with the worst records include Unilever (Aim toothpaste, Ragu spaghetti, Q-Tips, All detergent), which has no women on its board and is poor in minority advancement and charitable giving; American Cyanamid (Old Spice and Pine-Sol) and Texaco, both of which ranked poorly in most areas, including the environment and involvement in South Africa. "Quite low" in the ratings was Nestlé (chocolate, infant formula, Libby's and Carnation brands), which has problems in community affairs that reach beyond the boycott currently leveled at it for "dumping" infant formula in Third World hospitals.

What this boils down to, the CEP says, is buy Bounty over Brawny or Vanity Fair (by the James River Corp., poor in women and minority advancement); Cheer over All; Quaker Oats or Wheaties over cereals by Ralston Purina (not good in charitable giving, women and minorities); Hershey over Nestlé (hip commercials each, similar-tasting products, one company more decent than the other). Newman's Own spaghetti sauce, which doesn't advertise, over Ragu, which runs family-sitcom simulation ads, but ranks poorly on women's and minority issues. Pepsi, "one of the most improved" companies, over Coca-Cola, which "lobbies extensively against recycling."

Of course, the lowly rated companies disagree. "The evaluation, in most cases, is inaccurate," says a spokesman from Unilever, calling the ratings "rather arbitrary." A Texaco spokesman calls the CEP "ignorant of our outstanding cultural and educational programs. They ought to speak with the Metropolitan Opera and all the universities, social organizations and charities that depend on Texaco's philanthropic actions." "We didn't participate in the fact-gathering process," says an American Cyanamid spokeswomen, "so we don't want to comment."

It's commendable to try to break the lull created by advertising and the tacit consensus that most things on shelves are okay. And it's better to base decisions on facts than on vaguely recalled rumors. But all this presumes that shoppers—already in a compromised position, pretranced and tenderized—will interrupt their reflex action to read anything but prices, coupons, and maybe labels. Buying with booklet in hand may seem positively schoolmarmish. Shopping (pleasure principle) and thinking bad thoughts about companies (superego) are contradictory activities—a contradiction enhanced by the '80s "if you can't beat the corporations, join 'em" assumption that has blanched out this generation's will to make everyday decisions based on any political considerations at all. Buying based on principles seems like such a throwback.

But it doesn't have to be. Some of the companies covered may be actually half-listening, says the CEP's Leslie Gottlieb. "We're finding a fairly good corporate response. We get inquiring calls all the time from corporations not even rated in the book or mentioned in our awards ceremony [the annual America's Corporate Conscience Awards].

Shopping for a Better World is available at some bookstores or through CEP at 212-420-1133 or 1-800-729-4237.

December 20, 1988

Point of Purchase **121**

Forget the Dead Babies

Nestlé's PR Firm Spins Feel-Good Line

While continuing its often harmful infant formula marketing practices in the Third World, Nestlé S.A., the Swiss-owned purveyor of brand names like Nestlé Crunch, Taster's Choice, and Stouffer's Lean Cuisine, is looking for a good-citizen PR formula here. Nestlé has retained Ogilvy & Mather Public Relations—whose other clients have included apartheid boycott target Shell Oil, weapons manufacturer McDonnell Douglas, and the Tobacco Institute—to strategize its response to a renewed consumer boycott.

The *Voice* has obtained a confidential memo from the counter-ops at O&M to the big Swiss cheeses at corporate HQ on Lake Geneva titled "Proactive Neutralization: Nestlé Recommendations Regarding the Infant Formula Boycott." In juicy, corp-think detail, the memo lays out a plan to defeat the boycott with a saccharin image campaign—including getting a regular advertising slot on the controversial high school TV news show, Channel One. Feel-good ideas designed to win the hearts and minds of Americans—without Nestlé actually giving up its $1 Billion-plus infant formula market—also include: funding foster care for children with AIDS (the memo hints reassuringly that it won't cost too much); setting up a "National Homework Helpline," a parent-pleasing tutor-by-phone system; organizing a "racial awareness" program (never mind that Nestlé is one of the largest foreign investors in South Africa, according to the Africa Fund); and signing up any ex-president still kicking—Reagan, Carter, Ford, even Nixon—to sing the conglomerate's praises.

The boycott was resumed last October, when health-care and religious groups monitoring Nestlé came to the conclusion that it was not living up to the much-publicized agreements that ended the first boycott in 1984. The Ogilvy & Mather memo gives a glimpse of the COINTELPRO-like approach multinationals often take to grassroots protest.

Nestlé is the world's largest maker of infant formula, and before the first boycott, the company proudly shipped huge quantities to Third World hospitals to be given out as "free samples." Nestlé encouraged doctors to give away so much formula that by the time a new mother had run through her freebies, her breastmilk was in danger of drying up—making her a steady, paying customer for powdered formula.

That may seem like sharp trading, but in many underdeveloped countries, it's downright dangerous. The poor in Africa, Asia, and Latin America can seldom count on unpolluted water supplies, and feeding infant formula mixed with contaminated water to a newborn can cause malnutrition, disease, and death. UNICEF director James Grant has estimated that bottle-related diseases take one million infants' lives a year.

In 1984, Nestlé agreed to change its marketing approach, and the boycott, which critics say over seven years may have cost the company as much as $3 billion, ended. However, it eventually became apparent that Nestlé was still supplying the same amount of free formula as before—and that the company was merely getting more subtle in promoting it, says Action for Corporate Accountability, leader of Boycott II. "In certain regions, such as East Africa, Nestlé is actually increasing the amount of free formula," says Action director Janice Mantell. Like almost everything else between Nestlé and its nemesis, this issue is in contention. "The amount of free formula there remained the same," says Thad Jackson, Nestlé's boycott troubleshooter. "The percentage of free formula supplies went up, but only because it's measured against the sales, which went down."

Nestlé insists it is abiding by the World Health Organization code and the 1984 agreement by supplying only as much formula as the host country allows and the hospitals request. But, according to Action, Nestlé finds the loopholes, and it doesn't forget its friends, either. In Thailand, says Action, midwives who distributed more than 20 tins of formula were getting free leather OB-GYN bags. (Nestlé says it's discontinued free formula shipments to Thailand, but if abuses occurred, they weren't company policy.) In the Philippines, Nestlé has "donated" basinettes, air conditioners, and oxygen tanks to under-equipped hospitals and clinics, while "financial assistance" has made its way to individual doctors and other health care workers. Nestlé spokesman Jackson says, "The WHO code allows us to donate equipment to institutions and to send doctors to meetings as long as it's clear that the assistance comes from Nestlé." (This time around, American Home Products, the second largest supplier of free formula and maker of Anacin and Advil, is also a boycott target.)

But papering over a baby-killer image doesn't come easy. Nestlé hired the high-powered Ogilvy & Mather (Jody Powell is the CEO of its Washington, D.C., public affairs branch) this February to put the right spin on another infant formula fiasco that subsidiary Carnation stepped into. Along the way, "it was suggested," says O&M PR chairman, John Margaritas, that the firm try its hand at a campaign to blunt the boycott.

The six-part "Proactive Neutralization" program (does G. Gordon Liddy work for O&M?) is "discreet, carefully focused, and targeted," the memo states. "It is built around the idea of neutralizing or defusing the issue by quietly working with key interest groups." It covers "assessment and monitoring" of allies and enemies; training Nestlé employees to handle questions from friends and neighbors; media relations ("avoid *generating* more awareness of the issue"; and, most curiously, the "image campaigns."

The memo proposes to center the image campaign on a "Nestlé News Network" that would air on Channel One, the commercially sponsored classroom news show now being tested by Whittle Communications. After noting that Channel One could create "a target audience of *6.5 million* high school students" [drooling italics theirs], O&M goes on to say (mistakenly, as it turns out): "*There is an existing opportunity to be a (or* THE) *major sponsor of Channel One. The idea for Nestlé, however, is not to advertise, but to donate the 30 seconds of daily/weekly airtime for Nestlé sponsored additional daily news programming:* FOOD FOR THOUGHT."

The ad-sized "Food for Thought" could easily be spun off, the memo says, into a "Food for Thought Nestlé Satellite Assembly Series" (half-hour minidocumentaries shown during school assembly), "Food for Thought National Sponsorships," a "Food for Thought Speakers Bureau," and a "Food for Thought Conference"—a meeting of the "Nestlé High School News Advisory Panels." The conference could "create immediate national impact by retaining one or any of the four living ex-presidents, Reagan, Carter, Ford and Nixon to kick-off the session: AMERICAN PRESIDENTS ON FUTURE LEADERSHIP CONCERNS."

Of course, Nestlé—with $30 billion in revenues, the world's largest food conglomerate—is more interested in food sales than youthful thought. Channel One and Nestlé are a natural match. Both use free supplies to hook captive audiences early on: Channel One gives free video equipment to schools so they'll air its TV show in classrooms that kids must attend, while Nestlé gives free formula to hospitals so they'll distribute it in maternity wards where new mothers are more or less confined.

Some of O&M's more imaginative plans are designed to cover Nestlé subsidiary Carnation's ass during the boycott. Carnation, acquired by Nestlé in 1985, was to be Nestlé's entrée into the $1.6 billion U.S. formula market that the Swiss conglomerate has never been able to break.

Last year, Carnation introduced an American infant formula called Good Start H.A., but it got off to a rotten start. It's hypoallergenic (that's what H.A. stands for), but six cases of severely allergic babies who became ill with symptoms like vomiting or going limp were reported to the FDA. Severely allergic babies should use only *non*allergenic formula, but the labeling confused some mothers. Under pressure, Carnation dropped the hypoallergenic references from its label (but has retained H.A. in its name).

Carnation got into further trouble by advertising directly to the consumer, including a TV spot for its regular formula, Good Nature. Formula advertising has always been taboo for fear it would discourage breastfeeding, which is much healthier. (The TV spot flashes a token warning, "Not To Replace Breast Milk," in barely visible white letters on an off-white background—which is pretty good, considering they might have written it in cuneiform.)

O&M's solution to this formula fiasco? "Carnation Care"—funding foster-care programs for children with AIDS. AIDS tots always deliver more PR bang for the buck: "Majority of these organizations are at present in start-up phase and therefore limited amounts of funding can go a long way," the memo states. "Benefits": "Grass roots operation that can not be perceived as 'buying the public's love or acceptance.' " One of the "objectives": "help 'inoculate' Carnation from effect of Nestlé boycott."

An alternative dodge is the "Carnation National Homework Helpline." It would copy the American Federation of Teachers' Dial-A-Teacher program, which is staffed by volunteers and limited to just 10 cities. A national version would provide an "opportunity for Carnation ownership."

O&M raised, and rejected on its own, other possible programs: "Carnation Combats Cocaine" was "too 'negative' an area with no ownership opportunities. . . ." The "Carnation Racial Awareness Program" was nixed because of "potential for media criticism regarding South African investments and boycott issue."

"We did consider some of those things, but we didn't take any of them up," says Nestlé's Thad Jackson when confronted with O&M's plans. "It's hard to speculate why, but Channel One I'm not the least bit interested in. The idea just didn't hit me."

Changing marketing policies isn't Nestlé's idea of the very best. Annual revenues on infant formula worldwide are estimated at between $1 billion (Nestlé's figures) and $3 billion. Nestlé admits to racking up some $350 million in sales annually in Third World countries alone. And the profit margins in formula are deep—about 30 percent industrywide, according to *Forbes*.

Whether or not Nestlé eventually uses any of the O&M recommendations, if the recent past is any indication, they'll probably come up with more do-good smoke screens like them. Currently, the company's pasted its name all over the Nestlé/March of Dimes Women's World Team Championship—conveniently enough, the March of Dimes is another O&M client.

May 2, 1989

Uniform Standard

Du Pont is at it again—taking credit for our most intimate emotions. Most corporate image ads do this, of course—the corporate claim on our personal epiphanies is America's form of social realism—but by dint of its particular history, Du Pont has an ad leg up.

When we last saw the chemical giant and the largest producer of ozone-destroying chlorofluorocarbons, it was through the pathos of Bill Demby, the legless black Vietnam vet who, thanks to a Du Pont plastic used to make his artificial legs, was shooting hoops again with the best of them.

Now we meet "Tara Meyer," an ad concoction based on several real people who survived car accidents, one of whom soon after walked down the aisle for her wedding. Hey, dramatic contrast—use it!

As the Wedding March plays, the ad cross-cuts between the security of a church—lush space, sunlight-drenched pews—and the terror of the smash-up—a dark rainy night, resplendent in dry ice. "Tara Meyer's dream of a beautiful wedding almost ended two months ago in a car accident," the voiceover says. "Unfortunately, she wasn't wearing a seatbelt, and her face hit and shattered the windshield." She looks in shock at her male companion driving the car, her head hits, and we see a glass cobweb of cracks. But now, her father's about to give the veiled bride away (at Du Pont they don't know who Tara was riding with, but they're sure she didn't marry *him*). "But because the windshield was a new type developed by Du Pont"—on those last words the minister opens the Bible—"the razor-sharp glass stayed on the outside, away from Tara's face." As she finally lifts her veil, we melt with relief: She hasn't turned into the Bride of Frankenstein.

But suddenly more riveting than her scarless face or the magic glass (actually a layer of film used in "higher-end cars, mostly for GM") is the expression on her face. Her eyelids lift heavily, then widen with desire: She's seen fire and she's seen rain, which makes the passion she dissolves into seem all the deeper. *That's* the way to kiss the groom, *that's* the look I want on my face when I get married.

Du Pont was the best man.

In a second spot, a lone fireman walks out of a burning, higher-end house. His breathing is in Sensurround as if we were inside his oxygen mask. Meeting his fire-resistant Du Pont uniform, the flames flick away from his body like mosquitoes from Cutters, as he carries an infant to safety. "At Du Pont, we make the things"—close-up of the fireman—"that make a difference"—shot of the baby.

Thus Du Pont takes credit for young love, heroism, and even a baby's existence. The picture of the firefighter and the crying babe is reminiscent not only of this year's Pulitzer Prize-winning photo, but also of the 1855 John Everett Millais painting, *The Rescue,* in which a fireman carries two children to safety. Millais wanted to paint men in uniform but was irritated with the military vogue of the time. "Soldiers and sailors have been praised a thousand times," he wrote. "My next picture shall be of Firemen."

Du Pont's a lot like Millais. It too wants to show people in uniform, but not, certainly not, soldiers and sailors. After World War I, Du Pont was criticized during Senate hearings for profiting from "smokeless powder," the stuff that put the high into high explosive. Called a "merchant of death" by the media, Du Pont learned early on that the chemical industry had "perception problems." It became one of the first to launch a corporate image campaign.

"We've been doing corporate advertising steadily since 1935, using the same strategic approach, a problem/solution format," says a Du Pont spokesman. "Our research would suggest the effort must be working fairly well, because [the perception of Du Pont] has not been in general decline as it has been for the industry as a whole."

So Du Pont knows not to wear a military uniform. Rather, its heroes wear fireman outfits and wedding gowns, uniforms indicating institutional, conservative stability, the kind of things soldiers might go to war for.

But Du Pont still needs all the good-image boosts it can get. It recently gave up management of a polluted nuclear complex, the Savannah River Plant, where it had manufactured tritium and plutonium for the government since 1950. Under international pressure, it also agreed, slowly and grudgingly, to phase out 95 percent of its chlorofluorocarbons by the year 2000. One of its largest plants, Chambers Works in Deepwater, N.J., is also "one of the largest hazardous waste generators in the U.S.," says Kenny Bruno, toxic campaign coordinator of Greenpeace. "They've had an unbelievable amount of pollution and worker health problems. Because of the way they disposed of waste, they've destroyed two aquifers and they've discharged high levels of lead into Delaware River. This is a very toxaholic company." A Du Pont spokesman, Irvin Lipp, says, "We want to continue to cut down on emissions and we do each year. In any case, these are permitted emissions." As for worker health, he says, "The number-one business objective of Du Pont has always been the health and safety of our employees."

The ad trick, as always, is to point away from the corporation to the little people in all their against-the-odds glory. The essence of any corporate venture is lockstep group action, but the focus of most corporate advertising is on individual emotion—which they then try to possess. They don't *have* to take your money, your home, or your health—but they do have to take your moments.

May 23, 1989

Uniform Standard **129**

Where the Boycotts Are

In the dying days of the wussy '80s, grass-roots revenge has found its form in boycotts. Oil-spiller Exxon, nuke-maker GE, abortion-favoring TV movie *Roe vs. Wade,* infant-formula-dumper Nestlé, Madonna-dumper Pepsi—the recent flurry of boycotts, whether called by the left or the right, goes to the heart of what America's all about: buying things.

Boycotts and other economic pressures—shareholder resolutions, large pension investor demands—are on the rise. At least 120 national boycotts are currently nipping at the heels of American business (and that's not counting scores of local efforts), says Todd Putnam, editor of *The National Boycott Newsletter,* which has been chronicling boycotts from all sides for five years. Outright rebellion may be outré, but the sense that corporate elephantism encourages manipulation of consumers has been growing all along. "Boycotts are way up from the '60s and '70s," says Putnam. "After eight years of Reagan, I think people are feeling more than ever that the government won't do anything."

There are successful boycotts (the concessions made by Coors put it at the top, says Putnam), trivial boycotts (don't eat at McDonald's till they offer veggieburgers), and reverse boycotts (a fruit growers' association has pulled ads from some CBS affiliates over a *60 Minutes* segment about Alar and cancer).

And there are different boycott species, determined partly by their launch level of awareness. The Outrageous Event boycott, like Exxon's, is the rarest—publicity led the boycott, not the other way around. Organizations usually have to phone reporters for years to get an issue across. Those are the Social Injustice boycotts, usually protracted, low-profile affairs aimed at corporate policy: Burger King for buying rainforest beef (the two-year boycott was recently won), PUSH's past boycotts of Ford, Coca-Cola, Kentucky Fried Chicken to increase minority hiring and business.

Moral Mission boycotts, centering on cultural values, have no such problem: their issues are visceral and easy to understand. Actually, most Moral Mission issues can be reduced to one: sex on TV. These are the boycotts that cause even the networks to squeak, "Censorship!"

But TV-oriented boycotts do not always start from the right—the feminist group Media Watch has called for boycotts of Guess and Johnny Walker for sexist ads. Fundamentalists Anonymous is boycotting Pepsi for axing its Madonna ad when her separate sex-and-a-stigmata video came under religious fire (Pepsi, by the way, never pulled the ads in other countries—even the Vatican can tune in).

The latest boycott bad boy is Maxwell House coffee—for advertising on NBC's *Roe vs. Wade* despite "warnings" from antiabortion groups. So the Pro-Life Action League called for a yearlong boycott of the General Foods product; meanwhile, the National Right to Life Committee is encouraging members to flood General Foods with letters. The company is being singled out because it's big and, in NRLC's case, because "they were the only ones we were able to contact beforehand," says a spokesman.

Living by the political sword sometimes means having to conduct exhaustive searches to find the issue with just enough decibels of outrage. The Reverend Don Wildmon's group, Christian Leaders for Responsible Television, which has been monitoring the May sweeps for sponsors of shows using "excessive sex, violence, or profanity," will soon announce the worst offender and boycott it. Past Wildmon scalps include Mazda, which burned rubber pulling out of *Miami Vice* when he snapped "out!"

Moral Mission boycotts get good press—TV loves to cover itself. "Other boycotts you'll almost never hear of," says Putnam. "Tom Brokaw only just reported the Shell Oil boycott [over the company's South African investments], which has been going on for five years." But meanwhile, Terry Rakolta, whose letters to HQs scared sponsors into dropping shows like *Married . . . With Children,* was all over the tube. Having since formed her own organization, she's now looking for a boycott target of her own.

Boycotts have always been more leftist fare—starting with 17th century tenants who refused to deal with land agent Charles C. Boycott until he lowered their rents. But the right is taking to boycotts like the antiabortion movement took to civil disobedience. The TV-commercial-chokehold boycott seems as made for the right as struggling, organization-dependent boycotts do for the left.

TV is emulsified in many of the core values of the right. The modernism that TV is about—buying things to comfy up and insulate your life, while simultaneously exposing that insulation to others' different and sometimes objectionable lives—creates the tension that keeps the right's sphincter so taut in the first place.

Still, it's an odd spectacle to see the right going after advertising. They buy—and buy into—Glade room freshener and tricolored Aim toothpaste. The culture they oppose is not advertising's. While attacking advertisers can, sure enough (and fair enough), bully the media, their analysis breaks. Their boycotts would have you believe that advertising leads culture, even the free-thinking, artsy-fartsy culture they abhor. But advertising will say or do *anything* to make us think it's on our side—left, right, up, or down.

Corporations have both less and more to be afraid of than meets the eye. "The real impact of boycotts is usually not on the bottom line," says Jack Mongoven, a consultant to corporations under fire. "The real impact is on lost executive time and employee morale."

While boycotts are terrif—a kind of people's antiadvertising—their rising numbers can blunt their effect. "A lot of people are tired of hearing about all the products they shouldn't buy," says Putnam. To help straighten it all out, you can subscribe to Putnam's entertaining, irregular quarterly (*National Boycott Newsletter*, 6506 28th Avenue N.E., Seattle, WA 98115). Or you can do as he does: "Generally, if I see an ad on TV I won't buy the product."

June 6, 1989

30 Seconds Over Washington

Maybe it's just coincidence, but the major weapon systems that did better than expected in the last round of defense budget voting—the B-2 Stealth, the V-22 Osprey, and the F-14—all beamed TV commercials at congresspeople and staffers. Those systems that didn't fly as well—SDI, MX, Midgetman—did not groove to the tube.

Of course, other factors played a role, factors like lobbying, loss of jobs in home districts, the Stealth's resemblance to Batman merchandise, and the $19.95 *Top Gun* video that F-14 maker Grumman sent free to members of the Armed Services Committee and anyone on the hill who wanted it.

But the commercials were important in reinforcing those real-life factors. When the B-2 Stealth finally took off shortly before the voting, Northrop ads repeatedly replayed its dramatic ascent, as Washingtonians were assured that it is "America's most thoroughly tested new bomber." During the F-14 debate, the words "top gun" popped up— the legislators perhaps unconsciously nudged by the spot in which a male baritone intones, "It's the fighter the navy calls its top gun."

But even more than reinforcing issues, the fly-'em-high TV campaigns reinforced the mood that prevailed the last time major weaponry was portrayed in an ad—the Bush-for-president spot featuring a dufus-looking Dukakis riding an army tank and listing all the manly aircraft he was supposedly "against." "The real fear around here is that they're going to run an ad against *you*, an Atwater ad," says Representative Pat Schroeder. "That's the subliminal thing about these ads. Here are these glitzy ads and the real message is we're going to bomb you."

The ads were probably least influential in the happy fate of the F-14 and Osprey, which, despite defense secretary Cheney's desire to kill them, were propelled through by the fear of losing local jobs (New Yorkers for Grumman's F-14 and Texans for Bell-Textron's Osprey agreed to vote for each other). The ads had the most impact, Schroeder believes, on the Stealth, which came in with a $70.2 billion price tag for 132 planes. It had also been revealed that Northrop is under inves-

B2 or not B-2?

tigation for fraud in billing practices for various programs including the B-2. (Northrop says it is unaware of the investigations.)

"The Dellums/Kasich amendment [that proposed killing the entire B-2 program] would have passed if it hadn't been for the commercials," says Schroeder. "We had 205 votes on our whip count. But after the ads, the Aspin/Synar amendment surfaced with a 'this is our moderate position' " proposal. Dellums/Kasich was voted down 279 to 144, and the House eventually approved the Aspin/Synar measure that includes a spending ban on the B-2 until a cost-cutting plan is submitted. (The Senate measures are much more lenient; the two houses will go into conference to debate all defense systems after the August recess. Some commercials may be resurrected to greet them.)

The imagery of a flying chunk of steel masterfully controlling the vast emptiness around it may also serve as a role model for congressboys. Each aircraft lifting up, up, and away from the complexities and pressures of dealing with budget bickering, constituents' jobs, corruption scandals—those soaring birds showed how it *could* feel if you swallowed your objections and just voted for the damn thing.

We've all seen major defense contractor feel-good ads—about how the men and women who work for them are simultaneously team players and spiky individuals (GE, McDonnell Douglas), about how the omnipresent corporation is really God's subcontractor ("We're in the buildings you live and work in, the cars you drive, the planes you fly in," says United Technologies). In most defense feel-good ads, an aircraft may appear in the background, like a swoop of metallic smile. But these latest ads star naked weaponry, aim straight at the budget, and run only in D.C. (though Northrop also beeped it in its home-town, L.A., for employee morale).

Defense contractors don't have the Russians to kick around any-more, they don't have Ronald Reagan to protect them, but they do have offensive budgets coming out of their tail pipes. Like other "issue advertisers"—ads concerning abortion, animal rights, gun control, etc. are booming—defense contractors can and do take out print ads. But this extreme situation calls for the big guns—TV spots.

"These guys [legislators and staff] get inundated by lobbyists all the time," says Harold Heaslip, Grumman advertising director. "They can't remember if it was a guy from Grumman or Northrop who called 20 minutes ago. TV gives you a preemptive opportunity to re-state and summarize your case. You're closer to top of mind."

In that ad phrase lies the trick. The ads alone didn't change votes, but they kept the intended images pulsing. "Members of congress tend to get caught up in the technology," says Representative John Kasich. "The plane flies, they get excited, they see commercials—it almost be-comes magical. So when they fly this batplane around they say, 'We can't stop the technology.' "

The contractors deny that the ads are paid for by the very govern-ment funding that, through these ads, they're trying to retain or in-crease. "It comes out of corporate profits," they say. (Only Northrop would disclose a price tag: $109,000 for TV.) "But where do their profits come from?" asks Schroeder. "They come from government funds." Ninety-five percent of Northrop's business, for instance, is government business, the company says. "They write it all off on their taxes," she continues. "They get the taxpayer to pay for the planes and then for the ads. It's a double hit."

Maybe it's impossible that these weapon commercials really influence our representatives; congressfolk would never buy a B-2 in the same state of treacly stupefaction that the rest of us buy a Coke. It's too simplistic to believe that on such important matters they would operate at the symbolic, cartoony level of *neat bombers!* and *big kaboom!* Except that these are the same people who are now going *kaboom!* to those who desecrate what is only a symbol—the flag.

August 15, 1989

A Piece of the Wall

Hey, they're just being Prague-matic! Russian and buy some! Czech it out!

Until a political event is properly packaged as adnewsvid—with slo-mo, swelling emotions, and candy-bright colors—we can't quite digest it, with the end goal being to forget it. The hottest thing that the West has to sell to the East is the obsolescence of history. If advertising helps the capitalism go down, then these commercials—linking Pepsi, AT&T, Shearson Lehman, and Quintessence fragrances to the liberation of Eastern Europe—are capitalism's most satisfying burps.

Though these ads differ in technique (some use actors, others documentary footage), they all look remarkably similar. Not only because all feature the Berlin Wall, children, graffiti, and/or skull-breaking guards turned simpatico, but because most of these corporations view this "celebration of freedom" as their "holiday greeting." In each case, the company and its ad people talk about how "excited" they are to be "a part of history." And, since most of the spots were produced with breathless speed—Quintessence wrote storyboards *on the plane*—these ad folks could relate to those behind the Iron Curtain:

Breaking the chains of market research and agency bureaucracy is a kind of wild and woolly freedom, too.

These ads have something else in common: All this celebrating puts us in the mood to shop. Still, each ad gives its own twist to events that makes it suspect in its own individual way.

Pepsi plays the wall to Handel's "Hallelujah Chorus." As dozens of children chisel away at the cement, a big graffiti peace sign hovers above and, culminating the ad, a girl gives a guard a rose. (Can you imagine Pepsi using the peace sign or hippies handing cops flowers when America's Pepsi generation was protesting Vietnam?) But the narrator gets seriously confused: "In this, the season of giving, the gift of freedom is the greatest gift of all," he says. Did someone *give* them freedom? Hell no, they seized it, *man!* But the happy implication is that Pepsi, the first American consumer product to be sold and promoted in Russia, passed the torch. Last year, Pepsi ran a semiwhimsical spot linking itself to *glasnost.* Between 1789 and 1989 the tricolor has become the red, white, and blue of a Pepsi can. Some things about

Chiselers for Pepsi.

Western consumption patterns *are* liberating: We're supposed to have more fun, and the insouciance and excess of our products seem to bottle it—as long as the Third World is there with the raw material and cheap labor.

Investment banking titan Shearson Lehman Hutton made its spot pre-wall, in September, but the message is even more pointed. The spot starts with a teen skateboarding in front of a huge hammer and sickle sculpture. Shearson, the first company to use the word *capitalism* in an ad four years ago, continues to crow: "Signs of capitalism have begun to appear in the most unexpected places." And we see: young Chinese girls eating pizza, Red Guards chowing hot dogs, *Dynasty* on the tube below a portrait of Lenin, two stout *babushkas* who've set aside their medieval brooms to ogle their new sneakers— yes, yes, they can transform themselves from street-cleaning lowlies to up-to-the-minute, product-bearing gals! There's something insidious going on here: slices, hot dogs, skateboards, and sneakers—the same accoutrements that also make American outcasts feel like they're getting a piece of the pie. Shearson, which recently laid off 800 workers, is eager to expand into Eastern Europe.

AT&T has produced "a people spot." West Germans talk excitedly not just about the wall coming down or their joy in seeing East German relatives, but their joy in reaching their relatives *over the phone*. "And then I called my sister," one strapping lad says. "She couldn't believe it. She hadn't heard the radio, not the TV, nothing." Why, just weeks after showing how it saved the day for earthquake and hurricane victims, is AT&T claiming that it can reach out and free someone? "AT&T," says its adman, "is in the communications business, and we see this as a celebration of the freedom to communicate."

Quintessence, the company that makes Jovan, adidas, Aspen, and other fragrances, is the most artificial-smelling of the Eastern Euro-trashing ads. An East German grandfather crosses near the Brandenburg Gate, and his four-year-old, West German grandson immediately recognizes him. As they embrace, a teddy bear falls from *Opa's* bag, and an East German guard picks it up for him. The moment is moving, but how did these two, who presumably have never met, recognize each other so instantly? Victor Zast, VP of marketing, isn't quite sure.

"Perhaps they've seen photographs of each other," he says. "But, you know, as fragrance-makers our entire business is based on the idea that we let people's dreams come true."

Although capitalist propaganda has never been more truly spoken, the rest of the Berlin Wall ad gang hold their noses over Quintessence moving in on *their* turf. The Shearson VP agrees that Pepsi and AT&T are "relevant. But a perfume," she says, "I don't understand." But why are Pepsi, et al. interested in Eastern Europe except to open up more markets? In the spirit of giving, why not let everyone make a killing?

American advertising has often used the evil empire in one capacity or another. Five years ago, RC Cola played like Pepsi and Coca-Cola were Stalinist oppressors; Wendy's put on a "Russian Fashion Show" that goofed on the dowdiness of the same *babushkas* that we're now supposed to love. The country that was recently just one huge Brand X is now endorsing us as Super Brand A.

Eastern Europe is safe for advertising. But what corporation has the righteous-enough record to one day run an ad celebrating, say, the end of apartheid?

But there is some truth in this advertising: As ridiculous and manipulative as they are, the ads are saying that persuasion is a better way to run a nation than force. The East Europeans may want some of the rights of our system—free speech, entrepreneurship—but they don't necessarily want the results—homelessness, gulfs between rich and poor. Politically, they want to be Sweden; *tchotchke*wise, they want to be us. This is an entire civilization saying, "We want to be seduced." They're tired of being told to want what's good for them; they want what's bad for them. And nothing's badder for them than advertising.

December 26, 1989

A Piece of the Wall **139**

Don't Leave Romania Without It

Sammy Davis Jr. opened for Mikhail Gorbachev, Candice Bergen's horse reared high as Czechs yelled "Svoboda!" (freedom), and Mary Steenburgen contemplated Chinese hunger strikers. "The shell of an old world cracked, its black iron fragments dropping away, and something new, alive, exploded into the air in a flurry of white wings," wrote *Time* magazine, heralding its Man of the Decade special section—the stories, the words, the very type dropping away, and something new exploding into the air in a flurry of stylish, prodigal, capitalist white space: the American Express celebrity ads.

Ads piggybacking on East Euro Lib are tripping over themselves, like Pepsi's or AT&T's, which both flash some wall and product between newscasts. But the wiliest merchandising of freedom has been American Express's *Time* ads, vastly more subtle. AmEx bought all the ad space surrounding the massive Man of the Decade feature—the first time the magazine has ever sold it to an exclusive sponsor—and retained the right of first refusal to do so in coming years. Photographed in elegant hyperreality by Annie Leibovitz, the 14 pages of ads seem to do nothing more than to humbly bear witness to history, their meaning amplified only by the happy accident of their context. But the whole enterprise reflects what *Time* wrote in introducing Gorby: "Revolution took on . . . a quality of hallucination."

It seems only natural for AmEx to mix it up with the Decade Man. *Advertising Age* just named AmEx's two-and-a-half-year-old Portraits series the Print Campaign of the Decade, and, any day now, the company will bring out similarly intimate portraits in television form. They'll star Meryl Streep and Paul Newman (heretofore Newman has been one of those ad-celibate celebs who've pushed products only in the relative obscurity of Japan).

But AmEx's canny placement in the decade issue best represented what the American sense of politics is all about: celebrity and the only-too-bearable lightness of being.

The nine, mostly new, AmEx ads feature 12 famous people. Gordie Howe and Wayne Gretsky are chatting in a locker room; turn the page and Gorbachev's applauding. There's Gorby embracing Castro, Honecker, Deng, the pope, and Bush; keep reading and there's Barbara Jordan on a dusty road embracing the American flag. The short profiles of each de-communisted country are surrounded by art-director white space, which blends nicely with the more ample white space in which the celebrities are identified by name and the year they became American Express "members." So victory-fisted Soviet throngs face Jessica Tandy and Hume Cronyn in sunglasses and all smiles on the boardwalk in Atlantic City. Following a double-page spread of a Chinese student on a hunger strike is a double-page spread of a reclining Mary Steenburgen, looking like John Singer Sargent's *Madame X*. As each ad says, "Membership Has Its Privileges." Wilt Chamberlain and Willie Shoemaker do their sterling giant/shrimp pose to close this 38-page redefinition of the term "card-carrying" (Raisa reportedly carries a gold card).

AmEx says they didn't know beforehand who the man of the decade would be, but whoever it was (and anyone could've guessed), AmEx knew that his or her achievement would resonate with the achievers who always people their ads. "It's one of those rare opportunities where an advertising campaign directly fits the editorial positioning of an issue," says Kenneth Chenault, president of AmEx's Consumer Card Group.

And how well it fits. Celebrities have exchange value, they are immediately cashable. By definition, adored for something bigger than their particular selves, they take on an aristocratic, abstract quality. Why the hell is Sammy Davis Jr. (who kicks off the *Time* issue) doing a soft-shoe jig in the middle of a desert? Celebrities live on air. Neither do they spin nor sew. Celebrity is the ability to get people to lend you money. How perfect for a corporation that neither spins nor sews, but primarily services the lending of money. Which isn't far from the image of the Western economy. Like a big credit card company, it just gives you money. If you're smart and go with the West, maybe you'll become famous.

The Portraits campaign was devised in 1987 when the "Do you

know me?" series started to go stale, and AmEx's agency, Ogilvy & Mather, reversed the usual division of labor between ad media. Usually, print ads discuss a product's specific features, while the more emotional image-making is handled by TV. "We flip-flopped it," says O&M senior art director Parry Merkley, who created the Portraits series with creative director Gordon Bowen. "We took the features of the card and demonstrated them on television, and we took the prestige of the card and put that into the print."

Intriguing as they are, the print ads are all about vanity, which goes to the core of our culture. What Annie Leibovitz has caught in her remarkable photos—the hyperreal gleam is often achieved with strobe lighting—is the feeling that these people are doing what they really prefer to do in those rare moments when they don't have to do the thing they're famous for—Eric Heiden skates in swim trunks, James Earl Jones pets a bunny. Their fantasies finally unfettered by fame, they no longer ask, "Do you know me?" Rather, it's "I know you know me—now watch this!"

It's a quality AmEx hopes to catch in the TV extension of portraits. "TV will allow us to bring out even further that emotional dimension," says Chenault.

In the last few years, AmEx TV ads have served as very slick role models of how to spend money without seeming crass—especially for women, a market the company has aggressively sought. AmEx has woven its presence into the liberation of '80s go-for-it women even more than the liberation of Eastern Europeans. American Express doesn't shy away from making sappy and grandiose claims, like your everyday hawker. It's just that it looks so urbane while doing it. In one TV spot, AmEx even demonstrates how the card allowed one woman to give birth to twins! And that even outperforms Citibank's MasterCard, which, according to its spots, merely allows a family to adopt a little girl and helps a widow to survive.

If only American Express had offered Nicolae Ceausescu a "Do you know me?" spot years ago, maybe party membership might not have had its privileges.

January 23, 1990

The Face of the People

Companies are airing ads and odes to the new decade as if they were hyping a miniseries, perhaps one called *The '90s: A Return to Values*. Already the '90s means global, hope, green—it's a people decade. *Good Housekeeping* magazine has taken out ads declaring the '90s the "Decency Decade" (as if the last one had exposed itself, which, I suppose, it did). Sure, there's human wonderment over what the future will bring, but the rush to name that decade is also fueled by the urge to package *something*—a new and improved *feeling*—in order to sell it or at least its T-shirt. Greed is out—it no longer boosts profits.

But that's cynical. People 'round the world do say "om" together, i.e., they say "Coke." As the most recognized brand name in the world, Coca-Cola has a lot at stake in promoting Trekkie fantasies of one-worldism: We'll come to recognize our common destiny through the brands we have in common. And so Coke says it decided "to usher in the 1990s" with a new version of its 1971 "Hilltop" commercial, in which hundreds of teenagers from 30 countries dressed in native togs, stood on an Italian hill, and sang "I'd like to buy the world a Coke!" Only this time, the 400 or so folks include some of the original cast, now grown and singing with their children. The spot begins with the same blond British female, only 19 years later and with a teen of her own, warbling, "I'd like to buy the world a home and furnish it with love." (The five-month search by a detective agency to locate the original caffeine kids cost $25,000 alone.) "Hilltop Reunion" debuted on the Super Bowl in "QSound," which is supposed to be like 3-D sound if you have a stereo TV (for the last Super Bowl the company hyped a 3-D commercial, which turned out to be as flat as most diet sodas).

Coke has used the big, bountiful humanity gambit before: Three years ago, more than a thousand adolescents sang for the arms summit; earlier, Coke was a major sponsor of Hands Across America; and in 1977, a phalanx of kids aligned themselves in the shape of a Christmas tree and sang of Coke. The important thing for peace-loving corporations is to herd in *lots* of humans, of many colors, and, for the finale, pull back with an aerial shot from God's p.o.v.

The '90s as a corporate-sponsored '60s

In this, British Airways out-Cokes the cola. Like its '83 spot in which the island of Manhattan seems to land in London, BA's is this year's whammo ad.

Four hundred people in ruby-red bathing suits and caps swim out of what looks like an ocean, form into a pair of lips, and march across a desert like a kiss-shaped army of red ants. On a city street, people in blue compose a huge eye. Eyes, lips, and nose meet in a Picassoesque jumble on a salt flat. Like earthworks art or the giant symbols etched into the desert floor by the Anasazi Indians, the sight, filmed at remarkable locations throughout Utah, is entrancing, and is backed beautifully by Delibes's opera *Lakme,* remixed by Malcolm McLaren. But the sales hook is less Sex Pistols than Hallmark, as hundreds of folks of all ethnicities embrace each other as if the desert were an airport waiting room; a matron kisses a Chinese toddler, a black man hugs a blond cheerleader (she must represent America). "Every year, from all around the world British Airways brings 24 million people together," says narrator Tom Conti.

At the end, the facial features come together to form a 2000-person-large face — it smiles and winks and, at the last second, it becomes a globe.

This is capitalism with a happy face — and, global schmobal, a particularly blue-eyed one at that. What are the '90s? They're a corporate-sponsored '60s: product-enhanced peace and environmental wisdom and never a logo far away. Sixties values are now safe for corporate America. Once anti-ecology, multinationals are now "green." They're rejoicing over revolution in Eastern Europe (British Airways's ad agency itself, the largest in the world, hung a billboard on the Berlin Wall that read, "Saatchi & Saatchi: First Over the Wall"), but you didn't see 16-ounce Coca-Colas handed out during Kent State — which exploded the year before Coke's first "Hilltop" spot aired. What's gnawing at the heart of these Nurturing '90s spots is the feeling that the '60s failed. But if we follow the sponsors' lead, we can have the '60s and our carrot cake too, the '60s sans fear or any rough bumps at all. That's their job — to make life go down smoothly. BA's big face was dreamt up in the first place in order to "bring warmth and humanity to the airline's professional and technical image." (But sometimes the workers need to remind the big people to be warm: When *Chariots of Fire* director Hugh Hudson had the high school students who made up the face working long past mealtime, the kids got together and spelled out the word "lunch.")

Are the '90s going to be as people-friendly as these Hands Across Your Wallet ads would have us hope? The real theme, of course, is not bonding between humans, but between humans and brands. Despite all the hugging of ethnically diverse peoples in these spots, it's the homogenization of diversity that makes global marketing work. Though the face spot is pricey — approximately $2 million for the production alone — considering the 600 million people in 38 countries it will eventually reach, it's "one of the most cost-effective worldwide advertising campaigns ever mounted," BA says. That's the prime goal of global advertising: to use the same promotion for the same product in different countries, with possibly some minor tinkering. Selling product, not '90s enlightenment, is the name of the game. In certain British Airways markets, like South Africa, "some scenes will be changed," a Saatchi & Saatchi exec told me. "In some countries, you can't show blacks and whites together."

Peace.

February 6, 1990

Stay Hungary

The vernacular of East-West freedom continues to evolve, coddling and cooing us into a braver, newer world. Just two weeks before General Electric's annual stockholders' meeting, at which angry boycotters confronted the company for its massive role in nuclear-weapon production, GE brought out a new corporate image spot. Like the GE slogan "We bring good things to life," the premise is so brazen that it begs our cynicism. But, damn, if those production values—the very showcase of capitalism—don't seduce.

In a kind of adult version of McDonald's Moscow ad with its theme of "Food, Folks, and Fun," GE dazzles us with Lights, Love, and Liberty. We're in Budapest, Hungary. Everywhere are smiling people and lit candles. And lights, from street lamps to theatrical floods. They shine on the Danube, on a glorious ballet, they explode with every note of Liszt's "Hungarian Rhapsody." Elegant women and craggy old men let go a litany of phrases that, while perfectly audible, subliminally echo our own most intimate hopes: "Everything is changing. It's wonderful!" "It's a miracle! I'm so happy." "It's like a dream, a beautiful dream." And from an old woman, "I feel young again!" In other words, the good things.

The voiceover explains from whence good things come: "There's a new light shining over Eastern Europe. And in this spirit, GE has entered into a historic partnership with a company called Tungsram, Hungary's leading lighting company." Board member types shake hands over a conference table. "At GE, we're proud to play even a small part in helping the Hungarian people build what promises to be

GE pays extras to raise their candles high.

a truly brilliant future." On that humble note, a rousing finale builds, Liszt segues into GE's jingle, and hundreds of Hungarians raise their candles in a grand salute—not to their hard-won freedom but to the conquering sponsor.

Those candles make a thousand points. They say, "lighten up." They align our new Hungarian friends with a private-sector volunteerism (if not also with President Bush's predecessor, former GE spokesman Ronald Reagan). The wax also serves as a primitive counterpoint to all those West-Is-Best bulbs—a sly suggestion as to just how these Hungarians would be reading their *Wall Street Journals* if GE wasn't there lighting the way.

In fact, other than the lighting systems, there's hardly a modern reference in the 60 seconds. Ladies in floor-length gowns strolling gilded theater lobbies, folks high-stepping in native costume—this is ye olde Hungary, a lush, pre-commie one awash in royalty. Medieval-ish maybe, not in the ethnocentric superstitious way, but in an exotic, fairy-tale vein: New Traditionalism spun out on a geopolitical scale.

Almost as misleading is the ad's casual description of Tungsram as "Hungary's leading lighting company"—it's Hungary's *only* lighting company. Last fall, GE bought half its stock plus one share, giving it controlling interest.

Though expanding rapidly all over Western Europe, GE is an odd one to pocket coins behind the Iron Curtain. "They're making profits off both ends—lobbying for a defense budget to maintain the cold war *and* benefiting from the thaw in the cold war," says Nancy Cole, executive director of INFACT, the nonprofit group that since 1986 has led the boycott of GE. The company racks up a long list of nuke don'ts: It makes the neutron triggers for every U.S. nuclear bomb. It plays major roles in the development of the Stealth bomber, Stars Wars, and many other nuclear systems. "The taxpayer money grossed by GE for nuclear weapons work from 1984 to 1988 came to $18.3 billion," says Cole. GE has also left several radioactive sites in its wake and has been convicted of fraud involving government contracts.

INFACT has convinced some chain stores to stock alternative brands of light bulbs (until recently, Target sold GE exclusively). The boycott has cost GE at least $60 million in lost sales, INFACT claims. A GE spokesman would only say, "Sales and market share of all the products they have targeted have increased since the boycott."

While GE has brought freedom to Eastern Europe, Kentucky Fried Chicken is bringing East Euros *here* to foster a much more important freedom: the freedom to eat cholesterol.

A hefty *babushka* is immigrating to the U.S. to join her slimmer family—who immediately haul her off to a mall. Her eyes pop out, she trashes her old lady shoes for some Reeboks. But she doesn't quite get this freedom thing until she faces the KFC counter and orders her first bucketful. "For Leeza Venashenko, this is a very big day," intones the voiceover. As she chomps into a drumstick, he brings it home: "Today Leeza Venashenko is getting her first taste of America."

With McDonald's pecking at its chicken business, KFC actually aired a funny spot a few months ago. Ronald McDonald is grilled by congressmen, who demand to know what he can offer in the way of chicken that KFC doesn't already provide. "Toys," he says, "toys." Many people thought that spot was awfully mean to a national institution; it faded away. So KFC came up with the politically safe *babushka* ad, one that conceivably could help it boost drooping sales, as StairMaster Nation shuns fried foods. Deprived for so long, our Russian grandmother appreciates the grease—who are we to turn up our noses?

We're starting to see how corporate America is packaging the fall of communism in ever more subtle wrappings. It's presented not just as the validation of capitalism, but the people of the bloc also serve as role models for us—in their cute, pathetic little way, of course. They are at the vanguard of a mega-New Traditionalism that better illuminates the spiritual significance of ours. As they yearn to return to their happier, if sometimes benighted, ways we yearn to return to our Donna Reed America.

KFC's ad is also all in the family. PepsiCo, which owns KFC and Pizza Hut, is moving big into the Soviet Union. It recently doubled its Russian soda distribution in a $3 billion-worth deal—which also includes the opening of two Moscow Pizza Huts, in direct competition with McDonald's, which, by the way, serves only Coke.

As McDonald's, PepsiCo, Coca-Cola, GE, and other giant advertisers make us feel good about ourselves, they are balkanizing Eastern Europe: the commie bloc replaced by the corp blocs. Composed of consonant-crazed countries, the new bloc will one day spell freedom "GEKFCMcD."

May 8, 1990

Puff Piece

The success of a 12-year-old girl's antismoking subway ad attests to the existence of a primal anti-ad reflex. "Come to where the cancer is," the headline reads, over a crayon drawing of a skeletal Marlboro

Man riding through a cemetery of tombstones labeled "lung cancer" and "heart disease." Ads against addictions—whether to cigarettes, drugs, or TV itself—tend to be the most powerful, because they indirectly present addiction as a kind of constant, self-perpetuating ad campaign.

One measure of this primal anti-ad urge is that some 10,000 copies of the Marlboro parody poster have been stolen, apparently the largest number of ripped-off subway ads ever. Most were probably taken for Christmas presents, figures Joe Cherner of the Coalition for a Smoke-Free City, which sponsored a citywide school contest for the best anti-smoking ad. Cherner says he's been besieged by requests for Melissa Antonow's poster from hospitals, workplaces, the L.A. transit system, and the media in Europe (where the Marlboro Man *is* America). But by the time you read this, the pile o' bones cowboy campaign will probably be over, no longer razzing the largest category of subway and bus advertising—cigarettes.

In the ongoing controversy over cigarette (and alcohol) advertising, there is an alternative to the proposed bans that flirt with denting the First Amendment. It's counterads. Ads that go further than, say, the Isuzu liar or the Energizer Bunny spots that playfully acknowledge how advertising tries to put one over on us. The postmod mind occasionally requires such ad moments, as homage to its sophistication. But a good anti-ad goes backward, to the premodern moment of distrust and resentment. Yeah!

So when adman Paul Keye won the $28.6 million account for California's "Tobacco Education Campaign" (financed by a 25-cents-per-pack tax), he tried to convince Californians not to save their lungs, but to resent the cigarette marketers' manipulation of their minds. In one spot, a husky-voiced businessman brings a smoke-filled room full of bloated cronies to order. "Gentlemen, gentlemen," he huffs. "The tobacco industry has a very serious, multibillion dollar problem. We need more cigarette smokers, pure and simple. Every day 2000 Americans stop smoking. Another 1100 also quit—actually, technically, they die," he says with perfect pitch. "That means that this business needs 3000 fresh volunteers every day. So forget all about all that cancer, heart disease, emphysema, stroke stuff. Gentlemen, we're not in this business for our health." (The actor who made this speech sound better than it reads died two months ago of a heart attack, which his family believes was related to his former two-pack-a-day habit.)

A new California spot skewers industry flacks, showing them testifying before Congress with exactly the same words they utter daily: "Statistics can't prove a causal relationship between smoking and disease." "We're accused of trying to get people to start smoking. We don't. We try to get people to *switch*." The spot ends in Surgeon General type style: "WARNING: Some people will say anything to sell cigarettes."

It's hard to argue against people's pleasures, but it's easier to argue against the people who manipulate them. This is especially true for kids, whom Keye believes many cigarette ads are really aimed at ("Take a look at the Camel character—a muppetized, warm, huggy ectomorph," he says). "When we talked to kids about the health effects of smoking, their eyes glazed over," says Keye, whose agency also made the infamous "This is your brain on drugs" spot. "The average 10- to 12-year-old sees smoking as an act of individuality. But when we talked to them along the lines of 'Somebody's been playing with the front of your brain, it's not your idea,' they got interested."

Ads like these can be more potent than bans on cigarette advertising, which raise all sorts of First Amendment issues. (Actually, the Supreme Court has ruled that commercial speech is less protected than political speech. But the general assumption is, if a product is legal, it is advertisable—with some restrictions, such as limits on advertising prescription drugs.) If more states followed California's lead, cig companies could choke on their own ad dollars: The more money they spend (over $3 billion in 1988 alone), the more antibody ads they would necessarily create.

For a brief spin, this arrangement actually existed in America. In 1967, under the (now banished) Fairness Doctrine, TV cigarette advertising was considered a "controversial message," and the FCC therefore required broadcasters to provide air time of roughly one counterad to every three cigarette spots. When, in 1971, Congress did ban cigarette ads from TV (on the grounds that television reached so many minors, to whom the sale of cigarettes is technically illegal), the cigarette companies decided they'd rather switch than fight—going off the air would save them from the humiliations of the counterads.

Meanwhile, all the recent congressional attempts at banning or restricting cigarette and liquor advertising have gone nowhere. A just-released study by the Department of Education called for a ban of both industries' ads if, by 1992, an independent agency concludes that they target minors. The study also recommends that these advertisers finance counterads aimed at minors, though the department has no power of enforcement.

But the ad campaign that really cuts to the bone of it all is still in its infant stage. It's a series of paid TV spots called "Tubehead," in which people struggle to wrench TV sets off their heads. "Don't spend your life in the tube," the voiceover warns. Produced by the nonprofit Media Foundation, the spots are running only in Vancouver, Canada, but the organization plans to eventually bring them to the States. In its quarterly magazine, *Adbusters,* the Media Foundation links TV addiction to consumer culture and environmental destruction. But even they aren't for a ban on television—they just want to use it to run anti-TV addiction ads.

It all comes full circle. As Melissa, the girl who made the poster, says, "I got the Marlboro Man from a *TV Guide* ad. I wanted to reverse it and make the Marlboro Man dead."

December 11, 1990

Toxic Moxie

Whales leaping and seals clapping in a commercial is a sure sign of a mean green corporate PR machine. Star Kist, after being forced to stop killing dolphins in its tuna nets, is now getting green mileage out of letting them live. The company's latest ad features mama and baby dolphins nuzzling each other and arching out of the ocean, just like they do in the tiny pictures on its new "dolphin-safe" cans. But sea-loving mammals can lend *any* company a pristine, hearty look, something blubbery to counter a toxic, or decadent, reputation.

Take Absolut Vodka, which has recently gone eco and arctic. A four-page spread that ran in the December issues of *Interview* and *L.A. Style* depicts an icy world of sea otters, reindeer, polar bears, and penguins. The catchy Absolut moment springs out of a microchip implanted in the magazine (at a cost of about $1 million): Peel back the "lift and listen" tab and a woman's voice says, "Every animal and plant on this page is in danger of extinction, and every day you make hundreds of decisions that will affect their fate. . . . The importers of Absolut Vodka invite you to take the future of our planet into your own hands."

I know I'm supposed to say, "Wow," but for me the connection between alcohol, icebergs, and innocent animals just adds up to Captain Hazelwood. So potent is the thought of him at the helm of the Exxon *Valdez* that I almost forgot about Absolut's other gas-guzzling ads—the so hip sculptures installed on flatbed trucks that back up Manhattan traffic and undermine the 10 green tips printed under the polar bears (like "Don't leave the water running when you're brushing your teeth . . .").

You can almost bet on an inverse relationship between reality and ad: The worse a company's environmental transgressions, the more glorious its "celebration of the planet." In fact, Greenpeace has compiled a chart, "Polluters' PBS Penance," that lists companies, their "crimes," and the expression of their sorrow—usually sponsorship of a PBS wildlife show. Du Pont, for instance, may be one of the world's largest producers of ozone-destroying chlorofluorocarbons (CFCs), but it did underwrite *Discoveries Underwater* and now funds public radio's daily "Pulse of the Planet."

The inverse relationship in Du Pont's latest ad is even more mind-numbing: One of the companies most responsible for the ozone hole over Antarctica is literally applauded by some of the very animals that should be slathering themselves in SPF 30. While a seal lounges on a rock, a voiceover says, "Recently Du Pont announced that its energy unit would pioneer the use of new double-hulled oil tankers in order to safeguard the environment." As the spot breaks into Beethoven's "Ode to Joy," seals clap, duck flap, sea otters kiss, whales jump, dolphins arch, and penguins, the resident Antarcticans, chirp. "The response," says the VO, "has been overwhelmingly positive."

The animals are so adorable, the music and their movement to it so exhilarating, that they blow facts and numbers out of the water. It's true that Du Pont's oil subsidiary Conoco announced that it would make double-hulled tankers—before a new law required it. But Conoco has its own little landlocked *Valdez* situation. The company is paying $23 million to 400 families in Ponca City, Oklahoma, to relocate, because their homes have been contaminated with toxins from Conoco's huge refinery there.

And while seals may or may not applaud Conoco, toucans and spider monkeys are probably hooting at it. Their habitat, Ecuador's tropical rain forest—also homeland of the Huaorani Indians—is the probable site of the company's newest oil fields. Du Pont chairman Edgar Woolard, who calls himself the company's "chief environmentalist," is reportedly wavering over the final decision, in part because of the damage it could do to the corporate image.

Under Woolard, the company charged with being the nation's number-one source of toxic chemical emissions has been trying to play the environmental card. Du Pont swears it's going to reduce emissions as well as banish those troublesome CFCs. What it doesn't emphasize is that an international agreement requires all companies to phase out CFCs by the year 2000.

According to Greenpeace, "Since 1974 Du Pont has vigorously challenged objective scientific research on ozone issues [and] fought for delays in government regulation of ozone-destroying chemicals. . . . When the alarming documentation of the severity of the Antarctic ozone hole was announced . . . Du Pont and the CFC industry denied any linkage to CFC use."

As alternatives to CFCs, Du Pont is pushing HCFCs and HFCs. While the hydro compounds are less destructive than CFCs, they are, says Greenpeace, "in some cases ozone-destroyers, in some cases greenhouse gases, and in most cases have serious toxicity problems."

Pointing out the contradictions between green ads and the sludge-colored reality is getting eerily easy. But such ubiquitous advertising almost always snuffs out the occasional flash of contradictory info. It's not just that corporations can better afford persuasive images; they can also better control the opposition. This seems obvious, but while we're all focusing on outside forces of media influence—i.e., the Japanese buying movie studios—we miss the homegrown variety.

After the protests against Star Kist made boycotts sexy again, the *Today Show* asked Todd Putnam, editor of the *National Boycott Newsletter*, to do a segment. What would be the next big successful boycott, they asked him in preproduction prepping. Todd thought, and replied, "GE" (boycotted primarily for its massive role in the manufacturing of nuclear weapons). No, the *Today Show* people laughed, GE owns NBC and they couldn't get away with *that*. When Todd finally did appear on the show a few weeks ago, Deborah Norville's people brought out some boycotted props for him to talk about—Hormel meat, California grapes, Nike shoes, Marlboro cigarettes. GE, which also produces glorious, emotion-swelling ads (same agency as Du Pont), was never mentioned. And another opportunity to make a connection, just a connection, was missed.

December 25, 1990

Hawking War

What do advertisers do during wartime? They find, when possible, their own war dividend. Or they suddenly realize that their ads might be offensive and move them far from the war coverage or soften the tone. (Toyota: "We're not running any cutesy or humorous ads.") Or they do kick-butt research: "The people who were most in favor of attacking Iraq are also most inclined to be shopping for consumer goods," says market analyst Leo J. Shapiro in *Advertising Age*. "Hawks are driving this economy," he claims, and goes on to prove it with a series of graphs showing the relative strength of purchase desire among groups dubbed "doves," "mildly hawkish," "hawkish," and "superhawk." (But what assumptions lurk when hawks enjoy a luxurious three categories while doves get stuck with one?)

During the first week of Desert Storm, an uncharacteristic shakiness came over some advertisers—they even questioned whether ads dare air. Motivating their nervous maneuvers is the queasy question avoided by an affluent society at war: "Is *this*—the Real Thing, the Right Choice, the Right Beer Now—what we're fighting for?"

Some companies answer "Yes!" For the first time since the '88 election, blatantly patriotic ads have bolted out of the woodwork. The slo-mo, beery-focus style of the Reagan and Bush campaigns has finally found a hook on which to hang its helmet. Anheuser-Busch hauled out its "Here's to You, America" spot, originally created as a "salute" to the 1984 Olympians, and updated it for the Super Bowl. There it saw action on three fronts: (1) jerking beer tears; (2) reminding you that *this,* the freedom to pop open a cold one, is indeed what we're fighting for; and (3) soberly countering the bellicose exuberance of the Bud Bowl. (Bud denies a report that it pulled a Bud Bowl spot that included someone urging a quarterback to "throw the bomb!")

Budweiser wasn't the only company to treat the Super Bowl as a crucible for conflicting ad attitudes about war. While Pepsi fired its arsenal of good-time ads, Coke tried to take them out with a few more-Patriot-than-thou missiles, replacing its "Crack the Code" ads with sober messages on title cards. The voiceover explained that during the gulf crisis, "we feel it would be inappropriate to run our lighthearted commercials." It seemed a remarkable sacrifice—until the spot reminded you to "collect more game pieces with specially marked packages of Diet Coke."

Throughout the first war week, CNN ran a peacenik's worst nightmare—a montage of our men and women in uniform preparing for combat, set to "America, the Beautiful," and with a logo at the end: Boeing. Boeing, of course, produces many of the weapons systems now being used in the gulf, including AWACS, B-52s, KC-135 tankers, and Avenger air-defense systems.

But the spot, which ran for five days last week, was not created for the gulf. It resulted, curiously enough, from the threat of world peace that we experienced a year ago. "It was a very unsettling time to be in the service," says Elliot Pulham, ad manager for Boeing Defense and Space Group, citing the prospect of military layoffs. "So we made a spot and eventually ran it for the Army-Navy games and Veteran's Day. We're a very middle-American, patriotic company, and we believe very much in what they're doing." Boeing hasn't received the sort of windfall publicity won by Raytheon, maker of the Patriot missile (war footage of which is sure to be recycled into ads come defense-contract budget-talk time); but since the ad, Boeing has received hundreds of approving phone calls a day.

Self-interest is even bolder at Texaco. Pre-war, but post-invasion, it ran a series of 15-second Q&A conservation spots: "How can you save 12 percent on your gasoline bill every year?" one asked. "Have a regular tune-up," was the answer. After January 15, however, Texaco revised the campaign so that all four spots now ask a new question: "How can you help stop America's growing dependence on foreign oil?"

Texaco doesn't consider this crass, because, says a spokesperson, "they're not product advertising." But if I were the punch line of the second-best-known antiwar chant—"Hell, no, we won't go! We won't fight for Texaco!"—I wouldn't want to reinforce the connection between blood and oil. The spokesperson claims that Texaco is unfazed by its role in the peace marches. "There's a couple other companies that rhyme with that, and we're just better known."

But so far most of the ad industry is retreating. That's because in times of war, we re-see TV; the light it shines is refracted by shrapnel as well as the usual coins. Ads during wartime become offensive when they allow us to form new, unintended commercials in our heads. Normally, a red car rolling through the Mojave Desert is a beautiful thing; but now, any sandy landscape evokes a battlefield. The U.S. Armed Forces, for instance, has indefinitely suspended all advertising. When you hear "Be all that you can be," the Desert Storm-era reflex is to say, "Yeah, dead."

Ads that pitched Chips Ahoy! cookies as "richer than an OPEC nation" were pulled, too. Some companies—Procter & Gamble, GM, McDonald's—simply won't run ads during extended news coverage, while others are avoiding humor. GM has even predicted a whole new "soberness and fundamentalism in advertising." TWA goes further, vowing not to advertise until the war's over. This could mean a multi-million-dollar loss in ad revenues for the networks, who sent panicky memos to their sponsors. ABC, for instance, promised that "no [commercial] breaks will be scheduled immediately before or after scenes of action."

But perhaps the future of wartime ads lies in walking that line between offending sensibilities and putting up a strong offense. Dodge will keep "Johnny Comes Marching Home" as its theme music, but will literally turn down the volume. "We're not taking advantage of the situation," a spokesperson says. "We just didn't want to be too obvious."

Bowls Away! Halftime at the Super Bowl has always had a martial bearing, but this one, starting with a child singing to our troops, brought the war home in a way sure to make the rest of the world hate us even more. It was a Disney production, and the flags, the Bushes, and the big lug players kneeling in respect seemed to salute not so much God or country, but the castle from Disneyworld's Fantasyland, magically rising from the 50-yard line.

When hordes of children of service people "representing every one of our 50 states" were marched out, the connection between fantasy, war, and football rolled ever tighter—the viewer could make out only one black face among them. And as the song "America" heaved passionately, the camera pulled to an aerial view—much like the fighter plane p.o.v.'s we've grown accustomed to—so we could see the human-formed letters *USA* filling the stadium. Meaning began to form: the country as logo. The nation must've thought on cue, "Whadda target!"—except the weapon that's likely to drop isn't a smart bomb but another dumb ad.

"Norman Schwarzkopf—you've leveled five mosques, decimated 400 villages, and taken out the entire Iraqi offense. What are you gonna do next?"

"I'm going to Disneyland!"

February 5, 1991

Green Monsters

Seeing ads lace through war footage on the nightly news is to *almost* see that we are making war to preserve the American way of consuming. But such a revelation is quickly obscured by the very point of advertising: While most of us may be addicted to war news, we're also hooked on denial—and ads are nothing if not a paradigm for how to block out the bad and get back to the buying. Whenever a causal connection between, say, greed and destruction begins to break through to consciousness, ads march out as the rear guard that destroys the bridge.

Two weeks ago, more than 600 reps from the titans of industry, ad agencies, and PR firms acted *almost* as if they were ready to accept responsibility for the mess we're in and were going to do their darnedest to fix it. They were at the Crowne Plaza Holiday Inn attending *Advertising Age's* First Annual Green Marketing Summit, but their seeming fervor to do well by doing good was so intense they might've been at church for the day.

"Green marketing"—using an environmental angle to sell products that may or may not be so eco—drew a crowd of dubious do-gooders. Along for the ride were Mobil (Hefty trash bag fiasco) Oil, Union (Bhopal) Carbide, Dow (napalm) Chemical, Philip (cancer stick) Morris, G (nuke weapons) E, Du (largest CFC manufacturer) Pont, and even L'eggs (which sells itsy-bitsy pantyhose in giant plastic eggshells 'cause it's kicky!). Corporate PR apologists like Hill and Knowlton clinked nonstyrofoam coffee cups with folks from green mag *Buzzworm*, Friends of the Earth, and Scenic America (the environmental group that opposes environmental groups like Greenpeace using landscape-despoiling billboards to spread the word).

But only a few stars of the show tied environmentalism and energy to why we're at war. "How can you talk about toilet paper and light bulbs when a war is on?" Earth Day organizer Denis Hayes asked rhetorically. He went on to explain how they're completely related in a society dependent on oil and oil-based products and packaging. Joe Cappo, publisher of *Ad Age,* drew a comparison between Saddam

Hussein's "conscious decision to cause the largest oil spill in history" and, say, a publisher's decision not to use recycled paper.

But most of the summit focused on the more pragmatic question of what sort of guidelines should be instituted for green label claims, and who should regulate them—the Federal Trade Commission, the National Advertising Division of the Council of Better Business Bureaus (an industry-financed group that currently oversees ad claim disputes), or independent environmental groups like Hayes's Green Seal, which would slap a label on environmentally correct products. The controversy of the moment is, Is it misleading for a company to claim that a product is recyclable if no recycling facilities exist where the product is sold? The new conventional wisdom holds that claims should be specific—nothing like "environmentally friendly" or "safe for the environment"—although getting companies to kick that habit is like asking them to stop saying "new."

Differences in "philosophy," as businesses like to call their strategies, threatened the aura of planetary unity. Procter & Gamble ad manager and environmental point man Robert Viney stressed that until consumers change *their* behavior, industry can't do a heck of a lot. *Ad Age* columnist Bob Garfield scandalized the crowd by saying that for GM, fighter of emissions reduction, to advertise its dedication to the environment "is like John Wayne Gacy celebrating the International Year of the Child." ("Isn't that libelous?" one audience member gasped.) But in marketing it's just a matter of what you can get away with: The same week that P&G was looking good and green, the FDA told it to get rid of *Fresh* in its Citrus Hill Fresh Choice orange juice because it's made from a concentrate. P&G argued that "research showed consumers were not misled."

Still, the chant was "coalition." "Government can't [develop environmental politics] alone; business can't do it alone; individuals can't do it alone," said one panelist. "If we leave out one of those cogs, we're doomed to failure." And yet the coalition most mentioned was an all-industry one led by the National Food Processors Association and including 20 trade groups and a few of the major players like P&G, Lever, Kraft, and Nestlé. This month, they will recommend a series of labeling guidelines that they want the FTC to institute. Meanwhile, a group of 10 state attorney generals, which has taken a tough stance on fraudulent ad claims of all sorts, is also making recommendations to the FTC. Some corporate types don't care for this. "We believe since industry is the one to actually make the changes it should be the one to set the model guidelines for the FTC," said Melinda Sweet, environmental overseer for Lever Bros. P&G opposes independent environmental groups like Green Seal because, said Viney, research found that consumers are "less willing to accept little inconveniences or support funding for new [recycling] infrastructures if they can purchase a product with a seal and think they are doing their part." Yes, but that's exactly what companies like P&G have trained us to do for generations—to equate the brand label with all things good.

At best, it all sounded like the multiracial, gender-balanced team of teens who combine their separate powers of wind, fire, water, earth, and heart to create . . . Captain Planet!—the white cartoon hero of the TBS green cartoon show that was shown at the conference and inspired more people than anything else.

Except maybe for Texas adman Roy Spence, who delivered this unadlike sermon from the stage: "If you think it's a gimmick, get out right now. You trick 'em one time, they don't give you a second chance. Hard sell, soft sell isn't the issue. We created the disposable society—I did—any hands out there? [About 20 out of 600 went up.] We have to uncreate it."

February 19, 1991

War Is Bell

Running a war is like running an election campaign: The same man who gave us Willie Horton gave us Saddam Hussein. The "message of the day" strategy, honed to android efficiency in '88, now serves as the model for image coordination between Pentagon, White House, and State Department. So it's only natural that when a corporation takes the risky but potentially lucrative step of running ads to get good rub-off from a popular war, they hire a savvy political consultant.

NYNEX telecommunications has made the first TV ad designed to tap the war dividend (Boeing's patriotic salute to people in the service was produced long before the war and hauled out later). It shows our troops in the gulf and the folks at home connecting through telephone, television, and anything electronic. But NYNEX couldn't trust such a politically fraught project to its regular ad agencies. Instead, it went to the Sawyer/Miller Group, a political consultancy firm that has worked for Democratic candidates, including Dukakis, Moynihan, and Glenn, as well as the occasional secular client, like Drexel Burnham, that needs some high-level corporate strategizing.

NYNEX is a real trend-bucker for running a war ad at all. While many companies, dreading dismembered limbs popping up near their

But NYNEX didn't make this call possible.

logos, are placing spots as far from the war news as possible, NYNEX is jamming them right into the Pentagon briefings. What goes here?

The ad is a grainy, anxious montage of 15 shots in as many seconds: American soldiers in Saudi desert, women at home watching fighter planes on TV, woman on phone (in anguish?), computerized control panel, DJ on radio show, soldier on phone, and so on, all to staticky electric background noise until one woman utters the only intelligible words: "I want to know." Pull to (yet another) long shot of Planet Earth, and then to this solemn notion scrolling on screen: "Never is information more crucial to democracy than at times like these." Finally, the NYNEX logo silently appears, by now deserving the kind of respect we'd show the flag.

The impression is that through the sophisticated NYNEX network, our troops and civilians are able to stay in constant communication. In fact, NYNEX seems to be almost a *part* of the news, a vital cog in what's going on in the world today.

But here's the rub in the rub-off: NYNEX isn't involved in the war effort at all. The military doesn't use NYNEX equipment. And warriors can't call womenfolk on NYNEX. As owner of baby bell companies New York Telephone and New England Telephone, NYNEX by law isn't even allowed to go into the long-distance phone business. "Our involvement is our commercial," a NYNEX spokesman admits.

The commercial, however, "dovetails with our longer-range corporate image campaign that we're a leader in helping people communicate."

See, it works out so neatly! Although the bulk of NYNEX's business lies in its domestic phone companies and its Yellow and White Pages, it also has holdings overseas in consulting services, cellular systems, and directories, making it "one of the top 10 [telecommunications] companies in the world." The problem is that people think of NYNEX, if they think of it all, as some sort of local phone thing. It needs that sexy global edge.

Enter the war.

But using the mother of all battles to enhance corporate image is, PR-wise, as rife with land mines as the Kuwaiti desert. Hence, the political consultants, better equipped to face these dangers than a mere ad agency.

A memo from Sawyer/Miller to NYNEX, summarizing the ad's effect on focus groups, is a revealing look at what goes into such a landmine-sweeping campaign.

"The bottom line was very clear: reaction to the NYNEX spot exceeded all our expectations," the memo reads. "Rather than creating any of the negative responses we were concerned with, this kind of advertising has clear power for NYNEX. . . ." Sawyer/Miller's fear was not that NYNEX's claim as an electronic war hero would seem spurious. No, the challenge was how to use to NYNEX's advantage America's newly acquired addiction to the news (people are " 'feeling guilty' when they are away from the news too long," the research found, "but [are] also feeling traumatized by some of what they have seen") without seeming crass.

In this context, "traditional product commercials suddenly seem irritating and to some extent trivial," the report says. "The only commercials that seemed 'appropriate' to the new content of the news and the new interest in newsviewing, were those that acknowledged the reality that the news was communicating." Which is why NYNEX, rather than run from the war, decided to ride with it.

But NYNEX clearly didn't want to be associated with an outright emotional spectacle like Boeing's "America the Beautiful" spot, which Sawyer/Miller deemed "a very high-risk strategy," noting that if "support for the war diminishes in any way, the downside for Boeing will increase proportionately." For shelf-life, NYNEX needed to make an ad vague enough that viewers could read whatever they want into it and yet hot enough that they *want* to read it. How do you do that? Reflect their anxiety (with all that tight-wire pacing and indecipherable noise), and then quickly soothe them by referring to the cool, seemingly value-free zone of "information"—something everyone agrees is good. (Unless the military tells them they don't need to know it. And speaking of the free dissemination of info, remember when NYNEX balked at creating a separate heading for gay and lesbian organizations in its Yellow Pages?) Fortunately, the researchers found, the spot "created none of the backlash of reaction that the Boeing spot elicited. As one respondent put it, 'It appealed to our heads and not our hearts.' "

And in the end, NYNEX got what it wanted. *"Ironically,"* the memo states, *"the war actually seems to help people understand the globalism of NYNEX."* (Italics theirs.)

That's what we go to war for. But ironic nothing: NYNEX found a source of angst to grab viewers' attention, made it seem like they are *somehow* doing *something* about it, and there you have it—the happy accident of misery and merchandising working together again.

March 5, 1991

Watts Nuke?

For years, GE has successfully equated itself with goodness—"We bring good things to life," "We are the good things," its ads sing. Even when you know you're being manipulated, GE ads make you feel you can solve anything, that all you have to do is sit and watch them and the world will become an ever more beautiful appliance.

But in addition to light bulbs, GE also manufactures nuclear and conventional weapons—one-sixth of its $58 billion in revenues comes from defense contracts—and has left a long trail of nuclear waste and toxic sites in its wake. GE's alternating images—the hypervisibility of "goodness," the invisibility of radiation—create a particularly powerful strobe. Anyone who's been tainted by the destructive by-products of its technology is tainted again, in the ad-softened collective mind, as a naysayer, suspiciously lurking on the other side of the city on a hill that GE paints so well.

The worldview that GE presents is so alluring that the only way a good lefty organization can counter it is with some vaguely populist, Good vs. Evil image advertising of its own. So after years of leading a boycott against GE, corporate watchdog group INFACT is finally playing in the realm of corporate commercialism; on the fifth anniversary of the boycott, it premiered a half-hour video, *Deadly Deception,* that goes up against GE, image to image.

For the first couple of minutes, the video's clips of GE ads still exude the power to soothe and lull. But the gloss gets scuffed with the first populist hit about a baby, living downwind from the GE-operated Hanford nuclear facility, who was born without eyes, and another born without a skull. By the end, familiar jingles take on ominous meanings: "Wherever there's a glow/warmer than you know/we'll be there."

Taking a cue from GE, the video focuses on people. Hanford neighbor Tom Bailie, born with birth defects and now sterile, gives a tour of the area. GE operated the Hanford Nuclear Reservation in southeast Washington state for the government from 1946 through 1965. In the '40s and '50s, GE intentionally, as well as accidentally, released radioactive iodine there, hundreds of times more than was released at Three Mile Island, and probably with more radiation damage to thyroids than at Chernobyl. But unlike Chernobyl, warnings were never issued and no one was ever evacuated. Bailie shows you "Death Mile," where 27 of 28 families have suffered cancers or birth defects, all associated with high doses of radiation.

The secret releases were revealed only in 1986 under a Freedom of Information Act request, and the Energy Department admitted the extent of possible illnesses only last year. But GE still won't comment directly. "It's under investigation," says GE spokesman Ford Slater. "It's inappropriate for us to comment until the facts are known."

Then the video focuses on Knolls Atomic Power Lab, which GE still operates, in Schenectady, New York, and its history of radiation exposures to workers. Breaking down in tears, the brother of a refueling engineer who died of cancer at age 32 tells his story. A 30-year veteran who blew the whistle on falsified safety records only to be hounded out by GE tells his. (Recent GAO testimony, however, found "no significant deficiencies" at Knolls. INFACT contends "there are serious flaws in the study.")

The video points out the pressure would-be whistle blowers faced. A company newsletter warned workers that "unauthorized release of information" could result not just in getting fired but in "fines up to

$100,000" and "up to life imprisonment." Such threats are intercut with CEO John F. Welch Jr. prattling on in a speech about "people closest to the work know the work best."

GE would rather not talk details. "INFACT has made many erroneous allegations about GE," Slater says in a prepared statement. "We have no intention or interest in rebutting or debating their contentions on an allegation-by-allegation basis."

But INFACT, which led the original Nestlé boycott, says this one has so far been successful, partly because GE's ad image of "people helping people" provides such a juicy image to bounce off of. According to INFACT, their campaign has cost GE $30 million in sales from hospitals that have refused to purchase GE medical imaging equipment.

Recently, GE announced that it would pull out of the Pinellas Nuclear Weapons Plant in Florida, which it has operated since 1956. INFACT attributes the decision to the boycott; GE says it's a business decision made because, for the first time, the government demanded that GE be held liable for any future environmental clean-ups.

"The boycott has had no significant impact whatsoever," says Slater. "Since 1985, the year before the boycott began, GE revenues have gone up 79 percent from $32 billion to $58 billion. Earnings are up 87 percent."

Anyway, in producing nukes, GE is "simply following the nation's defense policy," Slater says. But, as the video points out, with the largest Washington, D.C., office of any defense contractor and with close ties to the White House and the Pentagon, GE helps make that policy. GE didn't do badly during the gulf war, with its "jet engines powering more than half of the military aircraft in use," says Slater. GE's ad agency, BBDO, is headed by Phil Dusenberry—who was also a Tuesday Team member for Reagan's '84 campaign. (Not so incidentally, BBDO also makes those glory ads in which penguins applaud another toxic big boy, Du Pont.)

Getting *Deadly Deception* on TV will be difficult. Take NBC, which is owned by GE. A few months ago, a *Today Show* guest was invited to talk about boycotts but wasn't allowed to discuss the GE boycott;

in 1987, NBC aired a documentary called *Nuclear Power: In France It Works.*

But INFACT will be showing the video on some local cable and public TV stations, and at religious, health care, education, and activist organizations. Major GE customers and shareholders are also being targeted. And last week, it premiered on a cable station in Fairfield, Connecticut, hometown of GE corporate headquarters.

June 25, 1991

Ad-Free Ads

Now that food labels are finally going to be less deception-friendly, as the FDA announced last week, why not the same for advertising? Ads that carry misleading health and nutrition claims present us with (at least) two dangers:

(1) Bodily harm. Ads proclaiming a product contains "No Cholesterol," as a TV spot for Dunkin' Donuts blared, are hazardous to your health, because they can leave you thinking the food will help prevent heart disease, even though its high saturated-fat content can raise your serum-cholesterol level. (The ad was eventually dunked because of "consumer confusion," says DD, as well as pressure from the New York attorney general's office.)

(2) Idiocy. When the Florida Department of Citrus promotes orange juice as "cholesterol-free," it's depending on and fostering a thudding dullness of mind. This is like saying, "Fly Eastern—it's dandruff-free!" Your easily tickled excitement is supposed to distract you from the non sequitur naughtiness. Idiocy-risk is also increased by turning the concept—*any* concept—into a celebrity: Whether the buzzphrase is oat bran or cholesterol, Madonna or Saddam Hussein, the good or the bad, the ads will say it, show it, flash it over and over into numb repetition until we eventually get tired of it and want to smash its little head in!

Whew! Well, we might get a bit of relief if a bill, expected to be introduced in Congress later this month, is ever passed. The situation is almost really simple: Ads may make misleading claims about a product's health and nutritional benefits that are not allowed on the same product's label. The Federal Trade Commission, which tends to promote the spirit of promotion, regulates advertising, while the Food and Drug Administration, which is finally getting tough, regulates most labels. The bill, sponsored by Representative Joe Moakley of Massachusetts, would require that health and nutrition claims in food ads meet the same standards as those for food labels. Like labels, ads would have to follow the guidelines of the Nutrition Labeling and Education Act (NLEA), for which the FDA last week proposed detailed regulations. (Highlight: Words like *lite, fresh,* and *low-fat* will have standard, more realistic definitions.) The Moakley bill, supported by a coalition of 25 consumer, health, and medical groups led by the Center for Science in the Public Interest (CSPI), could wipe that disingenuous smile off CSPI-targeted ads like these:

- A TV spot for Fleischmann's Extra Light corn oil spread starts off with a heartbeat-skipping scare: "Think of your closest friends. Now guess which one risks heart disease. Or is it you?" The solution: "A diet low in saturated fats and cholesterol with Fleischmann's Extra Light." "The problem," says Sharon Lindan of the CSPI, "is that Fleischmann's is high in total fat, which has been associated with an increased risk of cancer and obesity. The NLEA forbids claims like that on labels because the product includes ingredients that could increase the incidence of the disease in question or *another* disease."
- Stouffer's Lean Cuisine advertised that its frozen dinners contain "Never more than a gram of sodium." Sounds good, but at up to 900 milligrams (the NLEA requires sodium be measured in milligrams), they're virtual pillars of salt. In this case, the FTC went after Lean Cuisine, and the company dropped the reference.
- "New Lite Sausage from Swift Premium Brown 'N Serve Lite," the TV ad says, "—76 percent fat-free, 30 percent less salt, 100 percent great taste." Sure, but some of that great taste comes from the re-

maining 24 percent of yummy lard—a very high fat content (even whole milk is only 4 percent fat). It's the sort of misleading math that doesn't see life on the label, which reads "24 percent fat."

The FTC is opposed to the bill because, while it doesn't want to undermine the intent of the NLEA, it's "concerned that what works for labeling may not work for advertising," says Lee Peeler, FTC associate director of advertising practices. "Advertising does things that labeling can't do. It reaches out through the clutter and grabs people's attention. And labeling does a lot that advertising can't do. We're concerned about whether the bill would impose restraints that would make it impractical for ads. For instance, will an ad be required to discuss things only with a set wording, maybe 50 words to explain a claim?"

"This bill recognizes that there are differences between advertising and labeling," counters CSPI's Lindan. "It doesn't require every ad to list all ingredients. It's talking only about health and nutrition claims. Telling only part of the picture is misleading. You're not talking about whether the Jolly Green Giant exists. You're talking about the number-one and number-two killers in our country, heart disease and cancer."

The FDA and the FTC not only operate under two different standards—the FDA requires that label claims be supported by "significant scientific evidence," while the FTC asks for a vaguer "reasonable basis"—but the spirit behind the two agencies also differs. The FDA has finally become aggressive under new commissioner David Kessler—with such Dragnet-like actions as confiscating 12,000 gallons of Citrus Hill Fresh Choice orange juice when Procter & Gamble refused to delete the word *fresh* on a juice that actually comes from a concentrate. While the FTC has sharpened its teeth a tad lately, says the CSPI, it still suffers from "a philosophical hangover from the Reagan administration."

In fact, the latest *Adweek* "enemies list"—the 10 people who most stymie the free hand of advertising—is topped by Michael Jacobson, executive director of the CSPI (which *Adweek* allows is "backed by people who do good science and good law"), and includes Kessler, Moakley, Texas Assistant Attorney General Steve Gardner, and NYC

Commissioner of Consumer Affairs Mark Green. But nowhere is there mention of anyone from the one national agency whose job it is to crack down on ads—the list is 100 percent FTC-free.

November 19, 1991

In the Red Again

From behind the flickering screen, you can hear the sound of 100 admen screaming. Their creations are too happy, too nasty, too sexed, too desperate. Commercial culture under recession is Soviet in reverse: Instead of lines, we have sales, surplus inventory, markdowns, "free" gifts. Begging for shoppers, K mart stays open on Thanksgiving. My favorite little restaurant hires a stilt-walker to hand out fliers—does this mean it'll be closed by Valentine's Day? AT&T mails out $20 checks that people can cash—if they switch to AT&T before December 31! George Bush considers a one-time-only $300 tax rebate—rebait by rebate.

"BUY SOMETHING," Range Rover pleaded in pre-Christmas newspaper ads. "Buy a microwave. A basset hound. Theatre tickets. A Tootsie Roll. *Something.* Because if we all wait for the recession to be officially declared over to start spending again, the problem will simply keep feeding on itself. As for us, we're making a start. We bought this ad." (Or, as Bush tried to say, "Sock it to me!")

Ads rarely appear in the raw like this, but by year end, advertising the concept of buying—even buying ads—became the patriotic thing to do, as crucial to the economy as killing Iraqis was at the beginning of the year. Of course, buying things—along with buying the world that ads present—has long been the pacemaker that keeps the heartbeat of America going.

But this is the recession that squeezes white collars, too, and no one represents them better than ad people, the folks who write the songs that make the whole world shop. They've been undergoing massive

This is a commercial for Bugle Boy

The recessionary position

layoffs for years now, but now the bad news (including much of the following from *Advertising Age*) comes daily: After losing most of its American Express account, Ogilvy & Mather lays off 51. Huge advertiser Du Pont slashes its ad budget by $46 million. National ad spending for 1991 fell 1.5 percent (to $126.7 billion), the worst decline since World War II, according to Bob Coen of McCann-Erikson, who measures these things. (He says '92 looks better, but largely because the Olympics and the elections—the recession-themed elections!—will pump ad spending.)

Agencies are aching for new business. But in a sellers' market, prospective clients can make agencies jump through hoopla—requiring elaborate presentations that can cost hundreds of thousands of dollars. "A lot of agencies," one exec told *Ad Age*, "are spending themselves out of the business by going after every piece of business out there."

And brand-name products—the force that drives the ads that drive the media—are themselves in recession. In 1989, 56 percent of those polled by the Roper Organization said, "I usually know the brand I will buy and get that brand." By 1990, 53 percent agreed; by 1991, the number fell to 46 percent.

All this has placed advertising under a visible strain, inducing the sort of hyperthyroidism that can get an ad into trouble. Camel cigarettes insists it will not alter its penis-face Smooth Character campaign, despite the recent, well-publicized studies that show the cool cartoon figure appeals to children. (One study found that to six-year-olds, Joe Smooth is as recognizable as Mickey Mouse.) In addition to disputing the claims, Camel parent company R. J. Reynolds is rolling out a campaign that tries to convince teenagers not to smoke. Bumper stickers state, "Kids shouldn't smoke." That should do it. Billboards show cartoon kids sneaking a smoke in a bathroom with the headline "And you think this looks cool?" Actually, it does. Just not nearly as cool as Joe makes smoking look.

Old Milwaukee's panting attempt to outwild bimbo beer ads snapped back in its face. Because some female employees of parent company Stroh's are suing for sexual harassment—a situation, they say, encouraged by the ads—the beer can't even promote *Playboy* magazine's promotion of its Swedish Bikini Team. Still, it does get more desperate than this. Budweiser is so eager to regain its eroding market share that it's banning bimbos from ads—vive la différence!

These ads aren't in trouble just because they show too much skin, but because their persuasion is showing. Bugle Boy jeans, which once made ads that had humorous twists, now just shows supposedly humorous tits. "This is a commercial for Bugle Boy's new Color Denims," the titles read. "At least that's what we told Bugle Boy. They wanted to show a bunch of male models. We said showing nothing but beautiful women would work better." Above the titles, the ad is nothing but "beautiful women": a closeup of a woman in panties scratching her butt, a bikinied gal on the beach arching her back coitally, etc., etc. "In an extremely competitive environment," the Bugle Boy publicist told me, "you kind of go back to t&a."

Competitor Jordache uses recession as sex backdrop more pointedly: Against trucks and chain-link fences, a woman starts to strip to a hungry harmonica; a man with greasy hair does, too. They're in sepia and look like the Calvin Klein set, only less expensive. We don't have much money, but we can do it in the road.

Ads use this sepia-industrial style to seduce us not just with sex but with a salve for economic pain. The same agency that boosts Swedish bosoms—Hal Riney & Partners—also feels up our recession-era empathy for a different client, Saturn. While GM just announced 70,000 layoffs, Saturn (based on Japanese factory theory) is one of the few GM divisions doing well.

Past = great, present = bleak, future = bright, a Saturn ad declares. "Life was good, work was good," a male voice says of his past on the assembly line—that is, after he returned from Nam. Even antiwar protests—shots of which we see—didn't ruffle him and his car-crazy buddies: "It was the '60s and of all the things we could be thinking about, we still mostly just thought about cars."

Now that Riney has safely positioned his hero as a blue-collar Reagan-Democrat (Republican Riney also created Reagan's "It's Morning in America" ad), the ad pulls on the ripped sweatshirt of anxiety so that we can all relate. "But then the oil dried up, and it seemed that overnight something happened to the way people thought about cars." Footage of a woman shivering in a Rustbelt parking lot, a lonely coffee drinker at a diner. "It got frustrating. Then I decided to work for a company called Saturn"—then a horse runs free in nature (really)—"and build cars again but in a brand new way."

Other companies are also using the arty grim style that reflects anxiety in order to seem to solve it. Seiko and Bayer, like dozens before them, do it with black & white film, choppy camerawork, panicky pans, and—oh, shut up shutup shutupshutup!

And, McDonald's, you shut up too. McDonald's and Turner Broadcasting are "exploring" the possibility of installing TVs with programming and commercials—like Whittle does in classrooms and Turner does in supermarkets and airports—in its 8600 U.S. restaurants. At best, aren't TVs in McDonald's redundant?

But hold on to your hope. The times, they're like a coal train, see. We're down in the mine, dirty, smudgy, and clanging down the track of black-blue misery. The coal miners on our train are an exhausted lot—old men, worn women, one black fellow, too—except maybe for that blond youth toward the back. "They say the revolution's over," his voiceover speaks. "They say we'll have to work harder and harder just to stay where we are. They say the way things work now are the way they'll always be. But I say—they're wrong!"

Light at the end of the tunnel suddenly beams, matching the increasingly stronger light on his miner's hat. His face is suddenly cleaner than before. (An ad for Lever 2000?) "Everywhere you look people want to build a new world," a narrator explicates. "It's time to give them new tools. The revolution continues. Introducing the next generation of Apple technology."

What revolution? Even Apple can't mean the computer revolution, the one in which technology was supposed to be the savior? We're still talking jobs and housing. Like Apple's new business partner, IBM, which has deleted 50,000 jobs, plans another 20,000 lay offs, and is breaking up, as *Newsweek* says, "into a confederation of leaner, more competitive companies."

Sounds pretty Soviet again. But this was hardly the image a couple years ago, when corporations were rushing out ads to gloat over and/or take responsibility for the fall of the Berlin Wall. And what was all that for except to make the world safe for advertising, literally?

But now the ad industry is not reaping *its* peace dividend. Agencies are not just losing accounts—they're losing faith in the power of advertising. At the moment when the triumph of commercial culture should be peaking, ads are desperate and defensive. The victory over the Soviet Union cannot be properly exploited by an America without ad vision.

But while commercial culture is under pressure, it's hardly evaporating. No one's going to send Joe Smooth back to Arabia or the Bikini Team back to Scandinavia. For now, the ad industry still has the fundamentals of power. Unlike the doddering putschists who seized Gorbachev only to crown Yeltsin, Madison Avenue knows its way around a TV station.

January 7, 1992

In the Red Again **175**

The Off-Road to Rio

When an emotional sell is completely obvious and we *still* buy it, then what the heck does that say about us?

The emotional payoff in Isuzu's two ads for its Jeep-like Rodeo is so transparent—you can find your inner wild child if you let loose and buy their car—that it camouflages how the ad plays with the rest of the world (most of which is meeting this week for an environmental summit in Rio).

Each spot starts with *Wonder Years* kitsch. In one, an early '60s mom tries to rein in her young son by tying him to the backyard clothesline; still, the little devil dives into a mud puddle, splattering the camera itself. "They say our personality traits are formed at an early age," the voiceover muses dryly. "25 years later," the boy's a man and driving through mud, his blue Rodeo coated brown. The VO concludes: "It's never too late to have a happy childhood." In the female version (many Rodeo buyers are women), a classroom of children drawing in their coloring books is told by their teacher to "stay between the lines. The lines are our friends." One little redhead takes her crayon and, screeeech, outta the lines she shoots, infuriating teach no end. Grown-up translation? A charming freckly redhead now, she cruises the desert in her Rodeo and, grinning recklessly, zips off the highway onto what looks like the desert floor, insouciant, untamed, and free at last.

The spots began airing, very heavily, in March, and since then the Rodeo has broken all its previous sales records. Isuzu, if you remember, was famous for its "Liar" campaign. But after many years, Joe Isuzu's obnoxious charm failed to hype sales, and so today, Isuzu is pitching cars with the sort of glory stories it used to rib us were lies.

With a new ad agency and "a tremendous abundance of research," according to marketing director Dick Gillmore, Isuzu is playing its traditional Trooper to an older, more affluent crowd, while gearing the less expensive Rodeo ($13,200 to $19,500) to a would-be wilder set that "seeks adventure." "The car is an expression of one's ability to let go," he says. (But not too much. Isuzu's psychosocial research

Your inner child's driver's license

has dug up that "a consumer who spends an average of $18,000 for a car is somewhat unwilling to splash mud all over it." Future campaigns may be "adjusted.")

But the basic appeal is clear and now only too common. Since the late '80s, marketers have trotted out everything from meatloaf-based restaurants to "adult toys" to encourage baby boomers to roll around in muddy childhood memories. And that trend is part of a larger flattery: telling the television-imbibing millions that they are secret rebels, freedom-loving individuals who refuse to be squished by society's constraints. Corporate America is always advising us that if we just buy in we can feel like irrepressibly hip outsiders. As the jingle goes, "I like the Sprite in you."

But unlike most approved-rebellion ads, Isuzu's are specifically about the myth of *rugged* individualism—a rebelliousness best expressed in the Republican, free-enterprise sense. Underlying the Isuzu ads is the whole environmental controversy over off-road vehicles (ORVs include four-wheel drives, motorcycles, dirt bikes, and snowmobiles). Millions of acres of public lands have been denuded, eroded, gullied, or otherwise ravaged by what a 13-year-old government report likened to "mechanical locusts." Still, the environmental president signed a bill last year that would siphon some gas taxes to build more ORV trails in wilderness areas. And the conservative "wise use" movement, which is lobbying Congress for more acres, receives funds from motorcycle makers like Honda and Kawasaki.

Though "sports utility" automobiles are now the fastest-growing category in the marketplace, they're less of a problem than motorcycles—for all the money off-road car owners have plunked down to look semicivilized cool, only 25 percent ever leave the suburbs, Isuzu estimates. Not that the manufacturers don't encourage them to: Range Rover has a spot in which its ORV chugs down an almost 90-degree hillside, and an ad for Toyota's 4Runner slams it through a dirty rock 'n' roll ride and asks, "Are you getting enough roughage?" In another spot, Chrysler's Jeep hauls a bunch of wimpy marketing guys for an unnamed competitor high onto a desert plateau, as an ad director tells them that if they're going to claim their vehicle can do what Jeep can do, they really need to pose it on this plateau—all they'll have to do is helicopter their sissy machine up. As they drive off in *Jeeps,* the director sighs, "This is going to be a great commercial." (With this, Jeep takes up Isuzu's "ads lie" ad banner. The spot, says a Jeep spokesman, sounding like the fictional director, "is going gangbusters.")

Many of these car companies, including Isuzu, are members of be-nice-to-nature programs like the U.S. Forest Service's "Tread Lightly!" which is to off-road vehicles what "Drink Responsibly" campaigns are to beer. "We would never show our vehicle in an area of endangered species or anything," Isuzu's Gillmore says. The desert scene in the crayon ad was shot in Hungry Valley, California, "where this is permitted by the Department of Interior." Then he throws all meaning into reverse: "We're not implying anyone drive outside the lines. We're saying sometimes you want to go outside the boundaries."

Programs like "Tread Lightly!" are "useful," says Debbie Sease, public lands director for the Sierra Club, which is lobbying to stop new roads from being carved into the California desert. "But it's inconsistent with [many carmakers'] campaigns, which create these incredibly compelling ads that say, fun is going out with a large, powerful machine and tearing up the land."

This season, all roads, or off-roads, lead to Perot. Ads like these plant more fantasies of channeled revolution. They help soften the mind into swoony anticipation for an against-the-odds, doesn't-pussy-foot-with-"positions," rugged individual who claims to ride rough-shod over any and all lines. But most people cheering on Perot are not going to do anything "outsider," much less risk a "point of contro-versy" (like appointing a homosexual to the Cabinet), and most peo-ple who buy four-wheel drive vehicles never do leave the asphalt.

June 9, 1992

The Off-Road to Rio

Chapter Four

OUR **Four**

BODIES,

OUR

SELLS

At the End of a Sentence

Exactly what sanitary products are for, no one on TV has been able to say. Alone among commercials, those for "feminine hygiene," on air since 1972, have to communicate entirely in code. (Only portions of a napkin may be shown; forget tampons.) Even ads for incontinence pads, delicately phrased as they must be, frankly state their product's purpose: "bladder control." But a new Tampax ad is making personal hygiene history. A spunky dancer in a locker room says the word most commonly used to describe that time of the month. Says it three times.

Tampax isn't out to strike a blow for feminism: The last thing they want is to offend consumers. But their research shows that people prefer "straight talk." Fine with NBC and ABC, but CBS has rejected the ads. The word is "slang," a network spokesman says, suggesting "menstrual cycle" as a "clinically accurate" substitute. That sounded stuffy to the ad agency: "Tampax can change the way you feel about your menstrual cycle." So—damn the torpedoes—they went ahead and said the "P" word. Period.

April 9, 1985

The New, 1985 Crotch

Recently Clairol introduced a shaver specially for that area quaintly called the bikini line. "Until now," the ad reads, "your most delicate area was the toughest to shave." Oddly, the model in the "bikini shaver" ad isn't wearing a bikini, but a very high-cut one-piece. Maybe Clairol thought the misnomer would go unnoticed because the reader's attention is arrested by a looming gadget that looks startlingly like a vibrator with a razor at one end.

But more likely it's just another instance of one-piece high-thigh hegemony. This past summer marked the moment that crotchcutters, as some in the industry refer to these swimsuits, conquered completely—driving the more modest styles off the racks, forcing the deforestation of once-protected areas, and reducing thousands of women to walking the beach wrapped in towels. One such woman complains, "I feel like I'm wearing underpants that keep riding up." Once in a while you'll find a guy who doesn't like them either: "Women with hips can't wear them." But most people seem to agree with the glazed-eyed guy at Rockaway Beach who was staggering toward his six-pack: "They're *real* sexy."

The bikini was sexy once, too. But the novelty of flashing so much skin became commonplace, and by the early '70s the conventional one-piece made a stately comeback. Always more flattering for most women than the bikini, the maillot was now supposed to also be more erotic. More was less. Demure was allure. But about six years ago, as if to compensate for the cover-up (and to sell new suits), the one-piece was yanked in and up from below till it topped the hipbone and sometimes the waist. This one simple move has reshaped women's bodies, has actually created *new female body parts* previously found only on Playboy Bunnies and dance-class mavens.

New Turf: Dancers had the idea—you can make legs look longer only two ways—high heels or, where you must go shoeless, high thigh. It's not just showing more that looks sexy, it's showing previously unexposed territory, and the hip is one of the few remaining. Bikinis show hip too, of course, but they bisect it with the cloth of civilization. However, when framed by an ultra high-leg suit the area turns animal-like—crotchcutters create haunch. Some suits, skimping on top material and squashing the breasts down and out, create another new erogenous zone—what can only be called side cleavage.

Crotch Nouveau: But mostly, crotchcutters say "Crotch!" The longer-looking legs act as runways, enhance the build-up toward it; the torso becomes an arrow pointing to and ending in it. The New Crotch, with a younger and narrower (implying tighter) look, could not be more prominent. The torso suddenly seems one-third mons de Venus.

The Jailbait Look: The little suit makes these bold moves disingenuously. It's a way of showing hip and rear-end by making them pass as leg. Lengthy legs relative to the torso, flattened-down chest, like-a-virgin crotch—crotchcutters make grown women look 14 and 35, innocent and experienced simultaneously.

The Return of Barbie: The blueprint for this new anatomy was stamped on our unconscious even before adolescence by Barbie. Her El Grecoesque gams bend impossibly from the waist, not, like real girls', from along the "bikini line." Thus the daring doll laid the pattern for her owners' future fashion.

The Female Jockstrap: But another school of thought insists that women aren't imitating girls and certainly not dolls. Crotchcutters redefine the female shape with *male* overtones. The high-cut suit can transform the torso from hourglass to the "ideal" inverted triangle of the male body—broad shoulders tapering down to hiplessness. The narrower the crotchcutter's crotch, the more phallic it appears. In fact, one company has modified Calvin Klein and others' male-underpants-for-her and bills them as "female jockstraps." The masculine silhouette implies power. Queen Elizabeth I's stiff V-shaped bodice, which paved over her chest and ended in a point above her crotch, worked wonders for her aura of authority. Crotchcutters are likewise power suits: instead of dividing the body into two erogenous zones like bikinis, they unify and center it.

Our Corset: Some might argue that crotch décolletage is not desirable, that it makes you vulnerable to stares and impure thoughts. That's what they said about the cinched waist. It, too, was a place of intensified focus that rearranged the body's proportions, that women went to painful lengths to achieve (waxing is less heinous than corseting in part because it's only occasional). But the revisionist line on corseting is that it was actually progressive: *because* corsets were thought improper, at least initially, the women who dared don them were asserting their sexuality.

No doubt, crotchcutters cut it. But last summer may have seen their peak. If exposing the unexposed is sexy, it's just a matter of time before high-thigh becomes ho-hum. Some designers are already predicting the leg hole's slow creep down. But must we recycle the '50s for more coverage, or the '60s for less? Not at all. Now that male-style underwear has conquered women's lingerie, where can it go but to the beach? Where can swimwear go but to underwear? This month Norma Kamali, herself a pioneer of high-cut suits, is unveiling her new swim line: corsets and bras on top, girdles and men's briefs complete with flies on bottom. Mix and match. No need to expose your body— expose your underwear.

October 15, 1985

The Sound of Sexism

It's men that we hear in almost 90 percent of all TV ad voiceovers. Without ever researching it, ad people assumed that men are more powerful product pushers. That leaves actresses, already paid 10 to 20 percent less than men for the same work, out a lot of income, says the Women's Voiceover Committee of the Screen Actor's Guild. So

SAG commissioned a study, which showed that women's voices are just as effective in motivating audiences to buy, buy, buy.

After viewing ads for Listerine and Nestlé's Morsels in either male or female voiceover versions, test audiences (who often couldn't recall which sex was hawking the goods) chose those products equally as often regardless of which version they had heard.

Voiceovers must sound more authoritative than even on-camera actors, who play characters we're supposed to identify with, laugh at, or love. But VOs we *obey*. (In Japanese ads, on-screen actors rarely speak—words and thought descend from above.) With the power of invisibility, a voiceover is the superego of an ad.

The most desirable male VO is the gravelly voice of History, a stentorian bass like John Huston's in the new Dodge commercials. The attitude may be gently skeptical or deadly serious but the important thing is the gravel—it's as if the voice booms out of earth itself.

Interestingly, deep earth is the preferred VO for women, too. "They usually ask for the low-range," says Ziska, one of the few actresses who scores big VOs (Hanes, J. C. Penney). "It's a pleasing, soothing sound. And more authoritative."

But authority is more than how low you can go. Viewers might associate women's voices with another big boss. "The first voice we ever heard," Ziska says, "was our mother's."

September 30, 1986

A Hard Man Is Easy To Find

As part of chichi fashioneer Fendi's new perfume launch—which includes Bloomingdale's laying down carpet with the Fendi logo—we have this ad: A beautiful but bothered babe in a Fendi fur runs through a rainy Rome. Dream images flicker in her heated mind: She and a man—looking closely, we see he's a marble statue—are kissing, the camera spins, light bursts through their parted lips. She dashes into a sumptuous villa, flies down the stupendous spiral staircase, and, finally, confronts the objet d'art of her desire. The statue is supposed to command the presence of a Michelangelo, but the head looks like a schlock coffee-table statuette, less *David* than Dave. It's the woman's face—Streep structure, Adjani pout—that captivates. Glancing furtively to make sure she's alone, she lets her fur fall and stands nude, in silhouette. Now still and naked as a work of art, she's ready to join her perfect SWM.

The ad is part Pygmalion myth—the sculptor so in love with his ivory maiden that Venus brings her to life. And it's part *Cosmo* myth—*statues* make the best lovers: Rock solid, steady, they don't roam and don't give lip. Dave is the kinda guy a woman might take up with after getting burned by a real one; he's the next step after the Antonovich Fur ad selling "the I-finally-threw-the-bum-out coat."

But what we have here is a case of statutory rape. The ad has nothing to do with love, or love of art. It's too onanistic: As the woman makes love to an object whose reality is solely of her fantasy's making, "art" comes off as an inflatable fuck-me doll. And yet the ad is suc-

Fendi's perfect SWM

cessful in flattering women: Flesh-and-blood men, it suggests, aren't refined, aren't aesthetic enough for *you*. *You* are so sensual that, with a little help from Fendi, if not Venus, you can make a stone man melt. These myths create a luxurious mood—the joy of primping—the better to sell perfume by. They give you permission to say, "I'm just going to be selfish today." Done with real style, the Fendi spot, along with the Obsession and Coco perfume ads, is the elegant equivalent of men's beer commercials that say, essentially, "I'm going to chug this Bud and I don't givvafug what anybody says!"

March 17, 1987

Wipe Out

The complex knot of guilt, household cleanliness, and womanhood has been twisted tighter and tighter by advertising. Since a woman could wield authority only in the private domain, if she failed to stamp out dirt, she failed as a woman. Early ads portrayed her smiling through her chores—she was *happy* staying home. As middle-class leisure time grew, ads occasionally recognized that the point of cleansers was to get out of the house faster. But corporate survival required diversification—different cleaning agents for tile, toilets, glass, wood, walls. Whether or not they got the jobs done faster, their constantly advertised existence pounded in the idea that there were more jobs to get done.

Bon Ami, one of those products that seems to recede on the shelf, badly needed a fizzed-up image. Focus groups showed that women tend to buy the Comet or Ajax their mothers used; yet many imagined those products and their *users* as abrasive. (In fact, *Consumer Reports* found new-formula Comet and Bon Ami above average in nonabrasiveness.) So Bon Ami fashioned a unique come-on: pop psychoanalyzing the cleaning fetish. Not by examining advertising's influence—just Mom's.

Wipe Out **189**

Bon Ami: a better friend than Mom

A pleasantly rounded actress with an annoyingly cute froggy voice talks to you like you're hanging around her kitchen, a *bon ami*. Scouring a cappuccino maker, she talks about her mother: "Today she tells me if I really want to clean my cappuccino machine, I have to scrub it with that blasting powder she used. I said, 'Mother—to make peace with you, I had to give up a lot of old resentments, a lot of anger, a *lot* of hostilities—I'm not giving up my cappuccino machine.'" Another spot suggests shame, as if the house were one's body: "She says that my house doesn't *smell* clean"—our friend bangs her head against the wall. Finally, comes understanding: The actress relaxes with a cup of coffee and says sadly: "Cleaning things is my mother's way of . . . getting even." "Go, girl!" this psychospot cheers. "You're not frustrated like Mom (and you probably have better sex!)"

On one level, the ads simply push a product feature: Bon Ami's gentleness. On another level, they say sterile is for anal types; for you new, improved women, clean is good enough.

But cleanliness is still next to guiltiness. These ads are ambivalent: They encourage us not to feel guilty if our houses aren't as spotless as a

TV housewife's, declaring that standard out, flattering you that saying you're an independent gal too busy with important work to get hysterical over hygiene. Nevertheless, your good friend is always scrubbing *something*. (The question of why she's always doing it without a man's help is conveniently avoided by fudging on her marital status.) Her house is spotless, not an ashtray out of place—leaving you with the same standard but a more modern *attitude* to live up to. You don't have to feel guilty for not being like Mom, but just guilty enough so that New Woman approval comes through the purchase of Bon Ami.

December 1, 1987

Wild Thing, I Think I Smell You

Ridley Scott's previous ads for Chanel No. 5—a woman lies poolside as the shadow of a plane intersects her; a wealthy woman imagines corporate "Charles" asking her to "share the fantasy" as shadowy Chanel Airlines climbs the Transamerica building—have set up eloquent, surrealistic images. But with all the opulence, the invitation to share the fantasy was less shareable than enviable. The latest Chanel ad, however, draws on a fleshy real fantasy. It might be called The Ballad of the Wild Boy.

A classy dame in a red silk suit and a gray-haired CEO sort— husband? sugar daddy? mentor?—are up in the silver skyscrapers of Houston; but this time she kisses him and corporate clout goodbye. She can afford to. The lady in red (Carole Bouquet, the French actress who is Chanel's latest icon) leaves the tower of power in a Ferrari for a date in the desert.

As Nina Simone sings the loose, jazzy "My Baby Just Cares for Me," the woman stops at a gas station where the adolescent attendant

Chanel's flights of fantasy

gushes for her madly. Without encouraging him, she enjoys his crush—it fuels her drive. She gets out to gaze at the sun, and the shadow of the Chanel jet intersects her—obvious symbolism, but the remarkable thing about this spot is that you can feel her lift off. (Compare the Jovan ad, by *Fatal Attraction* director Adrian Lyne, that asks "What is sexy?" and offers lots of hot, but porn-predictable scenes as an answer.) Here, there's one long curve of anticipation, confidence, and flight. In the desert, those emotions are more purely focused, and any interference—boy or shadows—only enhances the meeting to come.

She's left the moneyed man and the yearning adolescent for something as far from her life as possible—a rough and tumble dude. We only glimpse the Sam Shepardesque cowboy she finally kisses, but the ad's more about women who want wild boys than the boys themselves. For civilized women, Wild Boys are often a primal object of desire. They aren't the common Bad Boy—i.e., your basic career-guy schmuck. The difference: If a Bad Boy (with a good-paying job) gets you pregnant, he'll pay for half the abortion and never call you again; if a Wild Boy gets you pregnant, he'll insist you have the baby, possibly marry you, and one day go out for that pack of cigarettes and never return.

But Wild Boys aren't merely macho—they're often needy, self-destructive losers whose rawness makes them win women's hearts: Natalie Wood and James Dean in *Rebel Without a Cause*, Stella and Stanley, Fay Wray and King Kong. Current Wild Boy: Patrick Swayze. Some women have seen *Dirty Dancing* 20, 30, 100 times on the strength of this wild one who makes good. That's another piece of the fantasy: It's not that women want to tame a Wild Boy into responsibility, but they want to trust him enough so they can lose their own respectability.

Of course, the fantasy and the ad have no more to do with Chanel No. 5 than with English Leather. But no product better contains fantasy than perfume—we can't see or touch it; it forces a different sense to play. The only problem is the patrician prerequisites the ad poses: If a woman wants a Wild Boy, she should be secure enough in money or class to go back when things get out of hand. Chanel, like any marketer, also says, "Afford the Fantasy."

January 5, 1988

Women Will Be Gals

Advertising's latest variation on the "new woman"—those who work but have been politically neutered of feminism—is to show them as relentlessly regular, unpretentious mensches. They are less likely to appear smack dab in the kitchen or the office cubicle than in the cracks between home and career—hanging out in employee lounges, lolling in the parking lot—in between times and places where grit gathers and life's real decisions are arrived at through collegial (and product-bearing) banter. These females are not shoulder-padded Women or sexy, silly girls—they are gals.

Like the three stewardesses in a Nabisco commercial who, grounded during a snowstorm, kill time in a staff lounge. "Garrity," a boxy brunette modeled on the down-to-earth Mary Beth Lacey, is doing a very gal thing—heating Shredded Wheat in the microwave. The principle of gal things (like mending hems with Scotch tape, wiping off your kids at a restaurant with a napkin dipped in the ice water) is improvisational wisdom—the zany misuse of commonplace objects for an ultimately practical goal. Like Carol Lombard, gals jiggle with humanity, but they're a little off the wall. So the cynic of the trio, a permed petite, says: "Garrity, that's Shredded Wheat, not a TV dinner." "Well," Garrity banters back, "that's how we do it in Nome." "I didn't know you were from Alaska!" the blond (and dumbest one) squeals, and there starts the goo and glue of small talk, eventually sinking into memories of how "Mom used to pour hot milk" on the Shred. The purpose is to remind us, as winter comes on, that the cereal has a

Relentlessly regular use: Bounce

"heritage" of being eaten hot—and it gives us permission to do this slightly unappealing thing again. It's got gal imprimatur.

Gals by definition are always balancing between being clunky and charming. The most glaring example are the two haimish hams, excited to death about a new product, Bounce with Stain Guard (you throw a sheet into the drier to prevent stains from sinking in later). Like a pair of stand-ups, this duo finish each other's sentences and are ethnically balanced: brunette Jew and (again, dumber) blond WASP. They're also balanced between being aware they're in a commercial and pretending they're hearing about Bounce for the first time. "You known when you're a shlump and you get stains on your favorite shirts?" asks the brunette. "Ooh, I hate that!" gurgles the blond. After a quick demo, she asks the TV audience, "Impressed?" "Yeah, they're impressed," finishes the other.

Why all the personality? A Procter & Gamble spokeswoman says Bounce's target consumer is "energetic and upbeat, different, for instance, from the Downy [a P&G liquid fabric softener] consumer, who is a bit older, has more kids, and has the time to wait around to put Downy in during the wash cycle." I.e., like the names might imply, "Bounce" is postfeminist, "Downy" prefeminist. The Bounce babes' hyperhappiness over a product signals that they love their family, but their wo-menschness tells you that they hold down jobs or, at the least, do not picket abortion clinics. But the right kind of almost-feminist is hard to find. While these gals tested well in local markets, their babble was found "offensive" nationally, and the spots may be pulled.

Gals have more fears than assertive yuppie females. In an Apple Macintosh spot, three secretaries have just sat down in a coffee shop when one of them announces that she's got to leave right now and find a new job. Her boss is going to sock her with a computer and she hasn't even "figured out the new typewriter yet." The actress sports TV signs of the working class: blatant dark roots, the sort of cameo pin that girls wore back in high school. A black friend with straightened hair assures her that computers are easy. A second friend with forehead wrinkles tells her that Bob Dion learned to use one. Despite her natural lower-class reluctance about being "negative," Roots smiles devilishly: "Bob Dion? The guy who still needs help with the copy machine?" They break into giggles, regular gals giving the world its comeuppance only at the expense of stupider guys.

Advertising flatters gals that, feckless though they may be, they really run the world. Ads may even get secretaries clamoring for this computer or that computer, but it's still the boss man who has the upper hand on the bottom line.

November 29, 1988

Flow Jobs

Some ads for "personal care" products are looking weirdly explicit. They don't shatter the cheekiness barrier like, say, the Playtex spot of a few years ago that allowed human females, instead of mannequins, to model bras; nor do they approach the Tampax profile in courage, like the ad four years ago that uttered—in a commercial first—the word "period." Rather, in that baleful tide of bodily fluids, some brands have found a way to be explicit without being frank. It's an awkward explicitness that actually evokes images more offensive than the words they dare not speak.

Like the Kotex commercial last fall, which at first looked like a spot for Bloomingdale's. Raving about her purchase victory, a woman says, you finally find the perfect sheets to match your bedroom. Not too pink, not too peach. But wouldn't you know it—the first night you use them, you get your period! (Though she doesn't say the word.) Maybe it was hoped that audience involvement in her shopping coup would freshen up the stained linens. But rather than getting us to think "period" (and what to do about it), we can't stop thinking of a big wet blood spill.

Granted, it's difficult to sound both modern, as befits anything claiming to be new and improved, and control-freaky, in obeisance to American queasiness. In a poll, Massengill, Tampax, and feminine-hygiene products in general were found to have the "most hated" ads.

But some of that loathing may have been due less to viewer embarrassment than to ad clunkiness.

This new explicitness has produced a goofy but off-putting hook for the new Luvs disposable diapers—now designed differently for each sex, in pink and blue. A little boy and girl are playing in a toddler-sized Garden of Eden. His p.j.'s show a large wet spot on his waist, hers on her behind. They're demonstrating "customized Leak-Guard protection"—because "boys get wet up front" and "girls get wet in the middle."

Just when unisex became old-hat enough to look retro comes a Reaganesque reversion to separation of the sexes. The explicitness of the wet spots is offset by reassuring pink-or-blue gender tidiness. As to whether differently aimed pee really requires a new product, the answer is mixed. "Parents have told us that overnight leakage at the waist for boys and at the legs for girls are the two biggest problems with diapers," says Procter & Gamble. But one mother with both a boy and a girl baby says, "Unfortunately, it's not just the front that gets wet even on boys, because it's not just urine anyway. When kids are running around in 11 different positions, you could use super-absorbency everywhere." So why not distribute the material throughout the diaper (and avoid producing babies with neocon edge)? There's less sell in that. P&G, which also makes Pampers, wanted a differentiating gimmick for Luvs. But it's not clear that unisex Pampers with "a second core" of absorbent material in the diaper's front two-thirds doesn't work just as well for both sexes.

As in the old days, the more scatological the product, the more euphemistic the spot. Ex-Lax conjures an image much more daring than mere "constipation," a word absent from the product's 83-year ad history. "Taken at bedtime," a voiceover says, "Ex-Lax is guaranteed to work. Gently. Effectively. By 8 a.m. or your money back." No proof is required. Of 23 million units sold in 1988, a spokesman says, only 23 users complained. But it's not like consumers are going to storm into their apothecaries and yell, "I didn't shit this morning!"

An antidiarrhetic ad flirts even more boldly with taboo imagery. A chubby-cheeked man on a long-distance bus has a bad case of the runs—but the bus has no bathroom! It's okay, his wife assures him, he took Imodium A-D. "Yeah, but just a little cup," he frets. "Perfect," she smiles. When they finally pull up to a rest stop, he's content to stay on the bus, thank you. "I'm fine," says the newly confident American.

By setting their stories to the familiar rhythm of ad singsong, these spots dull their own bite. They dare to cross lines that they themselves have drawn and end up sounding more offensive than they would if they just said what they're saying. But that would mean admitting something to really make them blush—that, goodness gracious, they're selling.

January 31, 1989

The Trad Trade

Good Housekeeping's print ads "The New Traditionalist"—the title tops off starkish portraits of mothers, their offspring leaning on them, copy about a "reaffirmation of family values unmatched in recent history" defining them—have the impact of a political manifesto in cashmere and tweed. The new TV spot is softer, merely declaring that in 100 years families haven't changed. The trend—the old-fashioned as fashionable, à la Barbara Bush—might not be so bad itself, but what's chilling about *GH*'s campaign for the trend is that it acts as a seal of approval: who gets it, who's denied.

"We're getting a lot of heat on it," says Carl Casselman, creative director of Jordan, McGrath, Case & Taylor. "It was never an issue except among feminists, who felt we were telling women to stay home and have babies. We're saying that's okay. But that's not all we're saying. We're saying they have a choice. It's a tough world out there."

NT kind of evolves from and still contains yup/prep/couch potato/cocooner/hip-to-be-square. But it's not just another marketeer's fun category. "We haven't been as sure of anything in 15 years," says a spokesperson for the Yankelovich market research firm, which "discovered" NT. "It's a combination of the best parts of the '40s and '50s—security, safety, and family values—with the '60s and '70s emphasis on personal freedom of choice. It's the first major change in the basic way we want to organize our society since the '60s." Defined simultaneously as "new" and "not new," New Traditionalism does cast a pretty wide net. "It crosses all age, economic, and education groups," she says. But it swerves out of the way of the underclass. They *could* be New Trad, too; it's just that no one knows: "We don't talk to the underclass," says Yankelovich.

Their invisibility is not insignificant. While NTs are hardly all Young Republicans, the press-released imagery is Bushian; it's the advertiser's understanding of a gentler Reagan materialism. *GH*, however, didn't jump on Bush's bandwagon; *GH* NT came first, says Casselman. Wholesome, family-oriented *Good Housekeeping* would "tend to apologize for what they were. We told them, you guys are what's happening." It's true that the print campaign was launched during the presidential campaign, but that was because they wanted to move it fast. "We knew someone was going to own this, and we felt it should be us." Upon reading "New Traditionalism" on Bush's lips, Casselman recalls, "We said, 'Holy shit.' " The same agency also gave us Quaker Oats' slogan, "It's the right thing to do"—another morally loaded line favored by politicians.

But the *GH* TV spot was launched to coincide with the Bush Inaugural. The commercial shows how five generations of families, WASPy lookers all, have lived in the same big old Victorian house, bonding over the same wedding, Christmas, and prom rituals, only their clothes and lampshades change. "Mothers haven't changed," says the voiceover. "Kids haven't changed. Families haven't changed. Love hasn't changed. What is fundamental to our lives, what really matters . . . hasn't changed."

The TV ad is more likable (though more debatable) than the print for good reason. The TV is aimed at consumers, who presumably want their emotional needs met, while the print ads are aimed at advertisers, who want the consumers' emotional needs defined. One emotional need in these uncertain times is for security. Simply insisting that nothing has really changed—divorce, abuse, drugs, etc. notwithstanding—does two things. It makes the traditional virtuous—it must *deserve* its longevity. And it presents a solution—*eternity* is the ultimate security.

Among the seven sisters, *GH* is on the far trad side. (*Woman's Day,* says a working mom, "is about how to make your floors look shiny when they're really not. *Good Housekeeping* is about how to scrape and dig the gunk off, and make it really shine.") But the problem isn't the magazine, or NTism itself—becoming a little NT, for lack of a better hook, is nearly inevitable when you start having babies. The distasteful thing is that the categorizing, naming, and publicizing of a social trend is colored entirely by the need to sell, whether it's votes for George Bush or ad pages for a women's magazine. When advertisers package social movements, they inevitably tell you *how* to become the thing they're defining, what look, what attitude, what product to buy. There is choice in New Traditionalism. But, though pushing "choice" as an attractive sales point, the very power of the categorizing tends to squeeze actual choices to the side. It fosters a choiceoisie. And the traditional thing suddenly becomes the right thing to do.

March 7, 1989

Cockers

So they're talkin' about how the girls were taller than they were at the prom 15 years ago, how dad's change used to spill out of his pockets when he sank into his favorite chair, and maybe kinda about the meaning of life, too, but all I can think is, why is the camera making me stare at their penises? And their butts? The camera has been poking around these parts for two years now, but only this new round of ads for 100 percent cotton, 99 percent middle-class white-guy Levi's Dockers really puts it out there. Maybe it's the cues: While another lap of luxury fills the screen, one guy actually pulls out a *tape measure.*

Is *sex* the secret that makes these ads for Dockers—the Levi's "casual" pant that unabashedly targets the baby-boomer boy—survive? Sittin' around talkin' does not always work wonders for ads. It got the nudgy Nissan engineers pulled off the stage with a hook; it blew apart Dukakis's spots, "The Packaging of George Bush." But these dudes dialoguing for Dockers are, apparently, very popular, or at least very tolerated.

Sales of the pants have tripled wherever spot advertising has run. Dockers shipments have increased from $1 million in 1986, when the brand was introduced, to more than $250 million this year. Dockers, says Levi's marketing director Steve Goldstein, have been "a spectacular success."

Denimsomething guys are to Levi's as Chicken McNugget eaters are to McDonald's: more market. "Men over 25 buy only one-and-a-half to two pairs of jeans a year, compared, say, to 15-year-olds who buy five pairs a year," says Goldstein. "So our marketing goal is to continue selling Levis product to these guys that is not necessarily jeans. And the answer is Dockers."

And to convey "all cotton," the ad's answer is "be real." Each spot was made with six to nine guys—actors, stand-up comics, and some people the ad agency just picked up—who didn't know each other beforehand. They talked and laughed about anything at all for six hours straight while the camera rolled. Then each chucklefest was edited down to 30 seconds.

Throughout, the camera whips across their crotches and butts. Oh, occasionally you glimpse a face—in fact, every ad ends on one as emotional punctuation: These pants are for *you,* a total person. But some of the longer, narrower props—a billiard cue, the tape measure—bring us back to basics. Granted, the symbolism isn't as blatant as, say, the comical, penis-faced dromedary in the Camel cigarette campaign. But I'm still floored that such thoughts never crossed their focus groups' minds, according to Goldstein. "Maybe if we were a soda commercial focusing on crotches we'd have complaints, but we're a pants company and pants companies should focus on pants." That's the idea— "to show the product in action."

Do I just have a dirty mind? Or worse, do I sound like Terry Rakolta, the lady who's forcing advertisers off raunchy shows like *Mar-*

ried . . . With Children? No, I checked it out with a few women, and they said, yeah, it's staring them in the face, too. (It is women to whom these ads are also lobbed: 60 percent of all pants for men over 25 are bought by women.)

But down, Terry, down girl. These spots are really much more About Men, in the *New York Times Magazine* column sense, than about sex. Sittin' around in baggy pants, these casual-wear yups go out of their way to tell us they're *not* studs, revealing how self-deprecating humor can be worn as a badge of class: "I was the school wuss," one guy says in an earlier spot. "I played golf." This time around, one guy complains, "Everytime I went to the school prom the girl was taller than me. I don't want to talk about it." The winning-loser image helps inoculate them against rampant smugness, a trick learned by *thirtysomething,* which this season made its two leads go jobless to wipe that fortune off their face.

Sittin'-around-talkingism has become the philosophical wine cooler of the leisure class. Any time they touch a "heavy" subject, they metabolize it into the lite version: "Well, what *is* your perception of life?" one guys asks a paunchy William Hurt type, who zeros in: "My perception of the meaning there is there it's I mean you know the meaning of life is answer the phone when it rings."

Laffs all around. The banter *alludes* to a time when we like to think we led "meaningful" lives, but the airbrushed patter gives us permission to leave all that behind—who has the time? What's fascinating is that these are "real" guys mouthing, in the media, the media-pollinated codes for the lite life.

These bleached-cotton conversations would not take place in Levi's 501 ads, informed by black bluesmen, rappers, and the street beat. (Only one black guy pops up in all of Dockers country.) But what 501 and Docker ads do have in common is that they give you the feel of their fabrics against your skin—and then they define the sociosexual way you feel in your skin.

The Docker ads are so effective that they make it seem unremarkable that six guys in the same place are wearing the same pants. Like blue jeans, these pants are nonuniform uniforms; they seem to be overnight classics. Even the word "dock"—though it's more docksiders than on the dock of the bay—buys them some quickie historical (even working-class) resonance.

The logo at the end of each spot, and over each back pocket, reinforces the image: "Dockers. Since 1850. Levi's." Of course, Dockers hit the racks only two years ago, and only to boost the buying behavior of a bunch of guys who weren't spendin' enough. But hell. Tradition isn't something we all share—it's something that admen create.

April 25, 1989

Ragtime

The image that really kicked off the mass pop environmental movement—and, after the flag, Willie Horton, and "Read my lips," the image that helped elect George Bush—was that of hypodermic needles and used tampons washing ashore during the summer of '88. But Earth Day was like two Advils for that really bad period. And now it's safe for tampon makers to go with the flow and push planetary as well as feminine protection.

Only last year Tampax was running spots for its Petal Soft Plastic Applicator tampons that featured MTV mod graphics and cheeky women crying, "I want my plastic!" What a difference a corporate-friendly Earth Day makes. The item is still sold, but without TV ads. Instead, Tampax is pushing its regular tampon with a feminist-super-charged environmental pitch. The product hasn't changed, but figure this: Feminism comes from the same root word as feminine hygiene, and environmentalism has traditionally been a women's issue (taking out the planet's garbage is an extension of an Earth Mama's household chores). And so Tampax, fearlessly braving snickers, has hauled out Helen Reddy's '70s anthem "I Am Woman"—in order to mention that its tampon is "biodegradable."

In a Leni Reifenstahl-like spectacular, Tampax parades a mélange of valiant-girl images. The line "I am woman, hear me roar, in num-

I am woman, watch me biodegrade.

bers too big to ignore" frames newsreel footage of WWII WAFs. "I know too much to go back and pretend" swings us to a today gal—a lady car mechanic who rolls out from under a car, makeup unmussed. From Rosie the Riveter to discus throwers to career heroines striding through airports heads held high, Tampax says there's a common string, as it were, to our terrificness. We are historical and modern at the same time. That New Trad appeal is made clear in the final shot: A young woman with big '90s hair romps in a field in a calico dress. "We thought you'd feel good knowing that more women trust their bodies to the tampon that's very, very kind to the earth," says a "Fractured Fairy Tale" lady voiceover, ". . . flushable Tampax tampons. Biodegradable since 1936."

Only weeks after Tampax's rebirth, o.b. tampons made their environmental debut. But like the plain, tiny item that it is, o.b. shuns the pageantry: "Me—I was only thinking of me," another pretty young woman muses as she strolls through a park. O.b. tampons have "no applicator, no bother. Then this environmental problem came along, and suddenly I realized with o.b."—here she discards a soda can littering the way—"no applicator to throw away means no waste." Wiser than Tampax, o.b. avoids that troublesome word *biodegradable*. We know too much to go back and pretend we believe that claim. Tampons (and their big sisters, sanitary napkins) don't present anywhere near the landfill problems that disposable diapers do, but they do leave their mark.

Contrary to the impression created, Tampax is not fully biodegradable. Being flushable *is* an advantage: Water-treatment plants may help break down at least the cardboard applicator. But in most plants, bulkier items, like the tampon itself, are screened out before they can be processed. They become part of the sludge that is either burned or put into a landfill. Already wet, tampons at this point may degrade somewhat more rapidly than other items in an airless, sunlight-deprived landfill, but no one's sure. A Tambrands spokesperson admits that "in some cases, the tampons will ultimately reside in landfills." But, he adds, "you still have a source-reduction advantage over pads." (With 60 percent of the tampons market, Tambrands can afford to dis pads; its one pad, Maxithins, sells poorly anyway.)

And, of course, environmentally concerned companies never mention that tampons—like pads, diapers, and most paper products—are bleached with chlorine, which forms poisonous dioxins. The problem isn't that dioxins enter women's bodies (tampons are further purified to prevent that), but that during the manufacturing process "dioxins end up downstream," says Greenpeace.

"We are strong, we are invincible," the Reddy-approved singer evinces. "We thought you'd feel good knowing . . ." the VO coos. There's the rub—it's about *feeling* strong, *feeling* good. If women feel they're strong, the company will be stronger. The corporate ecosell is to convince us that most environmental hazards are from the household products that are bought, consumed, and thrown away by women. Corporations ask us to focus on the throwaway stage, but to just trust them at the manufacturing stage.

Playtex, which sells only plastic applicators, is publishing ads warning women not to flush their applicators because they "can eventually appear on beaches." A Playtex spokesman refuses to say whether the company is finally going to get with the program and go cardboard. "We don't want to send signals to the competition."

July 24, 1990

Getting Olayed

"I have one word for you," I recently told a friend 10 years younger. "Moisturizer." Not "credit," "floss," or "cotton underwear." Those are obvious tips to enhance one's personal progress. The payoff of applied grease, however, is still underestimated. And so it's with one eye fixed and the other winced in self-recognition that I watch the Oil of Olay ads. Fear of aging, of female aging anyway, is laid right out there—but each Olay actress is made to seem quite the savvy Ms. for arming to the hilt. "Why grow old gracefully? Fight it with Oil of Olay," the nearly three-year-old campaign rallies, ever honing the killer tactics of dread and hope.

"There's the part of me that says I should be above being concerned about looking older," says an attractive, 35-ish businesswoman. "Then there's the *real* me. There's the part that says, 'Who cares about a few little lines?' Then there's the *real* me. There's the part that says, 'Oh, just grow old gracefully.' Then there's the real me that says—'Why?'"

By now an unpretty coyness descends upon her, but the point is made: When women hit a certain age, cosmetics becomes cosmology. Oil of Olay—the largest seller and one of the largest advertisers of facial moisturizers—has produced one of the most existential moments on TV. Oil of Olay (or O.O., as in uh-oh) sets up the schisms— real versus forced, safe versus sorry, pragmatic if painted-face feminists versus the kind who profess to find character in wrinkles. But then it provides this answer: Cher feminism, according to which plastic surgery is tantamount to controlling your own destiny. Sure, O.O. encourages us on the cowardly road more traveled—but that's because "today's woman proactively takes control of every aspect of her life—exercise, diet, and skin care," as a company spokeswoman explains.

Once the "real me" chooses sides, all that's left is to choose a brand. In a virtuoso performance of spinning gold out of straw, Olay helps her out. "It's important to keep your promises," the voiceover says. "If we promise it replenishes your skin in a flash"—and the camera flashes to a gorgeous gal, who completes the sentence—"It does." "If we promise tiny lines diminish on contact—" another woman says, "They do." "If we promise it can help you look younger," says a third, "It does."

Although after several viewings you're looking hard to find the actresses' tiny lines (you do), the rhetoric of the spot makes it soar over any nagging concerns that the ad is promising magic. Some viewers may recall that a few years ago the FDA began to crack down on cosmetic companies for making overwrought labeling claims—that products were "anti-aging" or could "reverse" aging, descriptions that were essentially physiological and permanent, and would throw the products into the category of drugs, rather than merely cosmetic and temporary. Companies were threatened with seizure of their products, and some responded with batteries of lawyers (Estée Lauder and Revlon still disagree about some of the restrictions, says the FDA). But most companies toned down their language: Instead of saying a cream makes "skin younger," it makes "skin *look* younger," or it "reduces the *visible signs* of aging." (For now, though, the term "anti-aging" may be used if a product contains sunscreen.) The Olay "Promises" spot plays off these debates—still hovering perhaps in the gal collective unconscious—as if to say, "You can't trust the *others'* outrageous claims, but *ours*—we promise."

The irony is that Olay's promises may sound extravagant (though no one's talking money-back guarantees), but in fact they are the least that any moisturizer should do. Anything that temporarily puffs up the skin—oil, water, or the dermatologists' favorite answer to overpriced potions, Vaseline—can make "tiny lines diminish on contact." Oil of Olay, the only major cosmetic company that did *not* receive warnings from the FDA, has always played careful and crafty with its words.

Like everyone else, though, Olay wildly inflates imagery: La Prairie has "Extract of Skin Caviar"; Estée Lauder, "Re-Nutriv Soufflé"; an Olay moisturizer is a "delivery system with time-release microencapsulates." The predictable reaction to all that is fake simplicity: Ultima II has a new line called "The Nakeds."

The bloated ratio of poetry, packaging, and price to actual thing has always been a cornerstone of the cosmetics trade. That's why it's cosmetic—the ads and labels do a job on us comparable to the one we hope to do to an onlooker.

If fear of aging is your weakness, you want to believe. I suspend disbelief over some cosmetic ads like I imagine other people do over beer or sneaker spots: We know they're hype, but they feel so good. My belief system even contains the notion that belief itself can help hustle the skin-care benefits into being—like some time-released microencapsulates of hope. Cosmetic advertising has its hooks in some of us even before they trill a misleading word.

Cosmetic ads are more like perfume ads, which are all fantasy. When you smell a perfume on someone else, unless you can identify the scent and link it to its ad, the advertising can't even begin to seduce you. (Unlike the image of most products—cars, clothes, kitchen cleansers—which bop again and again between the user, the ad, and the public, a perfume ad's hubba-hubba can be re-excited only for the user herself.) Once on duty, cosmetics, like perfume, must bravely stand on their own, cut off from their logos and tag lines—with only the consumer's commercial memories to puff them up, like a drop of oil does a wrinkle.

Meanwhile, Oil of Olay is spreading fear of aging to youth. Another spot features a novice wrinkle girl. "I never thought I'd get a wrinkle—till I got one," she says. "This is war!" Coming up is an ad starring 14-year-old tennis star Jennifer Capriati. Getting youth to prematurely age over crow's-feet is an Olay tack as much as mine.

But word is, advertising in general is going to gradually stop promoting age anxiety, if only not to insult baby boomers, who, as they turn 40 and 50, will continue to exert most of the buying power into the 21st century. "We are beginning to see a major shift," a Saatchi & Saatchi executive told *Adweek,* adding wistfully, "Aging will, I think, be mainstreamed."

October 2, 1990

Leggo My Ego

Whose ego is being flattered anyway? Men's or women's? You've seen it, heard it, and maybe even smelled Bloomingdale's sweating it out of every promo pore possible: Chanel's new men's cologne Égoïste. In the $1 million TV spot filmed at a Riviera-style hotel (actually in Rio), 31 gowned and long-gloved actresses open their window shutters, step out on their balconies, and scream in French, "Miserable one!" and "How could I have lived so long and be so disgraced? Show yourself, Égoïste!" If you don't get the French, you still get the gist: They're mad.

The object of their anger doesn't show himself. He just reaches his arm out to flash a bottle of the cologne and skunks back inside. Upon which the women howl, "Égoïste! Égoïste! Égoïste"—and (the cool part) in unison open and slam the 31 shutters against the lovely salmon-colored building. "Égoïste," says the voiceover. "For men." Or is it?

Directed by Jean-Paul Goude (creator of the big bad French bicentennial parade and Grace Jones), the spot's like all those overperfumed Calvin Klein ads, only, in French, more so. The introduction of Chanel's Eurotreacly fragrance has been heralded by a PR blitz that includes a video on the making of the ad and the setting up of an "Égoïste apartment" at Bloomies. But most striking is the Égoïste notebook. See, Chanel envisions the Égoïste man as a kind of entrepreneurial Ken doll with a full social calendar and many playmates. His journal was sent to the press, full of artsy sketches and such jottings as "All of me I give except myself," and "John W. is incapable of

Fickle Maiden forms

an original thought. I dislike him and his fake manners; he's such a chameleon. I am my own man. I can only be myself, always myself." On March 1, he writes, "Read a line from Nietzsche. 'What is the seat of freedom? Not to be ashamed of oneself.' " Though Nietzsche probably wrote that as the spirochetes were eating his brain, by March 11 our man in Rio is on a high: "I believe kindness is just a corrupted form of weakness." The women were probably flinging open the shutters to air out his odor. (The $50 scent smells exactly like insect repellent. Really.)

E, who's ambivalent about four women, leaves the diary at a fifth's. She returns it to him (i.e., it's sent to the press) with a letter that spins good ego: "I think of you as an 'Égoïste' in the very best sense of the word. Independent. Completely self-assured. Single-minded."

Maybe "égoïste" has nuances in French that it doesn't here. (Launched a year ago there, it's been hotcakes ever since.) And sure, there are positive aspects to egoism as well as negative ones (assholeist!).

But Chanel *wants* that lady-killer, world-dominating, arrogant edge. Though Chanel president Arie Kopelman insisted to *New York* magazine that "we've created a new hero for the '90s," E sounds very '80s, very Republican—just the sort of guy Ayn Rand might shimmy for.

This is all odd considering that women buy most men's cologne, some of which is even sold at women's counters. So why is Chanel selling to them by flattering a jerk? If it works at all, maybe it's because some women want to see themselves with a man like that. Or want to be like such a man. Over the years, men's fragrances have become more "complex" and "feminine," attracting women customers, many of whom buy the scents for themselves.

Or maybe women would buy a guy Égoïste as a joke, an expensive version of those T-shirts that say, "I'm With Stupid." But it's still incredibly flattering to men, and all around town they could be excusing their trespasses by saying, with charming half-crooked smiles, "I'm just Égoïste, baby."

One set of ads would seem to fumigate the air. To the children's rhyme "Did you ever see a lassie go this way and that way," shots of women's torsos in period costumes are shown, alternately sucked in and ballooned out with corsets, bustles, breast flatteners, and chest enhancers. The contortions are followed by this note from Maidenform: "Isn't it nice to live in a time when women aren't pushed around so much anymore?" Maybe, but are corsets really worse than having silicon shot up your breasts? In any case, Maidenform still sells plenty of girdles and padded bras. So much for "so much."

Another Maidenform spot, "Stereotypes," shows a fat fishwife, a bonbon eater, a prunish schoolmarm, a stripper, and states, "Somehow, women always seem to be portrayed like this. . . . While there are many stereotypes of women, there aren't many women who fit them. A simple truth known by all women, most men, and one lingerie company." The overstated modifiers aside, at least the spot's funny, though it's gotten some flak for perpetuating the stereotypes. (One of which turns up straightforward for Bud Dry. "Why do gentlemen prefer blonds?" the ad asks as the camera scans a blond babe. "Dumb question.")

Of course, Maidenform doesn't want to raise any real conflicts. "I don't know if I would say the ads are feminist, because people hear that as political," says Marilyn Bane, vice-president of advertising. "I think what we're really saying is Maidenform understands women, we know what you've gone through. No one has that position in the apparel industry." (Lily of France's headline for a sports bra ad: "The most support you can get for any woman's movement." *Adweek* writes that this "will appeal to the many younger women who regard feminism as something dowdy and spinsterish.")

The sociology of Maidenform's latest campaign is in reaction to its very successful previous one, in which Égoïstes like Corbin Bernsen and Pierce Brosnan talk up the intimacies of lingerie. The risqué move of making men the centerpiece of a lingerie ad finally helped to dedowdify the Maidenform image. But then research showed—guess what?—that the "era of glitz is over," celebrities are out, and companies that take a stand and push "values" are in. So as fast as you could say "I Dreamed I Went Shopping in My Maidenform Bra," the switch was made.

I don't know, girls. I just think we're being flattered—in a creepy way—when it seems we're being insulted, and pushed around when it seems we're being flattered. But then what do you expect? To borrow from Calvin Klein, between ego and id lie ads.

May 14, 1991

Demagaga

In a timely tale of politics, advertising, and alleged sexual harassment, there is the case of Hal Riney & Partners. Riney is the creator, and often the throaty, old-tyme voice, of many a commercial, from the bucolic (pre-benzene) Perrier ads to the bucolic Alamo and Blue Cross spots to the mock-bucolic Bartles & Jaymes campaign. Riney also created and narrated "It's Morning in America," Ronald Reagan's fam-

It does get worse than this.

ily-values, American anthem, which fathered the family-values George Bush ads to come. More recently, he made the Old Milwaukee spots featuring the "Swedish bikini team"—a supposedly wry riff on bimbo beer ads, which nevertheless pushes the large breasts up front.

Around the time of the Clarence Thomas/Anita Hill hearings, a former secretary at Hal Riney & Partners sued for sexual harassment, charging one executive with "excessive and lingering touching," and another with telling her to "talk in her sexiest voice for supposed 'voiceovers,'" and then playing the tape throughout the office. Riney himself is not accused of harassment, but of allegedly "creating a hostile work environment which condones and fosters sexual harassment." The case is complete with other women employees expressing disbelief that the men would ever do that. Riney's lawyer calls the suit "frivolous" and, noting its timing, "opportunistic."

Not that politically conservative admen who make sexist ads are all harassers. No way. If I said that, I'd be making Al Simpson-like leaps of logic, and besides, I'd be ignoring all the liberal groping admen.

But, considering that there's politics in all advertising and advertising in all politics, a much subtler connection lies between the mythic Thomas/Hill hearings and the more modest myths—the ads—that ran during breaks. After all, the people who will be writing the attack-dog and innuendo-filled political ads for '92—for which the hearings served as a dress rehearsal—will often be the same people who currently write the heartwarming consumer ads. Is Anita Hill the "product as hero" or Brand X? In a taste test, which do you prefer, Hill or Thomas?

What the hearings and a lot of advertising—even "nice" ads—have in common is the use of demagoguery, *everyday* demagoguery. Demagoguery, says Webster's, is about using "popular prejudices and false claims and promises in order to gain power." It's a volatile, seemingly outdated term, and nowadays if you aim it at anyone less virulent than Joe McCarthy you can be accused of demagoguery. But we see—and most of us use—it daily in more mild, entertaining, and widely accepted ways. It's in the slam-bam put-down of the talk radio host. It's in the ads that sweetly lull with bucolic scenes of an all-white, all-right yesteryear. Demagoguery Mean and Demagoguery Nice. Either way, its *effects* percolate throughout public discourse, from the safety of spouting small-talk clichés to the lines that characters in commercials use to ward off suspicion that they're not one of "us." ("How about those Red Sox?" the Japanese businessman is forced to ask the Boston businessman in the Fidelity Investments ad.) On the everyday scale, demagoguery burps whenever popular prejudices are used to gain power (or market) by floating often unspoken and highly fickle notions of "normal."

None other than former Reagan speechwriter Peggy Noonan demonstrated, albeit inadvertently, the tie-in between hearings demagoguery and the commercial variety. The same woman who made the words "kinder, gentler" coo out of George Bush's mouth wrote in a *Times* op ed about "the normal humans" who supported Thomas and how "normal Americans will carry the day." She pitted normals against "professional, movement-y, and intellectualish [people like] Susan Hoerchner, who spoke with a sincere, unmake-upped face of inherent power imbalances in the workplace. For Clarence Thomas, the straight-shooting, Maybellined J. C. Alvarez . . . [was] the voice of the real, as opposed to the abstract, America. . . ." Noonan's got it right: Name brands and buying into the commercial culture make you normal (another safety net Thomas cast when he announced that if all failed, he'd go back to picking up Big Macs and tossing footballs with his son). Alvarez, the self-declared "John Q. Public," said Anita was different, aloof, not a team player—and once Anita was beyond the bounds of normal, she could be remolded to fit anyone's prejudices.

Ads and the hearings both project narrow definitions of what is a safe black and what is a sane woman. Often mentioned as a silver lining from the hearings was the appearance of so many conservative, well-educated African Americans on national TV—educating white America that they exist outside of the sitcoms and commercials where, it's believed, they're merely the product of show-biz affirmative action. See—some black people are *normal*.

Women in ads don't have to prove their veracity, but they do have to respond at exactly the right pitch—not too aggressive, not too weak, neither careerist nor homebound, sexy but not slutty, and so on. It isn't *normal* to wait 10 years to mention an incident. Why, in a commercial, a girl with a lecherous boss would only have to consult with the water-cooler gals before cutting the creep short by handing him a bottle of Listerine! Everyday Demagoguery always has the answer. It doesn't merely use prejudice to appeal to a crowd, it tosses ambivalence and ambiguity—that is, the stuff that life is made of—out the window. Eating Quaker Oats is "the right thing to do." Coors "is the right one now." Pepsi is "the right one, baby, uh-huh." AT&T, which smears its rivals in a most reasonable, Arlen Specteresque way, is "The Right Choice."

We were all monitoring Thomas, Hill, and J.C. for the slight raising of a lip or the aversion of an eye that might give us clues not just to their veracity, but to their normalness. Because even if someone was lying, as long as he or she could confidently mimic the standard gestures of honesty, that would be enough to encourage our willing suspension of disbelief. No, more than that—it would encourage our ad-trained willingness to believe lies.

Demagaga **215**

Hundreds of times a day, ads offer lessons on HOW TO WIN! Even if Thomas didn't read *The Exorcist,* he watched TV like the rest of us.

Friend or Faux

One night, very late, a movie-star moment lit up the TV screen and affected me in no small way: Cher was doing an infomercial and she looked marvelous. To cut to the chase: I bought my first off-the-tube 800-number product—Lori Davis Hair Care shampoos, conditioners, clarifiers, etc. More on how they worked—or didn't!—later. For in this purchase lies a story of celebrity, power, and the sweet lure of artificiality that flavors them both.

I was probably as shocked as the next American to see Cher in an infomercial. Granted, this was not hot-pink Cher, but executive Cher in a beige silk suit jacket, taking the 'mercial by its tinny horns and toning it down. Though Cher's mission in a 30-minute endorsement is essentially the same as in her many 30-second jobs—to blend glamour with menschlike believability—the very presence of a *non*-has-been star in the low-rent district of "paid programming" gives the ad an extra boost that says, "If she's slumming for this product, it's gotta be good!"

My style swoon was also the result of Cher Cher everywhere—each Cher appearance multiplies the effect of the others. Here she is for Lori Davis; there she is for *CherFitness,* the exercise video that's outselling Jane Fonda's latest (for which Jane, too, made her first infomercial); there's Cher on the cover of *People* and in every silicon nightmare story; and, wow, is she there in the ad for the fake sugar Equal, her hair at its most glorious. Okay, it's fake hair, her publicist admits, but the *wig*'s glory carries over to the infomercial, influencing how we see her real hair.

Maybe, too, I'm particularly susceptible to hair improvement prom-

Her wig has no Equal.

ises. My hair of late has been "flyaway," "unmanageable"—all the '50s adjectives of commercial life. And since my hair is kind of on the Cher track, dark and curly (or on the Cher wig track), I actually thought I could make it look like hers.

"Did you ever look at your hair and want to cry?" Cher opens the ad. "Well, eight years ago that's exactly what happened to me." After dying her hair red for *Mask*, it was a disaster. That's when Lori Davis "miraculously revived my hair." Cher name-drops Lori's other clients—Julia Roberts, Michelle Pfeiffer, Winona Ryder, Barbara Hershey—reinforcing the lure of fame beyond resistance.

In the corridors of such glamorama, Lori herself is a bit of a shock. She's, well, a large woman, and with unnoteworthy blond tresses. But what a character!—the kind of hyperregular gal that famous people just love to be pampered and reprimanded by. Why did Lori devise these "pure magic" products, Cher inquires. Because, says Lori, other products "just didn't deliver . . . I got so frustrated and disappointed, and then I got mad, and you know me when I get mad!" Cher gushes, "Oh, yes, I *do*!"

Like most 30-minute ads, this is a multitextural experience. Cher's "best friend," redhead Paulette, makes a surprise appearance in a fresh curly 'do by Lori. "Paulette!" Cher screams. "It looks great! It looks really great!" "Real" people do before-and-afters, bolstering star clout with their own worker-ant kind. In a pretaped clip, Larry Hagman beckons Lori: "Come here, you little devil, come over here . . . give me a kiss." And Lori gets her own surprise walk-on visitor—Ted Danson, who gets down on his knees to testify, "I could lose my agent, I could lose my lawyer, but if I lost her [Lori] my career would be gone." It's all so impressive that you barely wonder, what are Hagman's thinning hair or Danson's hairpiece testimony to?

Whatever else she does, Lori serves as a stand-in for all us nobodies who never get to schmooze with the legends of our time. But on top of the fame fun, what makes this infomercial more mesmerizing than most is gal sensibility: Paulette, Cher, and Lori trading beauty tips, giggling over photos that magnify a single, dirty strand of hair a billion times, and simply having the luxury to talk about *nothing*, nothing but their hair. All the while you, almost sitting with them, don't have to do a thing, except maybe pick up the phone. That's the beauty of it!

So for two payments of $19.95, I received the basic kit of six products and many glossy brochures of instructions and enticements to buy more. The bottom strand: they were no miracle for me. In fact, the army of shampoos, conditioners, clarifiers, shiners, and hair sprays left my hair so dry that only cheapo VO5 (unscented) got it through the day. Just one item, a superconditioner called Lori's Perfection, seemed to have any effect over what you can get in the drugstore. But Lori's Perfection, an unreal chemical green, smells like extract of lollipop, maybe the no-cal kind made with the aspartame found in Equal.

The Equal ad is Cher at her most beautiful. It's not only a particularly lovely wig, but Herb Ritts shot the spot—a half-artificial/half-real setup that extends to her paid message: "It's kind of unbelievable that people in America are eating 40 pounds of sugar a year," she says. "I was told about it first of all by someone who was a nutritionist and said, 'Cher, you gotta make some change in your diet.' . . . You got the sugar, you got the pink stuff [Sweet'n Low], and you got the Equal. . . . I choose Equal."

But if the answer is Equal or Sweet'n Low, the question is flawed to begin with. Better questions are: Why do Americans eat 40 pounds of sugar a year anyway? Do you really want to substitute that with artificial sweeteners that may pose health hazards of their own? Cher, why not fruit?

Whether it's fake sugar, hair, or body parts, one side effect of artificial ingredients is feelings of inadequacy in those who don't fake it. The least the reconstructed stars owe the undone girls back home is the open acknowledgment that the game is rigged. That, of course, has always been one of Cher's draws—she's honest enough, sometimes, to admit her artifice. "You know, if I want to put my tits on my back, they're *mine*," she's been quoted as saying.

But in the process of being real about artificiality, artifice gains. The reconstruction no longer matters, it fades into "Cher." Her appearance at age 45 becomes a "miracle," "pure magic"—a modern possibility—and *that* becomes a real goal for others of us. But all the time we forget—because advertising and the system of celebrity have reconstructed the memory—that we can't really be Cher. An illusion we— okay, I—pay for in dollars and brain cells.

April 7, 1992

Operation Miscue

Maybe the only area available to move into beyond the two intellectual cul-de-sacs of the abortion argument—it's murder; it's women's rights—is symbol shock, industrial-strength imagery to cut through the grease of ambivalence.

It was only a matter of time before mutilated fetuses were hauled into TV commercials, if only through a loophole. Since by law TV and radio stations must air the spots of any federal candidate, Mike Bailey, a 35-year-old evangelical, decided to run in the Republican congressional primary from Indiana's ninth district just so he could get his *Alien 3*-style antiabortion ads on the air.

He won, in both ways: He slaughtered his little-known opponent, but more importantly, the fetal shots saturated Indiana and parts of Kentucky and Ohio, and Bailey promises they'll be back in the fall to do battle (and likely lose) against Democrat Lee Hamilton.

The ads immediately position themselves as tough look: This commercial, Bailey announces, "is not suitable for small children. That is because abortion is so evil it is not suitable for America." Then to ominous music, he shows pictures of large dead fetuses or tiny legs ripped off at the pelvis. At the end, the camera zooms, horror movie-like, into the black eye of a fetus.

Handy for the right-to-lifers, Bailey is an adman by trade. "I really helped pioneer a lot of the ad industry's shopping mall cross-promotions," he brags—a reference to handing out game cards to mall customers so they can win junk at McDonald's and Burger King. Now he's "pioneered" another cross-promotion: "No federal candidate has ever made the decision to include aborted babies in their television commercials—until now," he says.

What were all those midwestern viewers seeing? For the most part, very late fetuses, far past the 12 weeks when 91 percent of abortions occur. ("We have earlier ones," Bailey says, "but people would have thrown up at the dinner table.") Planned Parenthood of Indiana suspects that some may be miscarriages or stillborns, like the "Baby Tia" that a reverend pushed in everyone's face during Operation Rescue in Buffalo.

Early or late, the pictures come from a short video, *Hard Truth*, made by American Portrait Films, the prolife group that gave us *Silent Scream* in 1985. "We verified each and every aborted baby and baby part shown," insists APF president John Hocevar in a press release. Another release cites Judges 19:29-30—in which a woman is gang-raped to death and her husband cuts her up into 12 pieces, sending them to the 12 tribes of Israel—to justify "presenting the truth to God's people in a form which shocks them out of their lethargy. . . ." APF claims that showings of the nine-minute video influenced the Louisiana House in pushing its abortion bill, the most restrictive of all. The video, says APF, "has a 'cutting edge' that silences rationalizations and leaves pro-abortionists nonplussed."

And that's the goal of all symbol shock—leave 'em speechless, unable to resort to words or ideas. Because at this point in the abortion war the struggle is not only between competing images—baby-killers vs. woman-killers—but between each image and the more complex ideas it does mercenary duty for.

The dead fetuses can be be countered with the usual debate points: The same people promoting dead fetuses tend not to get as exercised about the suffering of living babies, or about killing living people; they may even applaud pictures showing scorched Iraqi bodies in jeeps or, for that matter, Rodney King getting beaten. But for the sake of argument, let's assume that at least some of the pictures are from abortions. And let's accept that dead fetuses are a consequence of later abortions. In which case, it's fair to show them: They're at the center of the debate. The thing to do is to not make these images verboten, even to ourselves. Consider, for example, how the French deal with RU486, the abortion technique of the future. At one clinic, women are asked to look at what comes out, partly for a sense of emotional resolution. Because RU486 is used only at seven weeks or less, admittedly what comes out is "tissue," very far from a fetus. But the point is that staring at the embryo is not approached in a confrontational way—the Indiana pictures are only shame-making if we agree to be shamed.

Shame works very differently in the Arthur S. De Moss Foundation's antiabortion ads running mostly on CNN. These fuzzy, warmhued spots, made by the rather secretive organization that funds groups like Campus Crusade for Christ, come on like a Hallmark ad, or like the child of Reagan's '84 opus, "It's Morning in America." (And guess what? They were made in part by BBDO CEO Phil Dusenberry, who helped make "Morning" as well as ads for GE, Pepsi, and Du Pont.)

For an estimated $14 million to $20 million worth of cable time, groups of healthy and mostly white young girls are shown in plaid skirts hopping up steps of their private school or dressed as kittens for Halloween. And though they sure look like actors, the narrator says,

"All of these children have one thing in common. All of them were unplanned pregnancies, pregnancies that could have ended in abortion. But their parents toughed it out, listened to their hearts, and discovered . . . that sometimes the best things in life aren't planned. Life. What a Beautiful Choice." A second ad shows a white middle-class couple that finally gets the chance to adopt a white infant because some other woman also decided to "tough it out."

Adoption is a wonderful option, but the "tough it out" cheer is as obnoxious as the portrayal of these adoptees as GE ad fodder—most children waiting for adoption are not white, not infants, and are often handicapped or sick. "Tough It Out" is a "Just Do It" for poor women, single mothers, and teenage girls who've just been coddling themselves for too long.

"You can almost hear [CNN] saying, 'Hey, there's no disruption of format from the Pepsi commercials,' " says Herb Chao Gunther, head of Public Media Center, which makes ads for progressive groups. CNN rejected two of the four ads he made for Planned Parenthood, "because our spots were grittier," he says. One showed a young woman fainting in a phone booth after an illegal abortion; the other featured the mother of Becky Bell, an Indianapolis teenager who died after a secret abortion. CNN rejected both for content, while Planned Parenthood pulled the other two because, it says, CNN insisted on running disclaimers stating that the views of the ads are not those of the network. CNN denies the disclaimer claim.

Meanwhile, the National Abortion Rights Action League's campaign applies unassailably patriotic symbols to prochoice ideas (fighting behind mainstream armor is a Bill Clintonian technique and, hmm, these ads are made by Clinton's Washington, D.C., media firm.) A sixtyish man identified as Jim Friedl sits all Schwarzkopfian bulk and says that his mother died when he was four of an illegal abortion. "I'm a retired marine and I believe antichoice politicians are threatening the freedoms I fought for. . . . Remember, when abortion is illegal, women—like my mother—die," he says. The pause before "die" is scripted, but a strong word in isolation is almost as effective as a fetal eye. In Buffalo, NARAL is running a spot that starts off with the Statue of Liberty (a part of NARAL's logo) and ends with the flag as a visual safety net to these risky words: "America needs policies that help reduce the need for abortion. Better sex education, effective birth control, contraceptive research."

After all these years, the problem remains the same: Though most people favor abortion rights, abortion carries a stigma, at least in the commercial environment of TV, that antiabortion does not. Says one woman with Planned Parenthood: "Their soundbites are very effective: 'You're a baby killer.' My response is 'You're a woman-hater,' but I know that's not as effective. We simply need to put something out there that's very human and not just for the politically sophisticated." She thinks maybe they've found it with a slogan that debuted at the Washington march: "I am the face of prochoice America."

Sorry, but that *is* politically sophisticated — and limp with '70s idealism at that. No one seems to have the winning slogan or image — coat hangers are better than "I am the face" but no longer quite enough — and you have to keep asking: At what point is a slogan or an image considered alive?

May 19, 1992

Fear of Buying

While the process of empowerment is key to all political progress, flicking around the *word* "empowerment" comes off like wearing a name tag at a dinner for four: ridiculous, self-serious, ultimately *de-powering*. And to use "empowerment" themes in ads designed to manipulate women should be a contradiction of such a high order that even manipulators would shrivel at the thought.

But, of course, they don't. If the ad industry can sell to women with guilt and fear (of not pleasing others enough, of not being perfect enough), it can also sell with fear of fear itself.

"You are born. And oh, how you wail," narrates Sigourney Weaver, no alien to empowered female imagery. On screen, an athletic femme

Hey, Reebok Girl—mmmwaah!

comes up for air from a midget pool and runs gloriously through city-scapes. "Your first breath is a scream. Not timid, or low, but selfish and shattering. . . . The rest of your life should be like that: An announcement. Just do it."

Despite the announcement, ads have been instructing women to fearlessly be themselves since before Nike was even born. In the late '60s, for instance, Clairol brought out a hippie girl, all straight hyper-blond tresses. "Who am I?" she asks, strolling on a ledge, flower in hand. "Myself. Silly. Serious. But me. I never want to do anything, be anything that isn't exactly me. . . . Even if I use *piles* of makeup, I still want to look like me. Same with my hair. I wouldn't touch it—unless I was absolutely sure I could get a color that says me. That's what I like about Nice 'n Easy. It lets me be me.

"If you say it sells the most," she concludes, "I guess that's why." In encouraging courage, advertising *must* simultaneously lure with the cowardice of the crowd.

And so women's guilt-and-fear (GAF) ads—still common on day-time TV—have always coexisted, often in the same spot, with go-away-guilt (GAG) ads. In fact, after the mid-'80s ad gush of executive gals who had it all (and instilled guilt in anyone who needed more than four hours sleep a night) came commercials that began to take back the fright. Some spots—like Elaine Boosler's for Fantastic—went out of their way to suggest that *im*perfection was the smart way to be. We buy that you're struggling, these healer ads said, so buy us.

Now, in the '92/'93 model, woman is imperfect but she *struggles* perfectly. She faces her soul, she knows she's the only one she can really count on, she takes no prisoners of sex. This attitude gets a boost from the anger and frustration over Willie Smith, Bob Pack-wood, the Swedish Bikini Team; inspiration from Anita Hill and Hil-lary; and continued financial support from the sales charts.

Nike says since its women's-empowerment print campaign began in 1990, it's had a 40 percent increase in women's business (and more than 250,000 letters of support). Maidenform ran an ad that pinned political buttons—"No Means No," "My Body My Choice," and, playing it safe, "Right to Life"—on women's chests as the tagline asks, "Isn't it great when a woman's mind gets as much support as her body?" In the wake of that and other pro-women ads, sales have not only seen "double-digit" increases, says Marilyn Bane, vice-president of marketing, "but our image-tracking studies have also shown an increased perception among our target group that we are contempo-rary and fashionable."

Currently, clothing, shoes, and cars (women now buy about half of all new cars) tend be the favored categories for GAG ads. Purchased for oneself, these products can be played right into self-empowerment. (Food and household items, which women more often buy with men and children in mind, can still be played for GAF value.) The latest empowerment ads tend to fall into different strategic categories:

Pounding, pissed-off woman: The best, Reebok's, features a woman smashing a talking tennis ball. First it takes on the animated face of an overdemanding boss, then a court creep who says, "Hey, babeeee, you gonna hog da court forever?" As the jerk-face ball makes sloppy smooch effects, she WHACKS him one. Reebok, it would like us to think, helps women put balls in their place.

The little-known Bodyslimmers lingerie brand got invaluable PR when Rush Limbaugh attacked its print ad for "male-bashing." It reads: "While you don't necessarily dress for men, it doesn't hurt, on occasion, to see one drool like the pathetic dog that he is." Rush, the goal of so many ads is precisely to make men drool. This is funny. Bow-wow.

Not coming out of the medicine cabinet: These ads let women vent steam while clamping them into traditional stances toward men. For Nyquil a whooping-cough wife gives the last dose of drug to her hacking husband because "You have a big day tomorrow." Her day may not be as important, but she gets the last joke: "I just hope my coughing doesn't keep you awake riddled with guilt."

Clairol hasn't changed colors since its hippie days. It's just added a light rinse of Madonna's I-may-be-in-chains-but-I'm-in-control theory of empowerment. "This is for my mother," says a brand-new brunette. "This is for my husband," says a new blond who defied his advice. "Any idea who this is for?" winks Ivana Trump, touching her golden he-hive.

Poetry is powerful: "These shoes," says a Nike print ad, "know all about bodies that move and mirrors that speak and they must move, *they must dance,* they must shake down the walls of this world in *wildest celebration.*" Offering itself as poetic priest or medicine man, Nike often talks up "celebration," which is empowerment with party streamers.

Reebok moves past its would-be haiku campaign ("I believe in howling at the wind," etc.) and joins the poetry slam: "It's when the beat of the music syncs up with your heart. When your legs are pumping and the only thing that can stop you is the apocalypse. It's where your head has ultimate power over your body. It's called 'Planet Reebok.' And we've built the shoe to get you there. The Aerostep Pro."

If you listen closely, you can hear that same segue from poetry rhythm to sales rhythm more and more these days. But a strong argument for such ads remains: If these companies are going to be selling themselves anyway, what's wrong with them using ideas that are at least ostensibly feminist, that are a small antidote to the Cindy Crawford Lycra parade, and that can maybe persuade *other* people with some good propaganda for a change?

Such questions were agonized over recently, at the ad industry's One Club in New York, by a panel of ad folks who make some of these very ads. "Pedantic . . . a bunch of garbage," Gary Goldsmith, whose agency made the Bodyslimmers ad, said of the Nike spots. "The fact that it's soft sell is hard sell."

"Why are we under so much more scrutiny than film, TV shows, or plays?" was a refrain from the men. "Because we're more insidious," answered Roz Greene of Altschiller Reitzfeld, which tries to make less-demeaning fashion ads for clients like Liz Claiborne. Unlike the artifice in film or TV shows, advertising's artifice is more purely determined by "business decisions," she said. And the results are flashed at you hundreds of times a day.

One athletic woman I know who finds the Nike ads inspiring, says she likes "the strength of the women, the urban settings. But I also feel yanked and seduced. Even as I realize that I'm being manipulated, something says, 'Abandon that and just be a consumer.' They make you want to say, 'It's okay to be stupid, it's okay to be manipulated.' "

In the conflict between resisting a come-on and wanting to accept it is a sexlike tension: If you give in and do just do it, i.e., buy it, the moment of purchase can be a climax at the cash register.

The choices seem forked and, to women, much too familiar: Give in and have sex with Nike, or refuse and be called shrill, sexless, prudish. But surely there must be a third way. Perhaps it lies in allowing yourself to feel the pleasure or inspiration of these ads, if they so grab you, but in *not* making the connection you're supposed to—*not* connecting "celebration" with Nike or fighting back with Reebok. If you are stirred, sublimate—discharge those feelings onto something else—not sneakers, not bras, not anything you can buy. Work out barefoot, meditate, read a book, overthrow the PTA, mow the lawn, do good deeds, wash that man right out of your hair.

Draw encouragement from these ads, enjoy them if you must. Only don't connect (the way they want you to).

April 13, 1993

Boys Under the Hood

I was away during the hubbub over what some men regard as the commercial equivalent of Lorena Bobbitt—the Hyundai spot that (essentially) tosses a male member out of a car for the whole world to laugh at. But I feel that whenever penises enter ads, I should be there.

The snippy little ad goes like this: Two attractive, business-class women waiting for valet parking at a chichi French restaurant comment on the ostentatious autos of their male cohorts. "He must be overcompensating for a . . . shortcoming?" they snicker about one guy. "Now *he* obviously has feelings of inadequacy," they giggle over another. Then, out of a plain, rather boxy Hyundai pops a guy with male model glamour—and their jaws drop: "I wonder what *he's* got under the hood." "If it's true about men who drive flashy cars," says the voiceover (namely Jeff Goldblum, nudelessly establishing *his* stature), "then if a guy chooses a car because it's durable and dependable, wouldn't, uh, the opposite be true?" The ballsy ad rubs it in with the kicker: "Solid, well built, and long lasting. Actually, we're talking about the car."

This ad is, uh, potent. Women—including some interviewed on NBC's *Dateline* and a Midwest college student attending a lecture I gave a few weeks ago—have said that because of this commercial they *would* consider buying a Hyundai. It's as if, with a juiced-up metaphor in the air, girls everywhere will be mentally positioning men on a chart titled "Penises of the Automobile Kingdom."

Which is precisely why the National Organization of Men protested, complaining that the message is, "If you're a well-endowed male, you're going to drive a Hyundai." Of course, advertising makes such mercantile equations between female endowment and product desirability by the hour, but without the media all aflutter. Female frustration over *that* is the fuel that makes this ad accelerate. And men know that snickering over their parts is one of our few weapons of self-defense: Though the ad targets women, who buy a slight majority of Hyundais, it was conceived and written entirely by men.

Into this Hyundai hubba-hubba came succor from the right, where mercantile equations of any kind are in favor. "It's revolutionary. . . . It's a great ad," Rush Limbaugh raved on TV and radio. "Most guys . . . would love to be driving a Hyundai if women are going to be thinking of him that way." On that he's right—the spot probably flatters as many guys as it flattens. (Have you any idea how much Rush would like the world to reconsider *his* unimpressive chassis?) And hovering over this increasingly televised nexus of penis size and male ego is Howard Stern's tiny tail pipe, the one he so loudly bemoans— giving others, in effect, permission to be small and proud of it.

In the realm of car advertising, this spot is part of what might be called Feminism: The Third Gear. In first gear, car advertisers actually cruised for women, as in a 1917 *Vanity Fair* ad: "The New KisselKar 4 Passenger Sedané . . . Strikes Every Woman's Fancy . . . Because it is distinctly a woman's car." Only later did the industry remove women from the driver's seat and place the more buxom of them on the hood as ornaments (a trend still alive today, as in a Sony Auto Sound spot— each time a dude presses a car's radio buttons, a different pouty babe materializes. It ends with the advice, "If You Play It, They Will Come"). But by the mid '80s advertising again began to direct ads *to* women. Only with proven purchasing power—women now account for 46 percent of all car sales and influence 80 percent—were gals allowed to mouth off, like the Hyundai hussies. (Or the Subaru siren who preceded them: Checking her car's oil with a long dipstick, she lamented, "Would somebody please try to explain to me why every guy I know has tried to tell me he knows everything about cars and . . . the '69 Mets?")

And yet all of Hyundai's feminist-toned genital jousting is really a fig leaf to cover something much more intimate: class shame.

The two high-class women waiting for valet parking, the Lady

Chatterly-like suggestion of the greater virility of men who don't drive Lamborghinis—everything in this ad is geared to help potential customers overcome the embarrassment of buying a Hyundai. At $7149, Hyundai's Excel is still the lowest-priced new car in the U.S. The humiliation is made even clearer in another spot, "Hyundai Anonymous." A man stands before a 12-step meeting sweating bullets. "Hi, my name is Tony, and . . . I'm a Hyundai owner." Instead of stoning him, the whole room bursts into applause. It is heavy stuff for any product to admit it is powerless over its image, and to come to believe that a power greater than itself (i.e., Advertising) could restore it to financial health. But the trick in each of the campaign's four spots is to make the source of shame into a source of pride—just as Tony turns tony.

Could Hyundai be overcompensating for a . . . sales shortage?

Yes, admits Hyundai marketing director Maurice Bowen. "We think our cars have come a long way since the $4995 Excel in 1986," but Hyundais are still regarded "as cars bought by people who can't afford anything else." It's too early to gauge sales, but, says Bowen, "advertising awareness has moved dramatically up since the ads first aired, and so far November sales are ahead of last year's."

Okay, now I feel sorry for Hyundai. So let's say it's true, that plain cars mean brass ball bearings. Still, why, besides price, buy a Hyundai over any other plain box? Because Hyundai's ad agency made weenie jokes in public? Maybe. Most corporations are awarded for far less. But remember the arbitrary relationship of a product and its image. Some people might now see a Hyundai and think of you-know-what. Other people, mostly in South Korea, might think of Chung Ju Yung, Hyundai founder and honorary chairman who was recently sentenced to prison for fraudulently using company money to fund his unsuccessful bid for president.

To kind of paraphrase my colleague Bob Garfield of *Ad Age,* who was on TV during the controversy and said that, for the record, *he* drives a moped, I'd like to say—in the spirit of swerving past all metaphors made to move merchandise: I like men who walk.

December 14, 1993

Chapter Five

SHOCK OF THE HUE

Down and Out on Mad Ave

Bigoted ads aren't a trend exactly, but it's certainly safer for such sentiments to ooze from the woodwork these days. Strong economically but weak imagewise, the Japanese are today's primary target of ad abuse. Because we think of them in relation to products in the first place, agencies can insist they're portraying the Japanese only as their client's competitors, no more, no less. So the ads cry out "tastefulness," while offending as they wouldn't dare other racial groups. In a new spot for Volkswagen (of all carmakers!), a big, friendly white guy carries on about how Nipponese car prices are rising higher, illustrated with a small Japanese man, baffled and rendered silent, rising slowly off the ground. The white guy waves off the floating Yellow Peril with a cheerful *"Sayonara!"*

That's one way to reassert power. Baiting gays is another. They may be more vocal than the Japanese, but what with AIDS, their prestige is not at high tide. In positioning itself as "a man's beer," Schmidt's is airing radio spots on how this isn't a brew "for prissy women" or "guys who wish they were prissy women." Or for hairdressers or interior decorators.

"We wanted to appeal to the heavy beer drinker and to approach the macho image in a lighthearted, Archie Bunker vein," says Hank Wasiak, president of the Geers Gross agency. "It was never intended to be offensive." Future ads, he says, may be less "alienating." Yet when WCBS withdrew the ads, the agency offered (and the station

233

rejected) a spot about how the beer's not for guys "who like to walk around (bleep bleep)."

Archie had Edith and his malaprops to put him in context. But these days, when our president tells similarly befuddled anecdotes and nobody laughs, the signal's out to tweak the weak.

June 24, 1986

Little White Lies

In an early Tarzan movie, the African porter tumbles off a cliff after a pack crate, and the worried bwana shudders, "Our supplies!" Blacks and other minorities are still indispensable plot devices, supplying

How the German Volkswagen proves it's American.

Guess who Canada Dry is targeting.

emotional gear the white hero can't quite haul. In ads, it's subtle. For Canada Dry, a tall white achiever wearing suspenders and fresh from the office, joins a pickup basketball game on a graffitied court, with young city kids, black and white. He might be an investment banker, but he's got a great rim shot, even while holding a can of ginger ale—a feat that allows him to bond with a black kid. In the last shot, however, our hero savors victory alone with the product.

The soda company was aiming at a target group "rebellious" enough to consider ginger ale as a beverage, not merely as the more traditional mixer, a spokesman says. So the spots feature people "doing things you don't expect the adult segment to do"—a woman chasing after a construction worker, the Wall Streeter getting down. "We call it impish rebelliousness."

Black jazz musicians and DJs help make the night more sensual for the beautiful white girl and boy in the new "The Night Belongs to Michelob" campaign. In a Dodge Dakota truck spot, Indians on horseback surround a cowboy in a pickup. Threat passes when the chief gives the nod: This truck is *all right.*

Minority actors do have some decent roles in ads, but they're popping up more and more often as product-pitching second bananas. Blacks make whites seem more egalitarian, more hip, even while achieving. For baby boomers raised to be sensitive about race, bonding with blacks—especially over a product—provides a guilt-reducing link to the "real world," a link severed in part by too much consumption. If yup definition lies in the desire to consume, then ads permit consumption of the minority figure's skill, soul, or immediacy to nature, as the race may be.

October 7, 1986

Constructive Engagement Ring

White House Chief of Staff "Diamond Don" Regan's reservation about sanctions against South Africa—"Are American women willing to give up their diamonds?"—is turning up in advertising. DeBeers, the South African company that controls 80 percent of the world's diamond market, is showing an elegant Japanese-made ad inspired by those famous hands on the Sistine Chapel ceiling. A woman reaches across the pearly void for a man's hand above. His is closed; hers is open, imploring. As she gently strokes his hand, it unfolds, and a diamond necklace cascades out. As God gave life to Adam, so man gives diamonds to woman. A voiceover proclaims: "More profound than words. Diamonds."

DeBeers doesn't believe it's offending women, and certainly not blacks. The company "has always been an outspoken opponent of apartheid," says a U.S. spokeswoman. "The former chairman, Harry Oppenheimer, went around for 40 years making speeches against it."

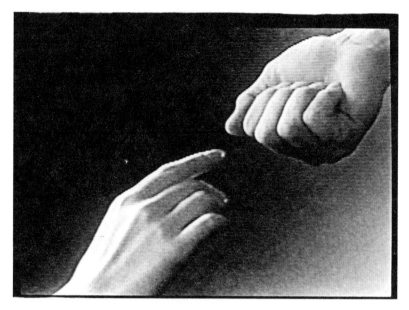

Please, sir, may I touch the DeBeers?

Antiapartheid groups are less sanguine. "DeBeers is one of the more liberal elements in the South African economy, but they don't support sanctions," says Cecelie Counts of TransAfrica. "They're able to profit because they benefit from the gross labor conditions in that country." The company's entrenched in South Africa's economy. DeBeers and Anglo-American Corporation (the two kind of own each other) hold 58 percent of all equities on the South African stock exchange

South African diamonds may one day go the way of gold coins: Overriding the president's veto, Congress recommended a ban on the gems if "significant progress" in dismantling apartheid isn't made. The master/miss relationship promoted in DeBeers ads may change, too. Perhaps to: "More profound than words. Sanctions."

November 11, 1986

Constructive Engagement Ring **237**

Cri de Coors

The Beer That Wants It Both Ways

As Coors has expanded with a line of light beer, it seems to have developed a case of political schizophrenia. Coors regular is the brew that boasts of being as pure and bracing as the Rockies. It's the suds of the rugged individual, of Mark Harmon's tough TV ads. This Coors, oft-boycotted, is embodied by company magnate Joe Coors, Reagan crony and Daddy Warbucks to far-right causes.

Then there's Coors Light and its Silver Bullet Bar ads (based on *Cheers*) full of "kookie," humanist types. Coors Light is so earnestly open that its press kit includes a booklet called *We're Glad You Asked,* about touchy topics like affirmative action. The lo-cal approach is managed by fourth-generation Coors scions Jeffrey and Peter, young, seemingly moderate and pragmatic. *Their* Coors seems like a parody of the socially conscious corp-with-a-heart: it sponsors a black rodeo, a Mexican cook-off, mammography ads featuring Cher, and, at Colorado HQ, a "wellness" center. The light effort has the giddy balance of the witticism by Joe Coors's pal James ("a black, a woman, two Jews, and a cripple") Watt.

Coors is entering the New York market in draft, bottled, and packaged beer. To mark the occasion, this week the company is breaking TV spots tailored for Manhattan, upstate New York, and New Jersey—back-slapping beer ads that lay on the local flavor ("Coors is the one worth drinkin', once you get through the Lincoln," goes the Manhattan jingle). They're the first thrust in a $25-million advertising, marketing, and PR blitz—worth it, Coors says, because New York and New Jersey account for 10 percent of national beer consumption.

Coors already spends more on marketing than any other brewer—$12 a barrel. It has to. The company has made some improvements: Prospective employees are no longer asked about their sex lives. And a black boycott, spurred by chairman William Coor's remark that blacks "lack the intellectual capacity to succeed," was ended by funneling $650 million into minority business opportunities. But Coors is still boycotted by labor, gay, and women's groups. While the company itself makes "socially responsible" contributions, Jumpin' Joe is still heavily involved in right-wing politics; and young Jeffrey is not necessarily too pragmatic for arch-conservative causes. He's a member of the Free Congress Foundation, which Papa Joe helped found and which recently held a conference on "Hope and Homosexuality" to consider how religious conversion might straighten out gays. (A Coors spokesman says Jeff wasn't involved in that event.)

The Gay Men's Health Crisis says Coors's New York distributor tried to give it $25,000 for the upcoming AIDS walk, asking that promo material read, "Coors presents AIDS Walk New York." GMHC refused the bread. "Did Coors make the offer because they really *cared?*" asks Marty Rouse of the NYC Coors Boycott Coalition, which recently convinced Googie's bar to dump its Coors down a sewer. John Meadows, Coors's director of community affairs, says: "It's my contention that the gay community is being used by the AFL-CIO." The union has been boycotting the nonunion brewery since 1977, and Coors is banned at city functions in Detroit and Boston.

The brewery's new light image may buy social respectability, but it's hard to believe that Coors's left hand doesn't know what its right hand is doing.

March 31, 1987

Gut Reaction

Only 15 seconds long, this ad would sleepily blend into the blur of ads for pharmaceuticals, but an ethnic curve ball pops it out. A Mexican family touring the U.S. is eating snack foods in front of a ringing trolley car: "We love visiting America," says the father. "Hot dog!" yells the son, about 10, holding up a specimen. "Fried chicken!" the mother chimes in. "Pizza!" celebrates the young daughter. "But," warns their patriarch, "we're glad you have Kaopectate." The spot closes on

Mom—the gender most likely to buy the stuff. "Kaopectate," she says, "the diarrhea e-specialist."

My gut reaction was that Kao scored a KO—reversing field on Montezuma's revenge is funny. Upjohn manages to avoid embarrassing itself à la Jimmy Carter and seems even sophisticated in its daring. But when the joke settles, it leaves a queasy feeling; like a stomach, social awareness starts to rumble.

The intent clearly was to make this group a counterpart of the perfect (North) American family of four, loaded with middle-class signifiers: sportswear, camera, nylon tote bag—Esperanto props that ID tourists the world over. But as the actors' broad accents wrap excitedly around monosyllabic words for fast-food, the characters become cartoons. They don't need sombreros. A 15-second spot virtually requires cartoon characters, but stick figures can't be expected to turn decades of a one-way joke into enlightenment.

"People have been bad-mouthing the ad," says Esther Renteria of the National Hispanic Media Coalition. "To be at the level where you could afford to bring your family here as tourists, you would have had

Recalling the stereotype reinforces it.

enough education not to have that broad an accent." She doesn't think the ad's funny. "For it to be funny, you have to recall the stereotype, and recalling it reinforces it."

Well, that's the gist of both humor and offensive humor; the ad rides uncertainly along that long, thin faultline. Unfortunately, other Hispanic-takeoff ads make this one look faultless.

Naugles, a Mexican fast-food chain in the West, ran a campaign featuring, says Renteria, "what were supposed to be Mexicans. They had terrible accents and terrible lines. The Hispanic actors who tested for the part turned it down. The company went ahead and casted Anglos for the role." The ads were finally pulled off the air.

This is the Hispanic version of the theme of *Hollywood Shuffle.* "We're usually cast," says Renteria, "as pimps, prostitutes, illegal immigrants, gang members, or gardeners." A recent study by the Center for Media and Public Affairs found that Hispanics are shown in one out of 50 roles on primetime TV—the same numbers found 30 years ago. (In the same period, black roles rose from one in 200 to one in 11.)

Together with its sibling spot—an English family visiting a dude ranch is also grateful for the diarrhea specialist—the Kaopectate campaign spans the media hierarchy of ethnic sensitivity. The *English* family gets stereotyped costumes as well as accents—but Brit jokes can pass. Not only can Brits roll with the punches, being mostly pale and English-speaking. But in the Handy Ethnic Cartoon Catalogue, the English represent fond memories of overdevelopment: class system in place, whipped cream peaking in a maraschino cherry of royalty.

Of course, neither the Mexican touristo nor the delicate-tummied English spots are aimed at those nationalities. They're aimed at white Americans for whom getting ethnic stereotypes confirmed is the only stink bomb strong enough to mask the mention of diarrhea itself.

February 9, 1988

Cereal Rights

Part of TV's banality is that everything appearing on it becomes more "okay" than it was before. Once an idea does a guest-shot on the tube, it becomes just a little bit harder to discern anything wrong with it. Buoyed by such prima facie goodwill, the ad for Kellogg's Nut & Honey Crunch cereal seems, at first glance, too banal, too cute to provoke antigay sentiment.

"Hey, Cookie, what's for breakfast?" a bunch of surly cowboys ask the wagon train cook. As Cookie pronounces the name as "Nuttin', honey," the dudes cock their guns. "It looks trivial, but the bottom line is one man calls another honey and guns get drawn," says Arthur Johnston of the Coalition Against Media/Marketing Prejudice, which is heading a protest against the ad.

At CAMMP's insistence, Kellogg's reviewed the spot. After much consideration, the world's largest cereal company concluded that reading the ad as antigay "is an unjustified interpretation," says a Kellogg's spokesman. The cowboys draw weapons because "the cook is saying there's nothing for them to eat."

Laughable as it sounds, Kellogg's deconstruction ignores its own ad: Cookie is flanked by four full bowls of cereal, the cereal box (of course), and a pitcher of milk. Two of the three previous vignettes in the same spot play on one character misunderstanding the kind of honey intended: A waitress vamps like Mae West when a customer orders Nuttin', honey; a rich lady looks like she's going to cough up her breakfast when her butler dares speak the word to her. The tenser cowboy scene winds the punch line even tighter, the better to remember it by. In the process, you can lose track of who's really getting punched.

"I don't think there was a cabal of people saying, 'What can we do to those queers?' I think they thought it was amusing," says Johnston. "They're having a real hard time realizing something's wrong." A boycott of Kellogg's, which refuses to pull the ad, is always an option, he says.

The seemingly vast space between good-time advertising and the bad-time real world easily collapses: A National Institute of Justice report released last fall stated that "homosexuals are probably the most frequent victims" of hate-motivated violence. The National Gay and Lesbian Task Force says reports of antigay violence and harassment have increased from 2042 cases in 1985 to more than 7000 last year. "These are only the tip of the iceberg," says a spokesman, adding that an earlier NGLTF survey found that nearly one in four gay men and one in 10 lesbians had, some time in their lives, been punched, hit, kicked, or beaten because of their sexual orientation. "That's the context in which the Nut & Honey ad appears."

There's a worse context: The ad looks like a cartoon version of the "homosexual panic defense." In a number of murder cases, male defendants have been acquitted or received reduced sentences in part by claiming they killed their male victim because the victim made a pass. "In almost every case where you have a gay victim, an effort is made by the defendant to discredit him and show he was asking for it," says Jacqueline Schafer, gay and lesbian community liaison in the Manhattan D.A.'s office. It's as if Robert Chambers got off for killing Jennifer Levin on the basis of her expressing *interest,* much less going to Central Park with him. Since there are usually no witnesses, the HPD can provide a neat cover for pure gay-bashing, without a "pass." That is, a guy doesn't necessarily even have to call another guy "honey" to get a trigger pulled. Kellogg's cowboys seem to have homosexual panic, and society offers the defense.

May 17, 1988

Rube Barbs

Lee Jeans came out with an ad last year that was so aesthetically up-to-the-moment that you almost didn't notice its greasy politics. An overweight, middle-aged black woman in a laundromat gently scolds a chiseled, college-aged white boy over his laundry habits, while a dewy-eyed white girl looks on. After reminding him that he needs soap, the black woman goes on to criticize his loading procedures: "You can't wash lights and darks together." Well, this ad doesn't either. The boy and girl, strangers at first, smile shyly at each other over his being bawled out. They're hurtling toward a "cute meet"; the nanny figure is just a prop—a Butterfly McQueen manqué—that propels the white young 'uns to bond.

It's just like in the movies—all those movies starring a white antihero and heroine and a black, Hispanic, or another "other" sidekick whose wacky ways spur the white stars' first eye contact. But the laundry spot is so artsy cool—jagged film cuts, classical music spliced in where you expect rock—that you do a double take: Is the ad really this snotty? Lee's current campaign confirms that it is.

In one new spot, beautiful young people gyrate over the foibles of those of a different class and age. To some wonderful zydeco, two young guys cruise the Southwest. At a diner, an old, wrinkled waitress reads the list of pies. What's that one before cherry? they ask. Rhubarb. Seeing that his pal doesn't comprendez, one kid says, in the perfect flat, self-righteous pitch, "It's a plant." The local at the next table explains, as matter-of-factly as if he's discussing the heft of a heifer's udder, that rhubarb is a vegetable. "It's about yea long." The boys share a laff when the waitress discovers, after all the hubbub, that they're out of rhubarb. There's that Andy Griffith word again! But you know that on "yea," the copywriters felt they'd hit their home run.

The boys' clean white T-shirt look, their willingness to "relate" to the locals through their bemusement, spell out a class aesthetic and attitude, sort of Ferris Bueller goes to Mayberry. Part of tourism is finding old people or other "authentics" to provide little interactions that can be bought cheaply, like postcards. Today's easy rider defines squareness as people who don't see the hipness of interacting with squares—squares are human kitsch decorating the path of the easy rider's personal journey.

But Lee's get worse. In another ad, a great gammed gal flutters into a large loft elevator to cool strains of Mozart's *Requiem* ripe to flirt with the young Michael Douglas type waiting inside. His eyes skim her Lee'd legs. The sexy situation is set: caged denim. But just before the elevator takes off, a plasterer jangles in with his tools, a déclassé guy polluting their paradise. "3's a Crowd," the title card interprets. Friendly as hell, he asks the girl what floor she works on. She barely pinches out, "Six." "*I* did that," he says. "I did the walls, the ceiling, everything. I'm on eight now. Moving up in the world. Hah!" Their coupling thwarted, the pretty people get tastefully ugly—she rolls her eyes, he commiserates over this weenie amid their carpaccio.

Whether the other is black, old, or blue-collar, the underlying contrast in Lee's spots is between the sexually active and the nonsexually active. Sexuals are young, lithe, and jean-wearing. Nonsexuals are too fat or too old to fit into Lee's. In fact, they tend toward uniforms: waitress's, workman's, or, in a third spot, cop's—they are not "free." (But nonsexuals have *their* jean; it's just in another set of commercials—namely Wrangler, Lee's sister company, whose new campaign is explicitly aimed at men who want a "roomier" fit.) Sexuals bond over the dead bodies of nonsexuals. Nonsexuals are simply bonded to their workaday roles; they're the natural wonders of the sexuals' world.

Lee, which is targeting mostly 18- to 34-year-old women in this campaign, could have gone the way of, say, Jordache, which recently dropped its cloying tormented-teen scenarios in favor of the outright sex of chicks humping brick walls. Jordache just ignores the nonsexuals. But Lee goes out of its way to haul them into its ads—to more sharply define and flatter its market against them. Adolescence and the early twenties are the age of snottiness. Spending millions to promote it is like handing an arsonist matches.

There is a theme other than easygoing, pastel superiority to these spots—it's frustration. In each ad, something—a cop stopping a kid for speeding, a stalled car—botches a goal. "We try to build in some kind of tension, an emotion that anyone can relate to," says a spokesman for Lee's agency, Fallon McElligott. That the tension usually results from old or dumpy folk wasn't planned, he says; it was just a part of the "situations we came up with." (Tension is indeed a subtext to all denim ads, because part of blue jean mythology is that no matter how fucked up you are, you feel good in your jeans.)

There are worse instances of ad snobbery than the Lee's ads. Last year, *US* magazine ran a headline, "Definitely Not Us," with a photo of fat folk sinking into lawn chairs at a trailer park. Its current, more tempered campaign, called "A Better Class of People," merely spoofs tabloid fan mags with heads like "No Nude Dude Ranches." That campaign is another Fallon McElligott product (though "Definitely Not Us" was not). Fallon also institutionalized the class-at-a-glance technique with its *Rolling Stone* "Reality/Perception" campaign, which serves up quickie social codes to separate the yippies from the yuppies.

The real message of Lee's identification with its first-worlders seems to be that without fashion, reality wouldn't happen. If a fashion-deprived person has eaten a rhubarb and a fashionable person never has, does that vegetable exist?

September 19, 1989

Addictions and the Drug War

It came as no surprise last week when President Bush offered the Media-Advertising Partnership for a Drug-Free America the White House to announce the results of its latest survey. The news, naturally enough, was that advertising works—which is nifty because probably little else in his drug war will.

The partnership is the group of 75 ad agencies that has produced, in the last two-and-a-half years, 56 TV commercials, 50 radio spots, and 106 print ads urging various target groups not to do drugs—or to *like* people who do drugs, at least illicit ones like marijuana, cocaine, and crack. Legal drugs like alcohol and cigarettes—still advertised by many of these same agencies—are not mentioned in this, the most massive public service campaign in history.

They've given us fried eggs and sweating rats, humiliated doper dads, snorting school bus drivers, young girls diving into empty swimming pools, and younger girls prostituting for a hit. Unlike spots for

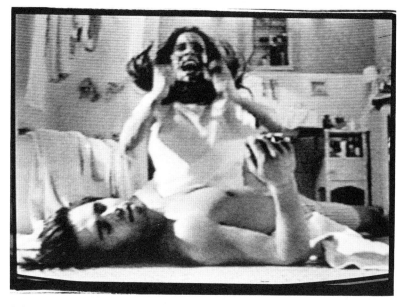

Ads as an addictive substance

cars or cereal, antidrug ads must load up with antisnickering devices. Their makers are very aware that snorting of the laughing kind awaits on just the other side of every visual pun, gross-out metaphor, and crying mama they film. Even CBS's own antidrug ad campaign, called "Stop the Madness" (conveniently featuring "members of the CBS family of stars") avoids the worst pitfalls of reefer madness. The ads must be cooler than the drug.

On their way to cool, however, they often trip over their own technique. Their cowbell sounds—grabbing you with "clever," punny slices of life; moving to what they believe is drop-dead rhythm ("This is your brain. This is drugs. This is your brain on drugs"). The ad people who are bringing all the tricks of the trade to bear on the drug problem—and specifically to one point: to prevent "first use"—are the same people who have so cheerfully, and lucratively, helped make this a culture of addiction in the first place.

Even so, such propaganda is semi-okay with me. We're getting propaganda all the time anyway, and deglamorizing drugs is useful counterpropaganda for the years of movie imagery and peer group posing.

But along with the antidrug message, unfortunately, come many other messages. It's not so easy to switch from a lifetime of selling to unselling, and the tension the effort puts on adsters shows in their spots. When mixed with drugs, every question of class, race, age, every "us versus them" on the plate can multiply out of control.

You can see this most clearly in the partnership's newest series, the African-American ads, written and produced by black agencies and targeting primarily black preteens and parents (a Latino campaign airing mostly on Spanish-language media broke last spring). The partnership's executive director, Tom Hedrick, says one reason these ads debuted only this October after more than two years of spots focusing on whites is, "We don't want to risk reseeding the myth that drugs are only a problem in the black community." The ads clearly try to avoid racial and class stereotypes, but types leak out anyway—through the dramatization, the acting, the very salesmanship of it all.

"Almost 400 years ago," one spot starts, "African Americans were brought to this continent in chains, stripped of their dignity, torn from their families. They never surrendered till they were free." Fine words, only trouble is they are illustrated literally, in a quick, *Roots*-like production, with fearful slaves popping their eyes. The metaphor of slavery does yield one very powerful moment—as the voiceover warns, "Don't dishonor them by becoming a slave to heroin, cocaine, and crack," a leather belt is yanked around a scarred bicep. But the moment is smudged when, at the end, iron chains that look like leftover *Star Trek* props are superimposed around the necks of two nodding-out men—giving them a junkie Amos and Andy look that could trigger racist yuks.

The grab-ya-by-the-balls graphicness, pumped by drug war urgency, is going to play differently to black and white audiences. Like the pusher in nylon sweats on the basketball court who, with snakelike arrogance, tells single mothers, "Mamas like you make my job so easy when you don't tell your children just how deadly crack is . . . I just *love* getting first crack at 'em." He may or may not get mothers to "tell junior about guys like me," but for some white viewers he's confirming the stereotype of menacing black youth.

Thomas Burrell, whose agency made that spot, as well as the black-targeted campaigns for McDonald's, Coca-Cola, and Ford, says, "We've got to make drugs unappealing and uncool, with the primary culprit being crack." The other way to do this is to make the antidrug messenger cool. Rap is the obvious and much-used answer. But all the fun that the partnership's rappers at least seem to be having undermines their rap. "Life is more important than material things. You don't need all the gold and the diamond rings," they sing while they play with the gold, the limos, the cops on a *Sesame Street*-like set. Antidrug rap (there are 18 new spots playing) works better on radio, where the visuals don't conflict.

One of the partnership ads supersedes the antidrug-ad snafus. Maybe because it stars a nine- or 10-year-old boy so sweet that everyone I know who watches it pouts out their lower lip in baby love. He's telling us what happened last night: "A noise woke me up. It was my older brother Ricky, he was going through my pockets looking for money. He grabbed my throat and threw me against the wall. He was high on crack. He was my older brother, man, and he was gonna kill me for some crack? I'm never gonna be like him."

"The primary focus of our campaign is black kids under 13," says Ross Love, chair of the campaign's African-American task force and VP of advertising at Procter & Gamble. "We want to create such a negative attitude among our young that they will reject even trying them."

The partnership campaign is as focus-grouped and press-kitted as anything by AT&T. "It originated out of marketing theory," says Hedrick, who worked for 15 years in marketing at two major agencies. "What we needed to do was the simple inverse of what we do every day—we needed to unsell. In a way, we look at ourselves as the competition of the drug business. Illegal drugs are an annual $150-billion retail business, by far the most profitable one in the world." Doing drugs, he says, "is like a buying decision—first your awareness of the product and its 'benefits' is raised. That should lead to an initial trial, and if that's successful, to retrial and eventually high usage.

"We know from long-term experience that the one thing we can change is willingness to make the initial trial. That's why we don't focus on drug users or addicts. Say you're a Johnnie Walker Black drinker for 10 years. My chance of getting you to change brands is very slight."

And so the bulk of the campaign is aimed at preventing "first use"; the real targets are "preusers"—generally preteens and teenagers—and their "influencers"—parents, siblings, friends, health care workers, and employers. Likewise, the ads usually focus on specific drugs rather than Drugs. "You wouldn't use the same ads for Top Job and Ivory soap," he says, "and you can't tell kids that smoking dope is going to kill them." The partnership believes in tailoring special messages to every group and every age for every drug.

The cost of such permutated propaganda has led to the $1 million-a-day obsession. With George Bush pushing them on, the partnership is asking the media to more than double its current donation of ad time and space to $365 million a year. By hooking up with this private sector, Bush can *look* like he's doing something about drugs: "Think of it," he said dreamily in his bag-o'-crack speech—"a billion dollars [over three years] of television time all to promote the antidrug message."

Whether or not the partnership has sold the antidrug message, they have sold the media. *The New York Times,* which almost never runs public service announcements, is contributing 100 pages a year to the effort; Cap Cities/ABC will devote $27 million this year, more than the other nets. (Cap Cities/ABC president Dan Burke is the brother of partnership chairman Jim Burke. Jim Burke, by the way, is a fellow Trilaterist of George Bush's.) Lately though, some media moguls are getting annoyed at the costs of campaigning; talk is circulating about how this could cut down on the PSAs for the homeless, the Red Cross, AIDS, education, and a dozen other causes.

But do they "work"? According to the partnership's new survey results, they do. In areas where media exposure to the ads is high, attitudes toward drugs and drug users continue to change at a faster rate than in areas where media exposure is low or nonexistent. This year, dramatic results could be shown only for adults (a 33 percent decline in marijuana use last year in high-media areas as compared to

15 percent in low-areas; a 15 percent decrease in cocaine use in high, compared to a 2 percent decrease in low). But with the all-important preteens and teens—where the goal is to prevent first-time use—only more modest achievements were recorded. There was a little less usage and a little more of the desired negative attitudes. More kids agreed this year than last year that "Drug users are aggressive, depressed loners who are self-centered, lazy, and have no future," says the partnership.

The flip side of "drug madness" is conformity anxiety. "The national intolerance can be internalized," says Tom Hedrick. "I believe in social censureship—not censorship—it's the most important force we have in society. It's more important than punitive action. The desire to be an accepted part of the group is extremely powerful."

It's also what drives a lot of advertising. "Drugs," a partnership press release states, "are perceived to make you feel good or powerful, make you less inhibited socially, make your sex life better, give you extra energy, and make you more popular." Sound familiar? Sound like the secret strategies behind ads for almost everything from Mercury Cougar to Michelob Dry? Our culture sells a series of addictions, short-term highs and blips that come from habitual buying and owning. But if you can't always get what you want, in material goods or status, if you try sometimes, you just might find drugs.

"For inner-city kids, I don't think any advertising would work," says a man who works in advertising and with teenagers in drug treatment. "What would work is a whole different view of society, money for treatment, real jobs. They sell drugs because they can make a better living at it."

One way to make viewers feel an accepted part of the group is to define them by what they're not. By leaving addicts so visibly out of the ads—or just using them as heavies—the campaign brands addicts and dealers as a class different from "us," a class easier to put in prison, exterminate, or both.

Also making "us" feel safe from "them," the partnership blitzkrieg villainizes marijuana while sparing alcohol altogether. Many substance-abuse researchers regard alcohol as "the most widely used and destructive drug in America" (so says the Bureau of Justice Statistics); alcohol accounts for 100,000 to 150,000 deaths a year compared to the 10,000 to 30,000 deaths a year for all illicit drugs combined. Cigarettes are deadlier still.

But then cigarettes and alcohol are still a source of vast advertising revenues. In fact, some of the same agencies working for the partnership also carefully research and target liquor, malt liquor, and cigarette ads to African Americans, Latinos, and women—seeking out, like any decent dealer, markets that haven't yet been fully exploited.

All human societies have used intoxicating substances for one purpose or another, usually shaped and prescribed by religious ritual. One of the very reasons drugs are a problem is because of advertising culture, encouraging the compulsive taking of *something*, telling you hundreds of times a day that what you buy can make you high. It's helped displace the kind of culture that could conceivably manage drugs. Maybe ads can counteract some of the quick-fix reflexes they create, but they can't attack the real roots of the problem any more than a fish can see the water it swims in.

November 14, 1989

Shock of the Hue

Short of pushing Darkie toothpaste (the Colgate-Palmolive product sold in Hong Kong that only recently, and only under pressure, changed its name—to Darlie), advertising still finds ways of maintaining white prerogative. "At Holland American, we're aware that perfection cannot be achieved overnight," chimes one TV spot, as an Asian waiter serves the luxury liner's all-white guests. "But we're trying."

Cruise lines are pretty clearly sold as a respite of colonial conscious-

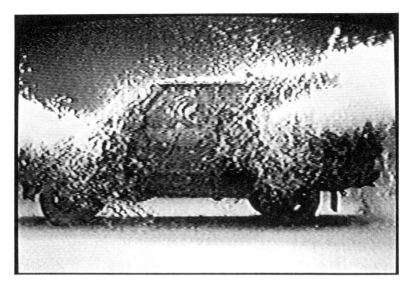

Range Rover cleans up.

ness, but there are also the slippery, are-they-or-aren't-they cases. These are often arty ads, where careless insults and stereotypes are so beautifully woven into abstraction and ambiguity they can hardly be seen. I'm thinking of an ad for Range Rover, the British-made luxury jeep that starts at $38,500. The ad is jewel-like symbolism itself. Against an all-white background stands a jeep smeared bumper-to-rollbar with mud. Jungle music backed by shrieking animals throbs as powerful blasts of water arch in sexy slo-mo over the jeep. As the mud dissolves, the jungle sound gradually, elegantly, turns into opera until we hear only a pure soprano, and the vehicle is, at last, gleaming white.

The concept is simple: Using the elements of sound and water, the ad makes a progression from muddy to pristine, from primitive to civilized. At first glance the ad just seems too urbane to be saying, "Out of Africa and into the opera house." But a *Lord of the Flies* frisson comes with four-wheel drive.

Of course, Range Rover is using this symbolism to make a point about the car: that, as a Rover spokeswoman says, "It's a unique combination of luxury and heavy-duty, off-road ability." Range Rover's previous TV spots have made this point more directly. (One showed your standard lush mountain road, but instead of the car coming down the pike, it shimmies straight down the mountainside.)

This season's particular choice of symbols is dicey enough, but considering that the car's history is about pith-helmeted, sturdy Brits making the world safe for colonialism, it crosses the line. The Land Rover was created after World War II and used for safaris and the like; the plusher Range Rover was developed in 1970 and just three years ago and made it to America. Its proud past is evoked more *genetically* in the print version of the mud spot: "It's a favourite vehicle of the British aristocracy. . . . Its pedigree is pure Land Rover. And it comes tested on tracts from the Serengeti to the Australian Outback."

Elevating whiteness was probably the furthest thing from the ad people's minds. And there's nothing inherently wrong in opposing primitivism and refinement—art does it all the time. But the assumptions that many whites hold in order to believe that blacks are inferior are the same assumptions that inform Rover's progression from jungle music to opera. Without any people in the ad it's just harder to see. Had the ad shown, say, a muddied Masai tribesman donning silk breeches and a powdered wig, it would have been clearly offensive.

Many stereotypes that advertising perpetuates derive from the knee-jerk sales reflex to "shock," to be provocative. Provocative ads often use visual puns or juxtaposed images. Yet, when race is an element of the pun, as in the controversial Benetton print ads and billboards, the social ice gets a mite thin.

For six years now, Benetton, the Italian-based boutique with 5500 stores in 80 countries, has featured a racial mix of children and adolescents in its "United Colors of Benetton" campaign. "Promoting racial harmony has always been at the essence of our company," says a company spokeswoman. "Since we're global, and we use the same advertising everywhere, it's only natural."

But this year Benetton got into trouble. Upping the shock quota, it virtually used arrows to point to the blackness of the black people in its ads: a black coalminer arm in arm and laughing with a white coalminer, who looks like he's in coal-dust blackface; the hands of a black man and a white man handcuffed together; the ample bosom of a black woman breast-feeding a white infant.

The ads have been criticized by both left and right. Here, the breast-feeding woman was seen as a wet-nurse mammy, and so the ad never ran in the U.S. In Paris, however, a Benetton store received a bomb threat from a right-wing group over this race mixing. Back here, people have protested the handcuff ad, interpreting it as a white cop arresting a black suspect. (I thought the Euro-idealistic Benetton was doing a spin on "none of us are free until all of us are free" mixed with a decadent jailhouse chic.) When advertising is ambiguous, context and who the viewer is change its meaning. Will all of this be on the Rorschach test?

The campaign involves "a little bit of showing off," admits Benetton's advertising director. (Benetton has shared the same adman/photographer, Oliviero Toscanini, with another poser, Esprit.) The effect, however, is that the black models are there for shock value, to make the viewer feel, how risqué of Benetton. The company has refused to pull the protested ads and says they haven't affected sales, but the next campaign will be "not quite as provocative," says the spokeswoman.

Actually, it's a laudable marvel that Benetton positions blacks so prominently in ads at all. "Most companies feel if you go overboard with blacks you'll offend whites," an L.A. ad exec (not associated with Benetton) once told me. "Their fear is that it's going to hurt their business, that they're going to screw up their image by being known as a black car, a black beer, a black toothpaste. They really live in dread of that."

Both Range Rover and Benetton use "African" for a little jolt of contrast; it's only that their value judgments differ—Rover whispers "primitive," Benetton chants "chic." It's like sitting in on a conversation between Ayn Rand and Picasso at Trader Vic's. If Benetton can lend its preppy fashion some soul with black models, then Rover can throw a little mud in your eye. Neither campaign really runs the risk of making the product seem "black." They're just looking for gold at the end of the rainbow.

January 9, 1990

Shock of the Hue **255**

Be-Twixt & Be-Tween

When I was in sixth grade and sitting in the back of class, Mr. Bradford told me to take the gum out of my mouth. I said I didn't have any gum, clamping down on the gum like it was mortar between bricks. As Bradford came hurtling down the aisle, I ran. He chased me, cornered me, and I finally had to give up my bubble of independence. Bradford, I believed, was everything repressive about teachers, but by junior high I felt that the kids were the bullies. They daily humiliated a math teacher, an old man who had a stiff classroom manner but was decent and wanted to teach, once hanging him by the legs out his second-floor window. The cool/square bloodbaths between students and teachers come to mind when watching some ads that flatter kids, telling them they're independent little system-buckers—so why not buy the things the commercial tells them to buy?

All poppin' fresh Max Headroom-like animation, the spot for Bubble Tape—six feet of bubble gum wound like a measuring tape—hilariously and ruthlessly skewers the egghead set. "Your principal can't smile," says the voiceover, as a balding man's tight face literally cracks. "Can't swim. Can't rap." As he awkwardly tries to dance in his black leather, he looks sickly s&m. Then the principal owns up: "I can't *stand* Bubble Tape!" Other spots take on Bubble Tape-hating math teachers, toupeed guidance counselors, and lima-bean-eating, polka-dancing parents. "Bubble Tape," the tagline goes. "For you—not *them.*"

The goading works. Introduced by Amurol (a division of Wrigley) in 1988, Bubble Tape is now the number-three sugared bubble gum seller. The spots are aimed at eight- to 14-year-olds—"tweens," as the industry calls them—and, although some boys have been known to chew the whole six feet, Bubble Tape mainly targets girls. "Girls are the main suppliers of gum," says Gary Schuetz, VP of marketing. "Gum is a social communicator. If a girl likes a boy, she'll offer him gum. If not, she'll say, 'I don't have anymore.' " He knows this because Amurol screens every concept before its 1500-tween strong "Candy Tasters Club."

From the clubsters, Bubble Tape learned that the way to kids' hearts is to give them something the authorities in their lives hate (even if the hatred is a marketing invention). "We took this idea, made it goofy and surreal, purposely overexaggerated it. We didn't want to upset adults," says Schuetz. "Now when we do consumer research, the kids play back two things—that it's six feet of gum, and that 'This is *our* product, this isn't for adults.'"

Moving up a few years are the ads for Pepsi's Slice soda. Featuring a simple line-drawn animated character named Fido Dido and the chanted words *Cool, Clear,* and *Crisp,* the ads are cool and crisp. Fido Dido's hair squiggles straight up, he wears a T-shirt with his face on it, and he carries a noncartoon can of Slice. As a human hand with a pencil sketches a suit and tie onto him, Fido yanks them off and breaks the pencil point with a karate kick, "proving," a Pepsi press release says, "that no one can force him to conform to the mainstream or take away his Lemon-Lime Slice," the two actions being equivalent.

Created by a former ad agency art director, Fido Dido was born not as a comic strip character or from a TV show, like Bart Simpson, but

Fido Dido can hawk for anyone.

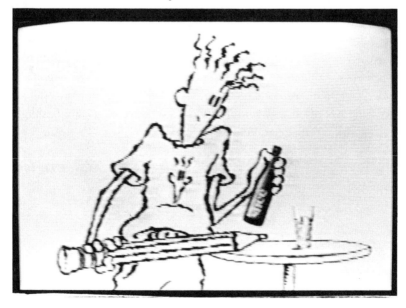

purely as an image to be licensed. He appears on socks, greeting cards, hair driers, you know, in 14 countries. Fido's a minor player here, but, says Pepsi, he has "a huge following" overseas, where he's been around for a couple years, having starred in ads for Slice's rival, 7-Up. In fact, they're identical to the Slice ads. Pepsi owns 7-Up everywhere but the U.S., and so when Pepsi wanted to use Fido for its domestic version of 7-Up, Slice, it simply drew in the new brand name. The original ads were created by McDonald's agency, Leo Burnett—which also makes the Bubble Tape spots.

Though he's the darling of multinational forces, Fido wants to change the world. There's a "Fido Credo," a sort of 10 commandments for the teen Esperanto personality: "Fido is for Fido. Fido is against no one. Fido is Youth. Fido has no age. Fido sees everything. Fido judges nothing. Fido is Innocent. Fido is Powerful. Fido comes from the past. Fido is the future." Fido sounds like a T-shirt–wearing (and corporate-safe) Jesus Christ.

Individualism has long been an advertising pitch, though much subtler than the sex or fear sells. In fact, Slice's Coca-Cola-owned nemesis, Sprite, *also* uses it. Sprite, the ads say, provides "the unexpected twist that makes us different," a theme usually illustrated by gals in layered clothes doing kookirooni things. Being just a *twist* different and acting whimsical—i.e., breaking loose by buying a noncola—is the suburban form of freedom-fighting.

Now with Slice and Bubble Tape leading the way, generic individualism is available in the junior version—and just at an age when most kids can't think without thinking about what everyone else thinks. Wearing IDs of our nonconformity on our coffee mugs and flashlight key chains, we are licensed to be different.

August 21, 1990

Rubber Sold

The recent confluence of AIDS-related ad news—Magic Johnson's HIV announcement and his corporate sponsors' subsequent fight-or-flight responses; Fox TV's decision to allow condom ads; the introduction of a major AIDS-awareness campaign, Ads Against AIDS (AAA)—made it seem, for a moment, that the right ads at the right time could foster a more enlightened mass consciousness about AIDS.

But how does an AIDS ad seize the moment? Is there a surefire method to hammer the message home—whether the message is to use condoms, to be careful, or to stop hating "them"? Does hard-scare sell better than soft-scare, is drama always more tasteful than humor? Some AIDS ads, like the one Martin Scorsese and Spike Lee did for the National Institute on Drug Abuse, have been so arty they only confuse. Others, like the new AAA spot showing junkies shooting up near the crotch, hit so hard they reinforce the stereotypes they want to stop. Recent events make us think there's a formula that's been missing all along. But will only the personal story of a superhero do it?

The last time opportunity knocked, the door opened, then jammed. In 1987, C. Everett Koop recommended that people, even teenagers, use condoms. Condom manufacturers spoke boldly of a new day on TV. But while their ads reached cable, independent, and affiliate stations, they never made it to the networks. Some advertisers wouldn't run commercials during the same break, the public got tired of hearing about AIDS, and AIDS became a drug addict's disease. Meanwhile, condom companies feared seeming crass—especially after a LifeStyles exec said, "AIDS is a condom marketer's dream," and his adman quit in protest.

The networks still operate with an imaginary mob of club-wielding citizens at their glass doors—at least when it comes to safe-sex ads. Mention of "protection" on TV programs is okay, but to use 30 seconds to encourage the *purchase* of rubbers makes the nets fear it looks like they're forcing the mob's kids to rut in the streets.

Magic Johnson may have changed some of that, at least for a while. After his announcement, shares of Carter-Wallace, which makes Tro-

AIDS ad backfires.

jans, went up $3. But it's not exactly like condom ads are back in the saddle again. So far Fox is the only network to accept ads, and even then only if they address disease prevention, not contraception.

Maybe because it mustn't seem mercantile, Trojan won't discuss its TV ad, won't even confirm it's running. Perhaps that's also why the spot is as straight as can be. A blond good-looking guy, in front of a bland background, tells the camera, "I'm 24, single, and I'm worried. I'm a nice guy. I go out with nice girls." Then he stares seriously: "These days, some pretty terrible things are happening to some really nice people."

That's quite a change from the Trojan Man series on radio. "The equipment manager thought he knew everything about protecting his players—until he heard from a man in a helmet!" the voiceover narrates. When the Trojan Man rides his horse into the locker room, the athletes sing, "Trojan Man! Trojan Man!" As he rides off he cries: "Remember—you're more in touch with Trojan!"

As far as safe sex goes, radio may tap pleasure; TV, only fear. For Fox, Ramses tried resurrecting a 1987 spot in which a father writes his son about "a whole lot of scary diseases I can't even pronounce"; but Fox rejected it because the package's "spermicidally lubricated" label was visible. LifeStyles also wants to run an old ad. "I'll do a lot for love," a woman says, "but I'm not ready to die for it."

PSAs on AIDS come and go, but the new Ads Against AIDS group is dedicating itself to spots that discourage ghettoizing AIDS. "People think it's a problem in New York and San Francisco, not in Norman, Oklahoma," says AAA's Bob Starr. But a campaign subgoal—to get people to stop blaming gay men—backfires thanks to the PSAs' shock-art tone. Flashing over the faces of adorable infants are the words "HOMO," "JUNKIE," "SLUT." "While we give special names to those infected with AIDS," James Earl Jones explains, "the AIDS virus has infected 1 million people. . . . Just as tragic, thousands have been born with this deadly disease, proving no one is immune. So instead of looking for a name that fits, let's find a cure that works." Sound thinking, but the impact of those words in big, bold letters deafens you even to Jones's voice and tattoos the taboo: Born a homo, die of AIDS.

Tom Waits narrates an ad with a more usable analogy. The pages of a phone book in a ratty booth flip in the wind as Waits rasps, "Say your local phone book has everybody's name in it, okay, including yours. Not let's take out the names of those 'other' people—you know, the hemophiliacs, the prostitutes, the gays, the IV-drug users. Is your name still in there? Are you feelin' safe? Don't. . . . 'Cause to AIDS, you're just another number."

But none of these ads would resonate much without the Magic Johnson effect. Which, of course, is double-edged: Though Johnson does endorsements for half a dozen companies, not all will continue to use him in product ads; some are trying to make us forget they're dropping him.

Converse will use him in product ads and will also run the first in a series of AIDS spots after Christmas. Not Johnson, but other "Converse athletes will talk about how they feel about AIDS as a result of Magic's situation."

Meanwhile, a Pepsi spokesperson was at pains to emphasize that

M.J. hasn't really done *that* many ads for them. He's more involved with PepsiCo as a partner in a Washington, D.C., distributorship. "His public persona has changed," says the spokesperson. "He's no longer Magic the athlete. He's Magic the community spokesman." As for future ads, Pepsi is "talking to Magic."

Whether corporations pick up from Magic a humanitarian imprimatur or cooties depends partly on how condom and AIDS ads treat the disease. Commercial culture—built on the easy-to-read symbol—has little talent for conveying something as complex as hate the disease but love the diseased.

December 17, 1991

Bash & Cash

Now they did it, calling us lazy and illiterate, saying we're short on the work ethic. I mean, white Americans have been saying that about black Americans for centuries—and now we're *all* supposed to take that kind of lip? This calls for a bash—bash that foreign hunk of metal, throw bonuses to employees who buy U.S. cars, even stick Pearl Harbor bombings into car dealer ads from Texas to Alaska. It's time to cash in on the fear and jealousy that's been heating up for years but didn't combust until the recession, the elections, and some big-mouthed Japanese leaders were all rubbed together.

The hurt and anger is so deep that for a moment during the news last week, I thought, some people actually *want* a war. Not a wimpy trade war, but a real, air-to-ground Nintendo war (oops, I need a non-Japanese product image for that, but I can't think of one). It's trite to say but still operational: We needed Iraqi hordes to replace the Evil Empire, and now we need the Invading Japanese to replace the camel jockeys. And even more than the marketable gulf war, Japan-bashing—born of our consuming lives—is ad-ready.

The most blatant example was right here in the *Voice*, in a cartoon

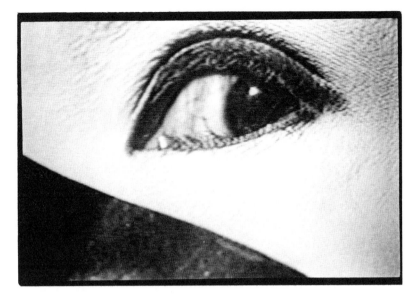

Nasdaq's nasty spot

ad from Danceteria: A squinty-eyed Japanese in Nazi uniform, says, "To the 66% of you lazy scum who *can* read this: better enjoy DANCETERIA now. When we take over we will close its decadent doors forever!"

Then there's the ongoing anti-Japanese rant of the tri-state Pontiac dealers. Over a big red sun, a voiceover narrates (and as if to prove we *are* literate, his words are written out on screen): "Recently, a leading JAPANESE politician described American workers as: 'a work force too lazy to compete with Japan.' . . . '30% can't even read.' WELL, excuse us. But the new Pontiac Grand Am has better fuel efficiency, a larger engine, and costs thousands LESS than a Honda Accord or Toyota Camry. Maybe THEY need a reading lesson." (Insinuating caps theirs.)

By using quotes straight from the pol's mouth, the ad would seem to inoculate itself against charges of bashing. "This is not screaming Yellow Peril," says Donny Deutsch, whose agency has made even more rabid Pontiac spots, such as the one that asked viewers if they like Japanese cars so much, why don't they move to Tokyo? "It's just smart marketing," he says. "It's on every newscast, it's on *Saturday Night Live,* it's on people's minds. Why shouldn't advertising be able to tap into what comedians and politicians tap into?"

Fair question. What *does* make an ad (or a politician) a basher and what makes it just an aggressive competitor? An ad bashes, of course, if it attacks the Japanese as a group; it's okay, however, if it can emphasize "buy American" without attack. "You'd rather walk than drive an American car . . . you wouldn't give an American car the time of day," says a spot for Buick Skylark, adding that this car is "going to change a lot of impressions about Buick." Fair enough.

Bash/not bash is also distinguished by an ad's relationship to facts. It's not just that Japan-bashing in general ignores certain facts—like the heavier British and Dutch investments in the U.S. or the high per capita Japanese consumption of U.S. goods—but that some ads fuel a mood in which facts themselves are offensive, as if they're intrusive little nits that exist only to suppress the downright *fun* of our anger. The fun-in-the-fury is expressed in the very word *bash*—as in both the "attack" and "throw a big bash" senses. Bashing is the only fun we get these days.

Actually, people *will* listen to some facts, especially if the facts can be used to absolve guilt. As one agency person who has worked for Chrysler and now Mazda told *Ad Age,* "The notion that patriotism transcends self-interest is absolutely nuts." And so advertising that makes people ask, "How American is that car?" should do well. As everyone probably knows by now, many "American" cars are made from foreign parts, while many foreign cars are built at U.S. plants and with a majority of U.S. parts. Toyota began advertising facts like these on TV before Bush's trade trip, with a rather bashful spot showing many noble American folk making Camrys in Georgetown, Kentucky. Toyota's also been running print ads to prove that it's a good U.S. corporate citizen. The company says it's been supporting charitable and community foundations for two decades, but only in the last few nasty years did it feel compelled to publicize the deeds. So in magazines it runs two-page spreads in old-time sepia telling how, for instance, a black American teacher, with Toyota's support, took her class sailing in Chesapeake Bay. "It was the first fish Jawan had seen that wasn't surrounded by french fries," the headline reads.

It's a little sad watching the Japanese twist and turn like that, but it's positively disgusting to see U.S. companies attack Japan for no reason other than to get attention. The stock exchange Nasdaq has been running an ad featuring a geisha girl doing a delicate dance of death to America while a voiceover reminds us that the Japanese stock market borrowed its technology from Nasdaq. If you listen really, really close, you'll realize that the ad attacks Japan only to get at its American rivals. "We're in constant competition with the New York Stock Exchange and AMEX for listings," a Nasdaq spokesman explains. "There are some issuers who have left us because they say, 'You're not as well known,' and we felt we better do something about it." They sure did. But being yet another person to whom the firm was not well known, I had assumed that Nasdaq—whatever it was—was just ruthless and racist.

Curiously, Nasdaq's agency, Messner Vetere Berger Carey Schmetterer, also made a fair ad for New Balance. "Mr. President: Here's one American-made vehicle that has no problem competing in Japan." There, New Balance is one of the biggest-selling sneakers—even though 80 percent of it is made in the U.S., compared with the primarily Asian-manufactured Nike and Reebok. So successful is this line that it will be worked into NB's first national TV spot ever.

But wait a minute. Doesn't Messner Vetere also handle the Swedish Volvo, which, unlike Toyota, Honda, or Nissan, has no plants here? Isn't that a hole in the flag of their whole Buy American theme? Answers an agency partner, "So?"

February 25, 1992

Buy-It Riot

Crisis calls for commercials. Over the next few months, you may or may not see new economic programs sprouting up in the inner cities of Los Angeles and other towns, but you will see the ads. "We can all work together" ads, "Intolerance is terrible" ads, even "Are you racist?" ads. Such PSAs have run before, but only occasionally—advertising almost genetically avoids any message more hard-hitting than Hands Across the Ghetto. Even with cities ablaze, they still may not go much farther, but in the ad flurry everyone and his local anchorperson will at least know you shouldn't call other people names.

The first few days of the L.A. riots were a commercial emergency, and ads were on the scene quicker than the police. Los Angeles TV and radio stations ran spots asking people to stay cool, including clips of Martin Luther King Jr. exhorting, "Build, baby, build." Tone-Lōc and N.W.A.'s Ren refused to mouth "stop the violence" in PSAs, but other rappers obliged.

Then *Ad Age* expanded the mission nationwide, running a front-page editorial—"A call to admen: Help stop riots." It implored companies (like sneaker firms) to make antiviolence ads, along the lines of the antidrug spots by the Media-Advertising Partnership for a Drug-Free America. That dubious antidrug ad blitz may serve as a role model for a campaign shaping up in Los Angeles. Last week, 15 top ad and media execs gathered to brainstorm ads that'll probably appear under the umbrella of Peter Ueberroth's Rebuild L.A. program.

Meanwhile, Mingo, a black agency, and the Ad Council will soon air the first of a series of PSAs on racism. They'll be along the lines of "we have to face what we've been denying—that discrimination exists—and we have to begin a dialogue," says a spokeswoman. Race suddenly has the media cachet drugs once did. "There is a window of opportunity right now insofar as media acceptance is concerned," says Ad Council president Ruth Wooden.

And though they've been in the works since the Crown Heights riot, 250 brotherly love posters were installed in New York City phone booths the week after L.A. The following words run down black-and-white backgrounds: "You have a tumor. In your brain. A specialist is ready to operate. He's black. Is that a problem?" . . . "Your son needs a new kidney. In 48 hours. They found a donor. He's white. Is that a problem?" A mite too drop-dead staccato (i.e., adlike) for me, but as a declarative sentence, "You have a tumor" does rather grab your attention. And then forces you to wonder if you're racist. But only under extreme conditions. Is that a problem?

"There's so many stereotypical ideas of what a black person is or what a white person is," says Doug Raboy, who wrote the ads and who, along with his agency, Smith/Greenland, makes up "Citizens for Racial Harmony," which signed and paid for the posters. "So when you can twist it and give it a surprise, that's good. It's also supposed to show how silly racism is."

NYNEX's TV ad tries to show how childish it is. A bunch of green and blue marbles confront a bunch of orange and yellow marbles; they argue in cute, babylike grunts. One blue and one orange marble finally break ranks and shake hands, so to speak. The marbles cheer, mingle in joy, and, as the camera pulls back, they have so mingled that

NYNEX saves the world again.

they form—what else?—a globe. The whole ethnic peacefest gets a big fat NYNEX logo at the end. (This from the company that ran pro-gulf war ads last year.) The spot was launched on Peter Jennings's (pre-verdict) children's special about prejudice, but the company bought extra time during riot week, because, says a spokeswoman, "NYNEX's mission is to help people communicate."

Unlike the marbles, Spike Lee's antiracism spot for Nike uses the name-calling words, though they're the joke ones. "I ain't playing ball with no ball-hoggin', gunnin', show-boatin', Nike-wearin', high-flyin', donut-dunkin', hip-hopping homeboy from Harlem," a white basket-ball player says to a black one, and so on. Spike ends on a note of peace and promo. "The mo' colors, the mo' better." The ad was filmed before the riots, but will be rushed on the air sooner because of them.

Ad people know they have the access to sell the right thing, but their industry has some major structural obstructions that militate against effective racism-bashing. Advertising and TV are too complicit in the larger process that leads to Simi Valley denial and South Central loot-ing. Most obviously, ads help perpetuate a system that doesn't allow many people to live the good life the commercials tell them to. (Though guilt over this is almost palpable in the rush of post-riot ad-vertising, that hardly means agencies will stop hyping the goods.) Ad-vertising has also committed thousands of sins of image—to name just one example, luxury carmakers who resist putting blacks in their com-mercials because it would communicate "low status." A system that justifies itself as a democracy of money, that runs on the concept that the market is fair—an idea for which advertising is the frontline and that the L.A. riots defy—cannot spend too much energy proving oth-erwise.

And because it's in the interests of commercial culture to get us to think more or less alike—in order to sell millions of people the same product—advertising has a tough time promoting real differences be-tween people. That puts it rather at odds with real racial harmony, which has to acknowledge *pluribus* before it can get to *unum*. Con-sider a current Ex-Lax commercial: A pretty woman with straight blond hair, the perfect median point between girl-next-door and model, further documents how normal she is by saying she jogs and swims but loves junk food. But even *she* sometimes gets constipated, she admits. "For regular people—who sometimes aren't," goes the tagline. If, as the very definition of "normal," she sometimes diverges, then it's okay for the rest of you to down the Ex-Lax, too.

Shit happens, and television is always there to push it aside. The happy ending, the cute meet, the never-ending glamour glow of the big people in the big world we watch on our TVs send poverty and injustice far, far away.

If ads are going to attack racism at all, they've got to go for the structural jugular. Increase the pitch.

May 26, 1992

Logo-rrhea

On the eve of a new political era made possible by Democrats who finally learned their marketing lessons, it might be beneficial to revisit Benetton. Benetton's ads do the opposite of Bill Clinton's—break ad rules rather than execute them faithfully. But by wearing their logo on their sleeve, they keep influencing the marketing of the everyday political, be it Malcolm X or social causes promoted by other corporations.

Benetton's latest ads aren't as jolting as their infamous spring litter—most notably, the photo of a man dying of AIDS in his family's arms. They're less likely to be seen as exploitative than sad: an electric chair, a smudgy Salvadoran girl holding a pathetic white doll, an albino Zulu adolescent who looks ashamed as other girls seem to shun her.

Only the last ad received the perennial Benetton controversy treatment. The company bought space for it in a Tina Brown issue of *The New Yorker,* but Brown asked for a substitute. It would rub wrong, she said, with the Malcolm X piece that week on "the racial-tension issue. This ad is seeming to address the same issue, but obviously in a very punchy, advertising way. We wanted to make sure we didn't seem to be mixing advertising and editorial."

Benetton refused. "To ask us to pull this ad because they thought their readers would misconstrue it in the context of the story sets up a dangerous precedent," says spokesman Peter Fressola. (The *New Yorker* logic also seems to say that there are so few ads and articles about black people that readers will assume they've been published in cahoots.)

But the objections to the campaign have less to do with the photos, which have all been previously published as news, than with the shock of the logo. When you see the green and white "United Colors of Benetton" slapped on the pictures, there are several possible responses: (1) You see only the logo; the picture recedes because the logo becomes a kind of lens, colorizing the picture with the whole history of ad exploitation; (2) You cease to be bothered by the logo, since you expect a tag on every tale nowadays; or (3) You see the logo as a sardonic caption: Poverty-stricken Third World girl with white doll from trash can—*United* Colors of Benetton, ha!

For years, I saw only number 1. It took a personal interview with Benetton's ad concept guy, Oliviero Toscani, to allow me to glimpse 2 or 3. To sell clothes in some 100 countries, he said, he must use pictures, not words. He could waste Benetton's $80 million worldwide ad budget to show more pretty girls in pretty clothes, or he could use it to further some social good. If viewers are sometimes shocked by the images, well, that's *their* Rorschach.

With this latest campaign, however, it's not the images that shock, but, as Fressola says, the "recontextualization of the image." The idea may be to generate discussion about AIDS or racism, but the ads do it only by ripping up your response to advertising itself. "Fashion magazine readers are in a narcotized fantasy world. I think it's much more insidious for Jewish children, for instance, to be hit with ads from Ralph Lauren, who is Jewish, and his images of Aryan perfection. But nobody's upset with that because it's fantasy. Our AIDS ad took AIDS out of the realm of abstraction and into the realm of the real."

But the rub is that Benetton ads often can't make their point without a spokesman or an article to escort you through the theory. (This is no problem for Benetton, though—the escort service is continual free publicity.) Critics of its AIDS ad in particular say, if you're going to exploit the image for a good cause, at least provide some sign—an 800 number to call, an organization to connect with—some way to act on the image. But while Benetton does give to arts and social organizations (including an AIDS hospice), they're looking beyond PSAdom. What they hesitate to say but clearly believe is that their ads are art, public art. All that recontextualization works at least as well as the billboards of a mysterious, rumpled bed that were all over New York last summer. Unlogoed and unsigned, they were art (mounted by the Museum of Modern Art) that passed as ads.

That is, the presence of a logo when unexpected (or its absence when expected) acts as a flash of consciousness—as a commenter, an interlocutor, a readjuster of the usual. What happens when the logo functions this way—the logo itself as artist, reorganizing the way we see things—is that our atomization becomes a little more accomplished, our sense of private and public is chopped and pureed in a media that Cuisinarts us, and makes it that much more difficult for us to sit in unambivalent judgment on what is an exploitative ad. And I've got to admit: By deciding to appreciate, if not necessarily *like,* Benetton's ads, I get a little payoff of feeling quite the radical—a prize in the Cracker Jacks that's also a piece of their marketing.

Meanwhile, Benetton made a huge image coup—and possibly preempted the sort of charges of racism that have hounded earlier ads, like the black nanny nursing a white infant—by getting Spike Lee to endorse their ads. For *Rolling Stone*'s 25th anniversary issue, Benetton bought the opening eight pages to salute their own ad photography over the years and asked Lee to write some text—paying him with a $50,000 contribution to his charity of choice, the United Negro College Fund Malcolm X Scholarship (perfectly timed to the opening of *Malcolm X*). He wrote some thoughts on the state of the world, recommending that "everyone get involved. And that's where the imagery involved in the Benetton ads stands head and shoulders above the rest. Let me first state that I have no illusions about them. Benetton wants to make a buck like any other company. In fact, we all do, but it's the route, the path we choose that makes the difference."

We're all supposed to accept that social change just doesn't get done these days without the right marketing plan—um, path. Benetton's own magazine, *Colors,* is a gathering of multiethnic musings that literally contains the company's clothing catalogue, like a baloney on pumpernickel sandwich. *Colors* has been out for more than a year. But only now, for its third issue, is it finally throwing a launch party. The reason is that this is the first issue to finally secure some outside advertisers. Says *Colors's* PR man, "It's the first serious issue."

November 24, 1992

Generation X-Force

When you hear "X" do you say, "Oh?" It's been at least X number of months since the media peaked over Generation X with major stories in *The Atlantic, Business Week,* and *U.S. News & World Report,* but the marketing to Generation X will be with us for, if we're really unlucky, a generation. The knotty relations between GenX and ad people, most of whom come from GenX's supposed nemesis, the Baby Boomers, are squeezing out ads that reflect the clichés of the day: that Xers are "cynical" and "media savvy," and soon as they smell your sell, they're outta here. Xers know they're valued only as a consuming concept—the 46 million people between the ages 18 and 29 who annually spend $125 billion. (Caution: X numbers vary wildly from article to soft-news segment—these are the ones the media most often grafts from other media. Furthermore, there's no Malcolm X in Generation X—except when an ad is deliberately "multicultural," the X of the media mind means almost entirely grungy white youth.)

All the hype can make you doubt if "they"—as a generation—exist at all, or if the much-publicized war between Xers and Boomers amounts to anything more than the latter preferring scotch and Walkmans while the former tilts toward tequila and Discmans (as the *Entertainment Weekly* ad sales force has so usefully discovered). Yet

If I talk like cool, you'll buy Subaru.

there are real differences between the generations: Boomers do have a more inflated sense of their own destiny, and Busters did come into a world depleted by recession, higher divorce rates, and a media monolith that's usurped institutions like education and government. But as Neil Howe and Bill Strauss lay out in their book *13th-GEN*, adjacent-generation warfare is nothing new; in fact, it got rather nasty in the 1920s clash between the X-like "Lost Generation" and the Boomful "Missionary Generation." The difference this time is the knee-jerk media attention—treating the Boomer/Buster categories like a Linda Evans/Joan Collins cat fight—and the knee-jerk marketing attention: This group is big and has discretionary income because a third of it lives with the folks. Get down and pander!

And so we have grunge-art–directed campaigns that say the word "generation" a lot: "What stirs the sole, moves a generation" is the headline for an ad featuring a grunge dude doing a little rock 'n' roll jig (for Giorgio Brutini shoes, apparently nicknamed GB*X*). Two G guys hold up a fish. "Work, work, work, work, work, work, work, work, fish. Take it easy," Southern Comfort advises. When Taco Bell wanted to promote its outlets' late-night hours to late-night Xers it ran the slogan "Get Laid at the Ball," uh, "Get Late at the Bell," illustrated by the speedy animation of MTV regular Bill Plympton. "The boomers are just not going to get this one," a Taco exec crowed in *Ad Age.* Meanwhile, CBS, the network with the oldest audience demographics, has its 20-year-old interns surveying their peers on how to stir X into CBS; and not one but two syndicated X newsmagazine shows, one called simply *Generation X,* are in the works.

Advertisers' guilt over doing another 180—from ignoring GenX to genuflecting before it—contributes to their dread that the generation will reject them. What else accounts for the self-flagellation among the mostly Boomer marketing people at a recent business symposium called "Why Doesn't the Fashion and Beauty Industry Understand the New Generation X?" The president of Merry-Go-Round, the 1500-store chain that sells $1 billion of merchandise a year to 15- to 25-year-olds, stood at the podium with this quote projected on the screen behind him: "Without constant research, I know nothing."

Or as Eric Conn, the 48-year-old ad manager for Honda and Acura, has said, "If I understand it, it won't work." In pushing the Integra to potential customers, about 40 percent of whom are X age and 30 percent are young Boom, Acura producted two distinct campaigns. For Boomers, the car rolls through a life-size Hot Wheels set (supposed to instill nostalgia), while for Xers a cartoon dog named Leonard mumbles cool quips like "Life is good. Mondo good." Conn explains the two-tiered approach: "Baby Boomers can still get ahead, they can still dig their way out. But the Xers, it's more like it's all been used up. They have a much more cynical outlook—you got to hit them with a little more irreverence for the system, a little more disdain in the voice." Hence, Boomer-but-bad-boy Dennis Miller as the voice of Leonard.

Carmakers in general are gunning for Xers—Geo, Saturn, Isuzu, Chrysler, Ford are all doing their X bit. Subaru's effort was the most obvious—and the most damning failure. Remember the Christian Slater-like kid who went on about how "This car is like punk rock" while other cars were somehow "boring and corporate"? The campaign did nothing for slumping Impreza sales, and the Wieden & Kennedy agency, despite its Nike rep, was canned.

One problem was its slavish posture before what research deemed "cool." In fact, a slave/master dynamic permeates most Boom/Bust relationships on the plantation of advertising, the two sides switching roles as needs demand. Boomers hold the real power—the jobs, the money—and Xers are supposedly highly resentful. But Xers feel, as the stereotypes goes, morally and stylistically superior, and so before their whims the Boomer bows.

But if you Xers are going to be so cynical, don't forget your friends, like the Nike or 501 campaigns, smart spots that, unlike Subaru, would never let their research stick out like some balding Boomer's ponytail. It's not that they surf a higher moral wave—they don't, they just use your cynicism and media-savvyness more cynically and savvily than you do. What does good pal MTV say behind your back when trying to lure advertisers in trade publications? It shows yet another grunger over the headline "Buy this 24-year-old and get all his friends absolutely free. . . . He heads up a pack. What he eats, his friends eat. What he wears, they wear. What he likes, they like. And what he's never heard of . . . well . . . you get the idea."

The real war isn't so much between generations as between those, of any age, who buy into a cramped package of stylized resentment and those who won't.

August 24, 1993

Generation X-Force **275**

Chapter Six
THE SPONSORED LIFE

On the Rox

The ad with clips from Steve Martin's *Roxanne* and people smiling for Diet Coke is confusing. Is Martin endorsing Diet Coke? Is the soda in his movie, sipped through that five-inch nose? Actually, Diet Coke doesn't appear in *Roxanne,* and Martin doesn't mention or appear with it in the ad. Diet Coke pulled a similar clip job with *Ghostbusters,* simply intercutting standard fun product spots with some of the film's footage. For the *Roxanne* spot, words from the "Just for the Fun of It" jingle are matched with the movie's visuals, and laughing moviegoers are shown wearing beaks like Martin's character, C. D. Bales, but we have no idea why Coke and *Roxanne* share the same 30 seconds. All we know is that Diet Coke and *Roxanne* are fun!

Tie-ins are as old as the shills. AmEx does it all the time with hotels and airlines. Diet Pepsi did it with its *Top Gun* takeoff. But Coca-Cola, which owns Columbia Pictures, sticks its cans into most Columbia movies and those by studios it owns a piece of, such as Tri-Star's *Blind Date.* In it, Kim Bassinger goes bonkers on booze, driving Bruce Willis away. The happy ending—she gets on the wagon and they finally get it on—is signified by the very last shot: While they're off camera, a bottle of Coke stands guard. *Blind Date* is an extended hook-and-bait ad for Coke.

Tie-ins are products endorsing products. Thrust together onstage, they validate each other: "I'm a good hot dog, but my close friend, the incredibly talented Cajun Mustard—here he comes now!—will tell you how great I really taste!" In conglomerate America, fused by takeovers and mergers of corporations as well as studios, advertising will

Not an ad

be more tempted to say, "Buy us, because we're co-owned." It could wham viewers with product power. But publicizing megaconnections could work the other way (the line "We're Beatrice" tagged to its multitude of brands turned viewers off; the company finally shut up). It could drive us toward "little guys" like Bartles & Jaymes (owned, of course, by the giant Gallo).

Blame this disjointed Diet Coke ad also on music videos spliced with footage from popular movies. The loose form of vids accounts for both their creativity and their shoddy use of symbols—real symbols will do, but so will anything visually charged, like movie clips. Videos prepared us to get mediums—records, performance, TV, film—mixed up, while takeovers and mergers prepared us to get companies and products mixed up.

At least it seems to have prepared Martin, who apparently doesn't think he did a Coke ad. His friend and *Roxanne* producer, Dan Melnick, says, "Neither he nor I regarded this as a TV spot. It's just an opportunity for additional exposure." (Martin does regular film promos, of course; a new one for *Roxanne* debuts this week. But the ad's air time came from Coke's budget, not the movie's.) "This is not a commercial," Martin's agent, Marty Klein, adds. "It's a cross-promotion. Steve's never done a commercial and never will. He was offered $2 million to do one and refused." But why risk such integrity by convincing yourself you're not hawking soda when you clearly are? "When you're marketing a picture, you want as much exposure as possible," says Melnick, as if "movie exposure" somehow neutralized "product commercial." *Roxanne* is doing quite well. Maybe the extra exposure helped. I'd like to think that when Martin makes Diet Coke sales, his heart's as pure as C. D. Bales's. But the ad was just for the funds of it.

July 28, 1987

Rock Rolls Over

'Rolling Stone' Courts Coors, and Everyone Must Get Sold

Perception: *Rolling Stone* loves rock and roll. **Reality:** *Rolling Stone* leads corporate sponsors on rock and roll raids. **Perception:** Coors is the brew for right-wing nuts. **Reality:** Coors is owned by right-wing nuts who use rock to shatter that perception. **Result:** *Rolling Stone* and Coors are getting married.

The big bash starts today (August 5) with *Rolling Stone*'s sponsorship of the Coors International Bicycle Classic, a 16-day, 1376-mile, televised race. *Rolling Stone,* the classic's "official magazine," has stuffed its August 13 issue with a pullout supplement and is distributing 250,000 extra guides to bike shops and spectators. In the '60s, *Rolling Stone* and Coors were as friendly as Abbie Hoffman and Mayor Daley. But the magazine, having gone mainstream in the '70s, is now helping to remold the music that created it into a handy marketing tool.

Rolling Stone's current cutting edge is corporate sponsorship of rock and roll. Last September, it began publishing *Marketing Through Music,* a monthly newsletter written for ad folks and company execs, encouraging them to use rock stars to hawk their products. *MTM* holds the businessman's hand through the sometimes ornery attitudes of rockers and talks to them in the smiling language of PR. July's lead story was on Run-D.M.C.'s Adidas sportswear line. "When they first started rapping . . . they purchased Adidas because they thought the brand made the 'deffest' (coolest) sneakers around." Despite the *Rolling Stone* imprimatur, *MTM* doesn't worry about selling rock out. That's the point. "Nike shoe company is announcing a revolution—in fitness, that is," the April issue glowed. "And what better way to herald this dramatic development than to use the original version of the Beatles' classic rock hit 'Revolution'?" (Last week, lawyers for the Beatles filed a $15-million suit against Capitol/EMI Records, Nike, and its agency for using the song without their permission. While Nike planned a press conference to respond to the charges, Paul, George, and Ringo said in a statement: "We do not peddle sneakers or pantyhose or anything else"—though Mr. Starr has been spotted in a wine cooler ad now and then.)

That *Rolling Stone* would publish a *Marketing Through Music* and hitch up with Coors itself is the quintessence of the corporate sponsorship boom. Ever since the Rolling Stones tour for Jovan perfume in 1981, corprock marketing has so enticed musicians and multinationals that most bands who don't already play ball with a company are dreaming up schemes to do so.

In this atmosphere, right-wing nuts and formerly rad media can benefit from each other. Both Coors and *Rolling Stone* suffer image problems. *Rolling Stone*'s old identity scares off advertisers. A clever we're-yuppies-not-hippies trade campaign is setting the situation straight—"Perception: Hash Brownies. Reality: Häagen-Dazs." Adolph Coors Co.'s reputation as racist, antigay, and in general the enemy of the good fight everywhere, scares off concerned guzzlers. But by spending $12 per barrel of beer on marketing, more than any other brewery, Coors is putting on the centrist lifestyle.

Paterfamilias Joe Coors just testified before the Iran-contra hearings that he donated, via Ollie North, $65,000 to the contras for a new plane. Coors cash helped start the archconservative Heritage Foundation. A boycott spurred by William Coors's comment that blacks "lack the intellectual capacity to succeed. . . ." ended in 1984 after the company agreed to finance a $325-million minority job program. (The Coors company filed a libel suit, still in litigation, against the *Rocky Mountain News* for quoting William "out of context." William said: "Nothing I said was to infer [sic] that the minds were not trainable, but only that they hadn't been trained in adequate numbers.") The AFL-CIO still boycotts Coors, the only major nonunion brewery. But by sponsoring black rodeos and Mexican cookoffs, and offering to underwrite what it wanted to call "Coors Presents AIDS Walk New York" (the gift was refused), the beer is looking like Rolling Stone Lite.

Recently, Coors discovered rock and roll. "For the young adult side of the market, it's taken the forefront," says a company spokesman. Coors sponsors regional club acts—its banner hangs behind, say, Big Twist and the Mellow Fellows in Chicago, who don "Coors wearables." On a larger stage, the Fabulous Thunderbirds will appear in a Coors TV spot shown out West. Meanwhile, the company's on the lookout for "up-and-coming new music groups" in New York.

Coors's loose new look has muffled the protests. *Rolling Stone* associate publisher Les Zeifman says, "My impression is that they've put that behind them and done a number of good corporate citizen things." (Publisher Jann Wenner declined to comment, referring questions to Zeifman, who says even Joe Coors's testimony about his contra support doesn't change his opinion.) The magazine is demographically dreamy for the nation's fifth largest beer seller—and the feeling's mutual. "The Coors Classic," says Zeifman, "is the smartest event sponsorship any marketer could associate with." Between TV coverage, special expos, and the pullout guide, *Rolling Stone* will reach hundreds of thousands of potential new subscribers with lifestyles similar to its extensively researched readers'. Young, affluent, usually childless, they have "their own personal interests at heart," says Zeifman, and can afford "that new expensive CD, that new expensive bike, that new expensive . . ." Because the magazine's typical reader "wants to be a trendsetter," he says, fashion has replaced music as the top ad category. Rock has evolved, with a little help from *Rolling Stone,* from a progressive vehicle to a lifestyle indicator.

Courting the likes of Coors is not as weird as it may seem. *Rolling Stone*'s marketing division created the six-page newsletter *Marketing Through Music* for the ad community, who had kept asking the magazine how they could tie their products into rock. Only about 1 percent of *MTM*'s 10,000 circulation is paid, and it doesn't run ads—so what's in it for *Rolling Stone?* "Promoting music as a marketing tool can result in additional advertising for *Rolling Stone,*" says *MTM* editor Dave Rheins, "because if a company is going to use rock and roll in a tour, they have to promote it, and *Rolling Stone* would be the prime outlet." Zeifman, who doubles as *MTM* publisher, adds: "It's already paid off." Since starting *MTM* and the Perception/Reality campaign, *Rolling Stone*'s ad pages have risen dramatically.

Rock and roll in advertising—which includes everything from buying rights to songs to rock star commercials like the new Tina Turner/David Bowie Pepsi spot—amounts to hundreds of millions of dollars each year, says Jay Coleman, head of Rockbill, an 11-year-old firm that pioneered the matchmaking of acts and corporations. Coleman guesses that corporate sponsorship, as much as it can be separated from the advertising that often accompanies it, comes to $70 million or $80 million a year. (One Rockbill client, Pepsi, spends more on rock tours than any company in the world.) A corporation may sponsor a band's tour, plastering its logo all over the place, or may attach itself to a specific venue (the Meadowlands and the Ritz are Anheuser-Busch, the Pier and Jones Beach are Miller). Less obvious than advertising, sponsorship is all the more potent, making the company seem generous, groovy, part of the act.

Dave Rheins figures there are several hundred bands, from obscure to established, involved in some aspect of music marketing. Miller Genuine Draft has promoted 60 bands in the last six years; Converse has another 27 out in the field. A short list of bigger matings: Chuck Berry/Christian Brothers Brandy; Aretha Franklin/Amoco and Kinney Shoes; Stevie Nicks/Sun Country Wine Coolers; Deborah Harry/Sara

Lee; Buster Poindexter and Kid Creole/Amaretto Di Sarono; Adam Ant, Grace Jones, Devo, Lou Reed, Sting/Honda motorcycles; Menudo/McDonald's; Pointer Sisters/Chevy and Diet Coke; Dweezil Zappa/Chess King menswear. Wang Chung cut a deal two ways on their hit "Everybody Have Fun Tonight," tapped first by Michelob, then by ABC Sports. The network—piggybacking on the success of an *ad*—bought the song and revised the lyrics: "Everybody have fun, that's right . . . ABC Sports reaching new heights."

Brand names have insinuated themselves onto back beats everywhere, making corprock seem not only inevitable, but ethically . . . so what? In this apolitical era, rock sings for anything—unleaded gasoline, Amnesty International, Republicans. Rock-for-hire has become so widespread that it's news when the money isn't taken. If it weren't for vociferous big-name holdouts—Springsteen, John Cougar Mellencamp, Billy Joel, the Pretenders, Prince, Dylan, a few others—would anyone notice there's a controversy at all?

Joan Jett has turned down "millions" to endorse beer, cars, coffee, and other products, according to her producer and manager, Kenny Laguna. While corporations seem gracious to underwrite performers, behind the scenes they can rough 'em up. Laguna says, "Some of these guys are so greedy, it's not enough to tell them no—they're mad at you. Twice Joan turned down a beer ad, and the product came back with a soundalike. If more big names like Springsteen refuse to do it, it won't be cool. No one will want to be the schmuck who sold out for a jeans commercial. To use all this love and devotion from the kids to sell them something—sometimes you lose track, but we're affecting society." Sponsored rock's long-term effect is that bands are validated as good members of society, nullifying any adversarial stance toward it.

"The rock and roll ethic used to be an attitude to live by," says Laguna. "To all those companies that tried to manipulate society, rock was there to say, 'Hey, asshole.'"

Would *Rolling Stone,* with its corp-sucking newsletter and Coors friend, ever publish an article criticizing sponsorship? "It's possible. Absolutely," says Zeifman. The mother magazine "is totally independent of anything the advertising department or *MTM* does." But at best, *Rolling Stone* reports just the facts. Writing that the $60-million Genesis tour marked "a new high in corporate sponsorship," the mag went on to quote, without comment, a Michelob spokesman explaining why they chose Genesis: " 'They're not controversial.' " The brand, he said, " 'was in a substantial decline for several years, but this campaign has turned it around.' " Zeifman applauds this as a "musical association so strong that every time you hear a Phil Collins song you think of Michelob." How great for Phil. Maybe one day every hit will jam a product into the listener's mind.

But except when an ad exploits a song deemed sacred, like "Revolution," most fans don't notice the corprock surrounding them. This is smart strategy, tastefully "presenting" performers, quietly injecting its presence. And to some fans, the music's even spiffier with a product thrown in. It's not just that a product looks more hip by rubbing up against a rock star, but the star gains some of the product's pop-cultural punch. By purchasing a brand advertised on TV, we buy a piece of the there-*is*-something-out-there television experience. Now, by rubbing up against a product, the musician throws off happy, TV-like sparks.

TV legitimizes rock, but it wasn't always so. Corporations once abhorred rock so much that they never would have considered it as an ad medium, which only strengthened the music's outsider cachet. But now that advertisers are desperate for mass outlets far from the commercial-cluttered tube, corprock is inviting outsiders—but not *too* outside—into the fold. This can take the form of bad flattery: Companies think enough of fans to cater to their tastes. For older baby boomers especially, rock marketing goes beyond stroking their nostalgia to stoking their vengeance. While many boomers think the music's a sellout, others have convinced themselves that it's a victory of their youth—multinationals are coming to *us*, our generation has something *they* want, they had to admit they're boring. We still have cultural power.

It's easy to accept corprock, because it seems knee-jerk idealistic and unhip not to. "Hip" has been redefined. Rock's contemporary hip-to-be-square attitude converges with the entrepreneurial, coke-snorting hipster of corporate culture. Like arbitrage, rock has always been a hustler's business, the argument goes; yelling out your needs— "Money (That's What I Want)"—*is* rock and roll. But the belief that corprock is harmless is soggy. It gives some susceptible fans permission to think it's cool to work for a corp, and question it less. Mostly, it confirms what young careerists want to hear anyway—that they can be hip and gimme-gimme at the same time.

What it comes down to is that corprock makes us stupid. It convinces us that links between products and stars actually exist. As *Rolling Stone* reported, Phil Collins himself said, "There is no good American beer." But he quickly added, "Apart from Michelob." We may not believe in product/star links, but many of us act on them, as Michelob's turnaround in sales proved. As for the bands, it makes them sad *and* stupid: They're used to fabricate the link.

One way to avoid looking like a chump is to truly love your product. Run-D.M.C. proudly wore the free gold chains and footwear and took the endorsement money *after* they wrote "My Adidas." A listener not used to such outright adulation hears the song as ironic. Real or assumed, irony seems the only cool attitude to be bought out by. It makes the band look like it's conning the corp, especially in Run-D.M.C.'s case. But as a lawyer who represents musicians says, "Most black bands aren't merchandisable until they cross over." Who's getting conned?

At a panel at the New Music Seminar July 13, "Merchandising and Corporate Sponsorship: The New Profit Center," the message repeatedly stated was mutual benefit. "Sponsorship works for both the artist and the company," Rockbill's Coleman said. But it's the company that holds a male prerogative: "If an artist is looking for a significant amount of money, artists are going to have to do more and more commercials. He's got to realize that if he's going to get in bed with these companies, he's going to have to consummate the relationship." No one in the standing-room-only crowd of local musicians, club owners, record people (and a Coors rep) expressed disagreement. What they wanted to know was "How can I get a cut of the deal?" When panelist Danny Socolof of Mega Inc. eeked what sounded like skepticism— "You're always compromised"—the room stirred. But the compromise was an okay one. "You're bound to turn off a certain portion of the audience, but then you're exposing yourself to a new and larger audience." The real compromise, playing safer music to please potential sponsors, wasn't mentioned.

Elvis did a Southern Maid donut ad in '54; Keith Moon flacked for the U.S. Navy in '69. But these are among the aberrations that corprock defenders always cite. Until '81, when the Stones toured under a perfume logo, rock was rarely heard in a marketplace other than its own. "Most people don't remember when music was a pariah in the television industry," said panel moderator Eric Gardner of Panacea Entertainment. That started to change in 1980, Coleman said, when "the record industry went into a tailspin and started cutting back. It needed more promotion but didn't have much money for that. So we came up with the idea of synergistic marketing, of corporate sponsorship, and convinced companies that contemporary music was the common denominator in their customers' lifestyle."

Music videos fast-forwarded the corporate connections. Madison Avenue could appreciate not only rock's drawing power, but also the musician's eagerness and skill at self-promotion. Rock bands routinely merchandise their own image, selling incredibly marked-up T-shirts, which themselves are ads. (The money in merchandising, in fact, is far greater than that in corporate sponsorship.) Music videos, by blurring the lines between commercials and performances, made it all the easier for rock stars to plug products other than themselves.

The corporate takeover of rock can be just plain insidious. DeBeers diamonds made a four-minute video-ad featuring the Long Island group Broken Arrow and distributed it to theaters showing movies that would appeal to 18-to-25-year-old males, presumably hot for engagement rings. *Music Through Marketing* handled this lead story without mentioning that DeBeers is South African, a titan that through its conglomerate web controls 58 percent of the money in that country's stock market. The kids who thought they were just checking out *Ferris Bueller's Day Off* get rocked into buying a piece of Pretoria.

In other words, anything can dance to rock. As Mike Aisner, direc-

tor of the Coors bicycle classic, says, "This is a rock and roll sport."
And he's right. Pay the tab and call it rock and roll.

Now when I say "Coors," I wanna hear you shout "Yeah!"

August 11, 1987

Jean Pool

Anti-ad ads—spots that seem to pull themselves through the rabbit
hole of their own artifice to say, "I'm a commercial"—ain't anti. Inside the self-consciousness is more self-consciousness. To an aghast
America, jean-pusher Jordache has brought back the whiny "I hate
my mother" girl. Just as you're ready to kick tube, the set goes blank
and a woman's voice says it for you: "I hate this *commercial!*" Wow,
finally. But then we see the woman: Doughy arms ballooning out of a
sleeveless, polyester housedress, she's reading a magazine—not even
watching the TV, like you are. But her teen daughter, topped by a
Pebbles Flintstone ponytail, grabs the remote control and turns the set
back on, protesting: "I *love* this commercial!"

As an original-ad boy asks about that first mother, "Was she hot?"
the "real-life," unhot mama shrieks, "That's disgusting!" and again
turns it off. Aiming the remote at the tube like a gun, the girl switches
it back on and says, this time with real contempt: *"I hate my mother."*

But it's channeled contempt. Jordache acknowledges audience hatred of the first ad, but only to assert that the first spot has become
part of our reality: These new characters experience the same TV as
we experience. In response, we can either hate that an ad has again
sucked out our sense of reality, or decide we kinda like it. The path
toward the latter, nuevo response has been made the more attractive,
just as the daughter has been made more attractive than the mother.

Jordache is also accelerating its riff on social issues. A black kid to
three white companions (including Pebbles) at a diner: "Man, there's
people starvin' on this planet and you're piggin' out!" A longhair re-

futes through his full mouth, "You sound like my *mother*," and imitates the maligned mom in a high-pitched nag: "There are people starving in Africa!" On the word *Africa*, Pebbles subtly nudges the boy—hey, in this company, isn't that, like, no?

There is a grain of truth here: the difficulty of saying anything straight and earnest against the force of peer pressure. But as long as Jordache's name is spelled right, it can use concern about hunger to move product. After all, the kid didn't say, "Man, there's people jeanless on this planet, and you're stockpilin' denim!"

A couple months ago, a 16-year-old reader wrote a letter to the *Voice* railing against Jordache's ad writer. "Those Jordache ads make teenagers look like pitiful ignorant scumbags. . . . He's only out to make a buck. Do you think he would stop running those ads if he heard that teenagers hated them?" Jordache reacted by asking her if she'd like to try writing some ad copy. Incorporating the opposition in this case didn't work out, but Jordache gave it another try with hunger.

With artifice more firmly in place, 4C's ads handle teen/parent chasms without milking spite. Showing only torsos and hands around a dinner table, "the Davis Family" spots are almost a throwback to '60s humor albums. Gruff-voiced dad says to daughter Melissa: "What does this boyfriend of yours do for a living?" Mom: "He's in high school, Jerry. . . . I'm sure he's a very nice boy, Melissa." Dad: "I know all about nice boys. I used to be one." And so on, while the Parmesan cheese silently gets knocked over, fought over, and accidentally shaken into Pop's hand.

The purpose, of course, is to increase awareness of this unflashy, stock item. "The dialogue is a kind of reward to the audience for having to stare at the table," the copywriter says. With the funny, hip image of 4C, "Sales are up and the client is thrilled beyond belief." If this keeps up, the Davis family will probably start talking about commercials at the dinner table.

March 15, 1988

Inner Tube

An ad aimed at kids warning them not to watch too much TV was all the stir on the news a couple weeks ago. Clips of the funky, animated spot provided just the kind of punchy featurette that warm-hearted anchors love to sign off with: "Couch potatoes beware," they chuckled across the country for at least a day or two. "The American Academy of Pediatrics has a new commercial. . . ."

The public service announcement is eminently likable. A boy and his little junk-food-binging sister are staring at the tube when it fizzes with the words: "TOO MUCH T.V.!!" The kids turn into tubby taters, their eyes into glazed red swirls—they've left the realm of the human senses to become electronic receptoids. "Couch potatoes— avoid this dread disease," the jingle taunts bravely. Glued to his Watchman, the boy raps out, "Leave me alone, just let me groove with my tube!" while the girl mouths (to the rhythm of Tommy-can-you-hear-me?), "Mama can I buy that?" (The TV sneaks in the related message: "Watch Out for Overeating.")

The American Academy of Pediatrics, which in the past has made spots on teen smoking, alcoholism, and suicide, was concerned that kids between the ages two and 12 watch an average of 25 hours a week of TV (more than any other activity except sleeping). They sent the spot to the networks, 400 stations, MTV, Nickelodeon, and VH-1. It has been accepted, but not yet scheduled, by the three nets and 37 stations. But so far, "Couch Potato" has been hotter as news than as a PSA.

"This thing has probably aired on every news show in the country," says AAP spokesman Jeff Molter. "For a while, we were just under the Mike Tyson/Robin Givens story." He's somewhat less surprised that the networks have agreed to air it. "It's ironic, but they didn't have a choice. They say they always believed that kids shouldn't watch a zillion hours of TV and they should watch selectively. Running these messages makes them look good."

In fact, TV occasionally makes forays to co-opt anti-TV sentiment. Two years ago NBC ran a series of 50 spots, in which famous and not-famous people would talk tube, pro and con. Ralph Nader even chimed in about "Nielsen rating tyranny" leading to "a formula that meets the lowest common denominator." "American Television and You" was ABC's dumber version. Of course, both networks wanted you to "think" about TV, not turn the damn thing off.

Recently, even the most tabloid-minded network, Fox, began running a PSA that gently encourages you to turn off the set and go out for a walk, reassuring you that "we'll still be here when you get back." This is one of eight spots made by "Life. Be In It. USA," a nonprofit educational foundation trying to foster healthier lifestyles. In Australia, where the group began 12 years ago, the campaign is such a hit that people go around humming the jingle, according to LBITUSA executive director Karen Wayne. The Aussie campaign has "98 percent awareness," and 46 percent say they've changed their lifestyle (more walking, more time to themselves) because of it. But as to whether it's helped cut down on TV hours logged, that question, oddly, was never asked. "They were probably afraid to ask," Wayne says, only half joking. The fact that the campaign is unthreatening,

Shown on a lot of TV

highly popular—*and* from his native land—made an "anti-TV" message safe for Fox owner Rupert Murdoch, who has exclusive use of the U.S. spots for three years (after six months, Fox stations may sell it to advertisers who can tag their seemingly do-good names to the PSA). Like the Surgeon General's stamp of disapproval on cigarettes, consumer warnings can function as just an excuse to continue the vice in question.

But the other question is, do TV warnings against TV make such good TV that they don't work? The Australian example is inconclusive. But there is the dicey logic that says suggestions to stop doing something are most effective if they come from the source of temptation itself. It's possible that, viewed enough, an ad like "Couch Potato" can remind even adults (especially adults, since TV infantalizes everyone) that TV is not life. But given that TV is total environment, it's more likely that the message would eventually become just another zappable annoyance.

The tube is an inner tube, in two senses: It's in your head and it's circular. It's as difficult to find a way in or out of it as it is to find the plastic tab on the wrapping of a VHS cassette. Like the Indian's Great Snake of the World, the tail of TV ("Turn if off!") is always being swallowed by the head ("Watch me say, 'Turn it off!' ").

Besides, couch potatoes are cool these days. The old term for dowdy stay-at-homes became vaguely hip about a year ago as a name for baby boomers who found liberation through their VCRs. Rather than embarrassing them, the label became a concept that aggressively distinguished them from the tainted yuppies (who go out every night and spend big); the label itself could even seem to organize habits into a "lifestyle." The AAP's ad runs up against the I'm-a-couch-potato-and-proud-of-it movement. Look at all the couch potato stuffed animals and toys. In fact, in typical übertube fashion, before the AAP can show its anti-TV spot, it has to work things out with a California man who, claiming to have rights to the tater term, plans to produce *Couch Potatoes*, a TV trivia game show.

November 15, 1988

Inner Tube   **293**

Desperately Selling Soda

There's never been a media buy like it. Madonna, the commercialized girl who's played hard to get for commercials, debuted the title cut from her still-unreleased album *Like a Prayer* on—whoa, *as*—a Pepsi commercial last Thursday. The ad was seen the same night in 40 countries, by 300 million or so people. A teaser spot running the week before and featuring an aborigine traipsing through the Australian outback (actually the California outback) to catch the commercial conveyed the pancultural ambitions of both soda pop and pop star: "No matter where you are in the world," the teaser instructed, "on March 2 get to a TV and see Pepsi present *Madonna*."

"We believe this is the single largest one-day media buy in the history of advertising," says Pepsi spokesman Ken Ross, figuring the two minutes of primetime planetary fame cost more than $5 million. And this wasn't just a Eurotrash media buy. Fans in Turkey, Indonesia, and even "war-torn countries like El Salvador" were also able to put aside their low-intensity conflicts to get down. (Despite Pepsi's earlier made-in-Moscow ad, called *"Glasnost,"* the Russians refused to air the spot.)

Even Michael Jackson didn't hit the cathode universe with such a bang. His Pepsi spots globe-trotted only after they had run in the U.S.A.; and his songs were huge hits *before* he used them to sell something he reportedly won't drink. Just a few months ago George Michael, a sort of Madonna with facial hair, almost beat her to it: Snatches of sound from *his* unreleased album popped up in a confused matador/superstar spot for Diet Coke. For her efforts—another Pepsi ad later this year and a Pepsi-sponsored tour—Madonna will make "short of $10 million," says an industry source, some of which will go to covering tour costs.

The faint pang of disgust raised by Neil Young's video parody of Jackson, Whitney Houston, Eric Clapton, and other corprock sellouts last year seems to have passed like a kidney stone. The sheer size and glamour of this ad, coupled with the built-in consensus that arty/vulgar Madonna was made for this kind of thing, has left questions of "artistic integrity" to Massachusetts liberals.

Like paying to pray

But the ad itself, if viewed as video, is so canny it cooks. It opens with something all us narcissists can relate to: watching home movies of our own childhood. There's Little Madonna at her eighth birthday party (actually filmed circa 1988) being viewed by the big real Madonna, looking peacefully lovely (in part because for once she's the spectator, albeit of herself). The entire spot is as recursive as a Rod Serling plot, which lends it the sentimental fantasy of most music video. Now Little Madonna, cine-magically transported out of vid-world and into full-color life, watches the famous Madonna on the black-and-white screen. The star goes back to the mid-'60s, singing and dancing on urban, interracial streets, where the kids don't moon-walk perfectly. There's Madonna back at her Catholic girls' school, a black-clad sylph with a crucifix in her cleavage towering over the linen-collared uniforms. Everyone marches in timid lockstep until they glimpse an old poster of the bleached superstar—and suddenly the screen is full of flying flocks as they dance with the lapsed brunette in their midst.

The lyrics have power ("Life is a mystery/Everyone must stand alone/I hear you call my name and it feels like home/When you call my name, it's like a little prayer"), and the music's hooky, but it doesn't really swing until Madonna lets the gospel spirit of the Andre Crouch Singers take over. (This is definitely the commercial version; the actual video, which ran on MTV the following day, is a much more daring mix of black soul and Catholic funk. Madonna is kissed by the reliquary of a black saint, gives herself the stigmata, and jitter-bugs in front of a row of burning crosses. Madonna is the kind of Catholic girl who forgets to wear a hat in church—or a dress over her slip. RAI TV in Rome, under pressure from Catholic groups, has banned the video.) [And shortly after I wrote this, Pepsi pulled the ad in the U.S.—and *only* in the U.S.—because of uproar over the video.]

At the end, Little Madonna, back in the B&W home movie, looks eerily from across time into the eyes of the real Madonna. As the child toasts her with a bottle of Pepsi, Madonna responds in kind with a can: "Go ahead. Make a wish." The tagline comes on—"Pepsi. A Generation Ahead"—and the loop is made: If Madonna Louise Veronica Ciccone could wish herself into stardom through the magic of video, a little cola consumer in Thailand or Paraguay can be like a star through the magic of advertising.

The ad is like a wet spot where all this season's hot TV topics have condensed: finding yourself by finding your "inner child"; depending on yourself (and not on men like Sean); the nostalgia of baby boomers for their 8mm wonder years; Catholicism as the fashionable ethnicity to come *from*, because it's new traditionalist yet earthy; interracial mixing as a symbol of mature hipness (not unrelated to the way TV white guys establish soul by playing basketball with black guys). In a *Rolling Stone* interview, Madonna said that when she was little, all her girlfriends were black and that she *feels* black.

All those very American themes would seem to make the ad too parochial to have the big, vague vavavavoom required for global marketing. What's a Tasaday in the Philippines to make of St. Mary schoolgirls in a chorus line? Actually, global marketing—crafting a commercial so that advertisers can use the same or nearly the same campaigns around the planet with little or no adjustments for language—was the big drive a few years ago. But it never really clicked—except with teenagers.

Marketeers believe that modern communications have spawned a "global teen," kids who have more in common with kids halfway across the earth than they do with other generations in the next room. Their percussive hormones drive them to Levi's and Swatch, Benetton and BIC perfume. Two new "global TV" shows—*Buzz* on MTV, which previewed Tuesday, and Fox network's *Revolution,* premiering in mid-May—are both rock 'n' roll "lifestyle magazine" programs that flash at a superfast pace. And they're both thirsting for Pepsi or Coke as sponsors.

Music is the universal language and all that, but more importantly, cola is the universal solvent. Fit for any lifestyle, its image mutable, cola is truly *fluid.* Aesthetically, at least on American TV, where hard liquor ads are banned, soda spots are the kickiest, and they've become the alcoholic content of advertising. Cola is the teen caffeine, accounting for 70 percent of all soft-drink sales. Pepsi, marketed in 150 countries, is still trying to catch up to Coke worldwide (the real thing outsells Pepsi two-and-a-half to one internationally). But their two corporate cultures share world hegemony, and to these titans, it's no longer enough to be just an *American* artist. Madonna has sold 75 million records worldwide—according to some, she's the most famous woman in the world. Naturally, Pepsi wants to use her to ensure its universal solvency.

As Madonna told *Rolling Stone,* "I like the challenge of merging art and commerce. As far as I'm concerned, making a video is also a commercial. The Pepsi spot is a great and different way to expose the record. Record companies just don't have the money to finance that kind of publicity. As it is, the music will be playing in the background, and the can of Pepsi is positioned very subliminally. The camera pans by it so it's not a hardsell commercial."

It's the *subtlety* of the sell that corporate-sponsored rock stars are increasingly judged by, not the fact that they're selling at all. For years, Madonna refused to do an ad—except in Japan (for Mitsubishi), like other big stars (David Byrne, Woody Allen, Paul Newman) who feel advertising would be crass here but is okay there, where they don't have relatives. One factor in Madonna's decision to do the Pepsi ad was the guarantee of exposure. "I wouldn't say [the long list of countries] was a prerequisite," says an industry source, "but there was discussion with Madonna's management and Warner Bros. about the number of people reached, or GRPs [gross rating points]. There was discussion of media weight."

The sense that the inevitable destination of all celebrity journeys is a Pepsi commercial validates the Big Shill of celebrity. Only the networks forged by the multinational soda pop vendors are vast enough to provide a stage for celeb/aristos like Madonna; only they heft enough media weight. We were always supposed to love Madonna *because* she luxuriates in media hype, writing jingles for teenage abandon. A Pepsi promo video has *Billboard* exec Sam Holdsworth kind of saying it all: "She's a commercial character. She's changed her persona three or four times in her career already, from the vamp ingenue to the punk to the techno girl to the who knows what, and I think Pepsi's done the same."

But in the next breath, he inadvertently spells out what's wrong with the sense that corprock is inevitable: "The whole push in promoting artists nowadays is how do you reach people, how do you reach people that either haven't heard of them, or haven't heard a particular album, or whose image hasn't really penetrated. And that's what advertising is and that's what promotion is, and I think that's what artists are really more and more about these days. Because it's an electronic medium, music's not a personal medium, and to be an international artist you really have to fly on that higher media plane."

In a press release, Pepsi lays its plans for world domination bare: "The groundbreaking deal is expected to change the way popular tunes from major artists are released in the future. Traditionally, new songs have been made public through heavy radio airplay. In an innovative twist, the Pepsi-Madonna deal uses television to provide unparalleled international exposure for her new single."

But if that's the way to enter the pantheon, then what does that make Pepsi and Coke? They are the medium through which the word is passed. They are universal, speaking no language and all languages. And each art/ad is like a prayer unto them.

March 14, 1989

The Afterschlock

They were just waiting there, unclaimed, virgin events. Hurricane Hugo and the San Francisco Earthquake, like the Olympics and the World Series itself—they were just *asking* for someone to make commercial tie-ins. But the neat thing is you never know whose logos are going to turn up on whose funeral. Who'd have thought that for Disaster '89, it'd be Burger King, AT&T, and Nissan?

Corporations tell you—and themselves—that they're in the disaster-ad business out of concern and compassion for the victims, and if some of their heavily promoted good deeds translate into goodwill for themselves, well, *shucks*. Anyway, disaster chasers are under strict orders to be "tasteful" and not spray-paint the smashed cars with their 800 numbers. But one clue that shareholders go before sharing can be seen in the way catastrophe commercials echo the companies' regular campaigns.

Burger King's everyday ads are based on its new, wild-boy wannabe slogan, "Sometimes you gotta break the rules." It's the kind of pop-toid conscientious objection that is supposed to Pepsi-up the company's dullard image and sales with techno-fantastic wackiness, like the guy on TV reaching out of the set and into another TV to grab a BK Double sandwich. Breaking a make-believe border is "breaking the rules." Now the slogan is recycled for tragedy. "When disaster hits and people need help, sometimes you've gotta break the rules," says BK CEO Barry Gibbons, who pledges that for every Doubles sold, the burger outlet will donate 25 cents to the American Red Cross to help the Hurricane Hugo and earthquake relief efforts. Gibbons looks very sincere with his hair blowing in the wind, but he's truly brave when he reveals, through his very accent, that Burger King is now part of a vast British business empire. (BK has been owned by British retail/restaurant megathing Grand Metropolitan since January, and the Brits in general hold twice the U.S. investments as the Japanese do.) Gibbons ends the spot with this wisdom: "Sometimes breaking the rules means giving something back." What's that rule? Isn't giving something back supposed to be the rule—the one that everybody breaks?

Burger King, which expects to raise "millions" for the Red Cross (and that much more for itself), does obey a couple marketing rules here: (1) the item chosen for the disaster tie-in, Double sandwiches, is the one currently getting a massive promotion anyway; (2) to its credit—as well as to its sales savvy—BK sent "burger buses" with free sandwiches to earthquake victims in Oakland. They also distributed free blankets and, logos blazing, Burger King sweatshirts. The feedback to Gibbons's spot "has been fabulous," says a spokeswoman. "More people are certainly coming and buying the Doubles."

But at least BK is giving something. AT&T and Allstate insurance are just congratulating themselves for doing what they've already been paid to do.

It's "the most hellacious thing I ever went through in my life," says a woman in an AT&T ad. But she's not referring to the morning after she ordered the *wrong* intraoffice intercom; she merely survived Hurricane Hugo and lived to tell AT&T about it. The spots feature the familiar catastrophe footage but with Hollywood production values and doses of *America's Most Wanted*-style slo-mo. The AT&T tie-in builds gradually, from the logo on a repairman's T-shirt to an avalanche of praise for the company keeping phone lines open. One AT&T lady, speaking of the quake effort, weeps: "It makes me feel like I'm part of a big company, and a big community."

But what's really weep-worthy about these 'cane and quake spots is the way that AT&T found real-life disasters to echo the multitude of career disasters and in-home humiliations that await anyone who fails to make the right choice and buy AT&T.

Of course, AT&T isn't alone in wanting to have its quake and bleed it too, and disaster ads are hardly new. Allstate insurance, running a Hugo ad in which a claims adjuster hands a woman a check for her ruined house on the spot, made tornado, explosion, and hailstorm ads throughout the '80s, and is planning a quake sequel. You can argue that disaster is their business, but all sorts of companies are now hitching rides on nature's violence.

When Nissan learned that Ronald Reagan was making a spot for the Red Cross, it arranged to donate TV time—provided Reagan was preceded by this scrolled message: "Due to the earthquake in San Francisco, Nissan is donating its commercial airtime to broadcast American Red Cross emergency relief messages." (The ad raised $400,000; Nissan spent $600,000 to air it. Why not just give this greater sum directly to the Red Cross?)

Making the sign of the Cross in your ad can help ward off charges of crassness. And it was the Red Cross that nudged all those, like Reagan, who wanted to make an earthquake-only spot to remember Hugo, too. If the dominant culture favors the quake—it followed more movie scripts, more classy real estate was lost, and it was a 15-second shocker, while Hugo took a week to spend itself—Hugo left more devastation. Hugo killed 78 people, the quake, 63. Red Cross relief efforts for Hugo will approach $50 million; for Loma Prieta, $10 million.

The earthquake may give bigger box-office bang for its bucks, but together the two acts of God outdraw all other long-term, chronic disasters—homelessness, AIDS, rotten schools, carcinogenic air—and if corporations don't pull quite as hard or as publicly for them, it's understandable, marketingwise. Natural disasters present the perfect politics—i.e., on the surface, none—for a company to attach its good name to. Natural disasters affect all classes (although rarely are the effects equal—from Watsonville to St. Croix). Natural disasters are ready-made for TV, and now for TV ads. The shorter the duration of the threat, the more engaging the tragedy, and nobody can sell anything with pictures of poor people except the Catholic Church.

With rock 'n' roll and sporting events becoming as cluttered with corporate sponsorship as TV itself, where else can an advertiser go?

The untrammeled rubble of physical destruction is the promising new land.

November 21, 1989

Hip Hop

If all the battery spots featuring unstoppably cute, jerky-motion toys are pretty irresistible, the Energizer funk bunny, wearing Ray-Bans and beating a snazzy drum through three convincing mock ads, stands ears and whiskers above the rest. Even ad people are giggling over the possibility that the different drummer will splash out of the still ponds of an Infiniti spot, shattering the narrator's sanctimonious calm.

The pink bunny is literally making a commercial breakthrough. He descends partly from those two-piece ads sandwiched around unrelated spots and partly from Joe Isuzu takeoffs. The rabbit has what it takes to make both baby boomers and babies ooh and aah—he fakes out ad formula, and, being a cuddly animal (not to mention a toy), he reassuringly follows the surest of formulas.

First we see E.B. (Energizer Bunny, as Eveready is gooingly marketing him) quickly rehashing last year's spot—banging his drum while the duller bunnies behind him freeze into silence. "Nothing lasts longer than the Energizer," the announcer says. "They keep going and going and going. . . ." But this time, E.B. marches out of the commercial and into a production studio as a cameraman mumbles, "Stop the bunny, please."

Then follow what seem to be regular ads. To soft classical music, tuxedoed and begowned dinner guests are waited on by servants. The camera scans the mansion's opulence, focusing first on a portrait. "The painting, Renoir," the voiceover reveals in hushed tones. "The vase, Ming," he says, as the shots tastefully overlap. "The wine, Marmoset. When only the best will do, serve—" and blop! the pink rodent traipses across the table, whirring his drumsticks and knocking over

This battery sell keeps going and. . . .

the china, as the appalled guests frantically grab their goblets. "Still going," the voiceover continues. "Nothing lasts longer than the Energizer. They keep going and going and going. . . ." (The last line is sure to be mimicked on playgrounds everywhere.)

Then comes another ad—maybe for "Nasaltene" spray with "fast-acting mucunal" or for "Très Café" in which a lady coos to her host over the "fresh-brewed coffee." "Oh, thanks," the host chuckles. "But it's not fresh-brewed. It's new Très—" when the hare hustles across the coffee table. The spots have all the pauses and intonations of the real thing, but their punch line whacks a little populist bop as the bunny tramples on pretension like Harpo does at the opera. (The agency, Chiat/Day/Mojo, is coming out with more parody ads this week and even running the rabbit through a real Purina Cat Chow spot—Energizer's owned by Ralston Purina. But would they ever mock something as deserving as Infiniti? *That* would be too cool.)

Brandishing all the emblems—Ray-Bans, the *Saturday Night Live* ad spoofiness—to signal that he's thumbing his nose at convention, E.B. pushes those baby-boomer buttons like so many channels on a remote. But he has something else going for him: He's a rabbit.

A subtle rabbitmania is spreading through advertising, with ads for everything from Grape Nuts to Pepsi sporting cottontail pitchpets. For a "low-interest category" like batteries (unlike cars or food, batteries evoke no emotion at all), rabbits are a fuzzy-warm stand-in. Rabbits (which is *almost* an anagram for "batteries") are sparky and persistent, just like a battery ought to be. If, like Bugs, rabbits are smart-alecky wise guys who steal carrots from your garden and make you love them for it, then rabbity batteries can somehow pull energy for your radio from outta nowhere.

Eveready's Energizer, in fact, snitched the pink bunny itself from its competitor, Duracell, and that company's hopping mad. After all, Duracell invented pink bunnies—sweet ones with snare drums and without shades—to represent longevity back in 1975. They moved on to other toys and are currently running ads that would rank most-cute if it weren't for E.B. One spot features battery-run boxers whose "sweat" beads all over their hard-plastic bodies until one KO's the other; in another, two jazz musicians play dueling trumpets, until one runs out of juice. But in the mid-'80s, Energizer was thrashing around, advertising with charged-up people like Mary Lou Retton and Jacko, the Australian screaming man. Finally, last year, Energizer brought out the updated, beat bunny to show that Duracell's Copper Top doesn't outlast the Energizer. (Nor does the Energizer outlast the Copper Top. This is called "brand parity," when the only real difference between products is their ads.)

A Duracell spokesman says that Energizer's use of a pink bunny "is admitting that their strategy over the years has been confusing consumers. They're trying to capitalize on something that did have meaning and that was Duracell's image." He takes some solace in the fact that the three-ad E.B. affair is an expensive 60 seconds long. But Eveready is now cutting costs by airing only the mock spots without the intro piece. The Duracell folks also tried to relish recent publicity that the $14.95 E.B. toy Eveready spun off for direct-mail sales is a distinctly low-tech, *batteryless* stuffed animal.

The battery battle is fierce. Duracell leads Eveready in alkaline battery sales 40 to 36 percent (according to Duracell; Energizer, for all its formula-busting ads, won't talk). Profit margins are high, estimated between 30 and 40 percent, and the rewards are getting larger. As the nation keeps buying more adult electronic toys and miniaturizing and portabilizing all of them, the $2.7 billion battery market has climbed from 1.6 billion batteries sold in 1983 to 2.9 billion in 1989.

Batteries reproduce as fast as rabbits, but their prolific droppings are much nastier. Batteries—including the mercury-leaking "button" ones, the cadmium-containing rechargeables, the lead-laden car kind (not made by Duracell or Eveready), and, most numerous, alkaline batteries, which contain small amounts of lead—are a chief source of heavy metal contamination of air, ground water, and landfills. According to the Waste Watch Center, the largest sources of mercury in the solid waste stream come from the things that make cameras flash and watches tick. In the boombox age, the same rule applies to batteries as to bunnies: You love 'em until they squat in your lap.

December 12, 1989

TV in Its Underwear

Thirty-minute commercials are growing like algae on late-night TV. They're as relentless as 550-TOOL ads, only wholesomer, as fake as professional wrestling, but without the wink. "Victoria Jackson's Beauty Breakthrough for the '90s," "Richard Simmons's Deal-a-Meal," "The Adventures of Marge and John," a sit(in-a-contour-chair)com for Craftmatic beds. Car wax, memory systems, woks, stain removers, piano lessons—suddenly they're all deemed worthy of a 30-minute sellathon.

Like advertorials in magazines, these infomercials try to blend with their surroundings. Many use a talk-show format, with the show's host "interviewing" the company's spokesperson. The studio "audience," usually wearing T-shirts with the product logo, applauds wildly when the ink blob disappears with Di-Di Seven or the Aura car wax still shines even though the hood of the Rolls has been set on fire.

There are testimonials, celebrities, and, most realistically, there are "commercial breaks," ads within the ad, that tell you how to order the product. "We'll be back," the hosts assure.

Languid with time and production values, and slightly oily to the touch, infomercials are television lounging around in its long underwear. They may be unkempt, they may not have left the house for days, but infomercials—at least the more inspired of them—have the soul of *The 700 Club*. "What about the person sitting out there right now, who is just about to swallow some pills and end it all?" Richard Simmons, the most financially successful infomercial mogul, asks the woman who went from 900 pounds to 650 with the help of his Deal-a-Meal plan and videotape for three payments of only $29.95. What would she like to tell them? Among other things, she'd say that Simmons is "Saint Richard."

It is easy to make fun. When the lady on "Harvey's Smart Kitchen" demonstrated a truly amazing food blender, she exclaimed, "It's perfect for singles, families, and newlyweds." But when she made mayonnaise fluff into being from nothing but an egg, oil, and the aerator attachment, my TV companion and I really did say out loud, "Look at that!" And she said to Harvey, "Look at that!"—and for a moment we four were one in America.

Long-form commercials were banned in the '60s when the FCC restricted TV ad time. But in 1984, the Amazing Reagan Deregulation Machine chopped and diced those restrictions, and as the number of independent and cable TV stations grew, so did the number of infomercials. Half-hour ads are now a $450 million annual business, expected to rise to $1.6 billion in two years.

You may wonder how any company, especially schlock shops, can afford 30 minutes of ad time. But late at night and early in the morning, a half hour may cost only—depending on location and station—$100 to $15,000. For stations, that can be extremely lucrative.

And they're not exactly schlock shops. Infomercials are produced by high-tech operations that often develop the product as well as pitch it. "You could ask which comes first—the product or the show concept or the star," says Dick Kaylor, president of Synchronal, the largest infomercial distributor, with 30 to 40 spots for as many products airing at any one time. "You could look at any starting point and answer 'yes.' We may have a budding celebrity who [wants publicity] and we come up with a product for them."

Infomercials vary from glitzy to tacky, but the basic sales technique is usually a clunky kama sutra of withholding and thrusting. They hold back information—the price, the phone number—until the suspense builds—and then they hammer you with harder-sell commercials within the commercial. "The shows are designed so that if you tune in at any time you don't miss the commercial," says Diana Espino, Synchronal product developer.

Craftmatic is perhaps the vilest of the infomercializers, targeting the old and infirm with chairs and beds that they claim help everything from edema to wrinkles. Craftmatic's contour chair business, which uses shorter ads starring Art Linkletter, has faced legal actions in a number of states, following hundreds of complaints concerning false claims about medical benefits, deceptive pricing, and high-pressure sales tactics. This week the Small Business Committee of Congress is holding hearings into what might be called disinfomercials.

Shoddiness aside, is there any difference between infomercials and regular ones besides their length? Isn't the slower pace and the program format just another way that ads lull you by temporarily disguising their identity?

The real offense of most infomercials over garden-variety ads is that their need for slack-jawed viewers is so naked. When they do work, it's because they tap into our ever-thumping desire to give in, to relax, to accept the whole big buyable world. With every minute more you watch, the algae grows. "So say, 'Yes, I've worked hard all my life! Yes, I deserve to pamper myself! . . . Yes, I want to be as relaxed and healthy as possible.' Don't . . . let dollars stand in your way. Say yes, yes to Craftmatic."

May 22, 1990

Lemon-Fresh Apocalypse

For the year-end wrap-up on *This Week With David Brinkley,* Sam Donaldson and George Will sat at the feet, virtually, of historian Daniel Boorstin and asked him, futurewise, what gives? Refusing to play geopolitical horoscope, Boorstin talked instead about the opposite, "the danger of extravagant expectations . . . something that, if I may say so, Sam, we learn partly from our American democratic rhetoric, which is the rhetoric of advertising, which depends on extravagant expectations. . . . [We're] inclined to assume that if we get rid of [Saddam Hussein], then the problem will be solved . . . just as we believe, in Eastern Europe, that if we get rid of the Soviet dominance, then there's going to be democracy all over Europe."

Soon followed GE's 60-second exercise in extravagant expectations (or "XXX"), the spot that salutes itself for bringing freedom (along with light bulbs) to Hungary. Despite the ethnic and economic dislocations unleashed by communism's fall, this ad of bright, joyful, waltzing folk has been burnished into our brains and will remain for years as *the* image of capitalism, the Great Emancipator. Game over, we don't want to know any more, it's "the end of history."

But for a real XXX, how about the end of the world? In the Year 2000, according to mythologies both sacred and secular, something very, very bad will happen (apocalypse or some form of eco/nuclear destruction), and/or something very, very good will happen (the Rapture, or Dawning of the New Age). Either way, 2000 is the hoop of fire for the planet to jump through; it backlights the '90s as the do-or-die decade. Was it merely in reaction to the greedy '80s that the '90s were (prematurely) deemed green and socially conscious—or was it out of fear of the big deadline in the sky?

"Margins for error are impossibly narrow in these last days; anything we do has repercussions at millennium's end," or at least that's the perception, which may or may not become self-fulfilling, writes Hillel Schwartz in *Century's End.* "For one hundred years and more, we have looked fearfully toward 1999 as the year of unappealable verdicts, then hopefully toward 2000 as the year of pardon and jubilee."

And so the marketing of the millennium has already begun. Maybe we're not thinking about it too much yet, but corporate HQ is. It's never too soon to start planning for history's closeout sale, which fits perfectly with the überpitch of every ad message: "Buy now—there may be no tomorrow!" But while advertising will surely link heroic companies with the prevention of all sorts of major disasters, the ad potential of the millennium lies less in the death and destruction part and more in the salvation part. The Calvinist sense of predestination, of an elect, becomes an econo-Biblical notion of "target markets." We are God's yuppies.

The banal seeds are here among us now: From Farberware's new Millennium line of pots and pans ("from nonstick to never-stick, the Dawn of a New Age") and Elizabeth Arden's Millenium (sic), the skincare line for older women ("look 10 years younger") to 2000 Flushes toilet bowl cleaner, Max Factor's 2000 Calorie Mascara, and the weird-as-heck new soap, Lever 2000. With the ever-present whimsical ad wink, the TV spot says it will clean your "2000 body parts."

But those are the bargain-basement knock-offs of the millennium— destruction and rebirth are so much richer than that. The many cusp-'o-the-'90s ads about the environment and making the world safe for capitalism are just the beginning of a larger, spiritual sell that we'll see pumped from now until at least 2001. Expect in coming years more ads aligning the sponsor with one-worldism, like AT&T's Universal charge card, sloganed "One World, One Card"; with multiculti hugfests like Coca-Cola's City on the Hill (the Hilltop Reunion ad); and with human glory, like British Airways's spectacle in which about *2000* extras form, from God's aerial p.o.v., a gigantic smile face that winks and then turns into a globe. And look for still more long-shots of Planet Earth that, at the end of a spot, turn into animated eyeballs, balloons, teardrops, bubbles, and, of course, logos.

The one thing that may save us from the millennium milkers is their very oversell. The best you can say for the American corporate ad reflex is that it eventually flattens out every emotion it pimps. We already get excited *and* bored daily with apocalyptic impulses—every ad holds a faint glimmer of millennial promise, assuring us that the product can change our lives for the better, providing a little spritz of Rapture.

As I say this, I realize that a straight line exists between me, ads, and my country. And so I would like to explain . . .

How I Am Like America:

1. I, too, am ruled by extravagant expectations. In the same way that if we get rid of Saddam Hussein everything will be great, so I believe that if I get rid of my noisy neighbors, or fall in love, or buy a red down parka with a *Doctor Zhivago* hood, everything will be great.
2. That is, my country and I have no sense of long-term planning. Instead, we have apocalyptic fantasies—where if we don't accomplish or prevent something *big* before our self-imposed due date, we're dead. But like lines in the sand, deadlines shift. Long before President Bush, I set January 15 as the date I would make a major assault on changing my life. But then I realized that, like our troops, I wasn't ready yet.
3. Our procrastination under God does not equal liberty and justice for all. America and I tend not to deal with our problems until it's too late. Kuwait? *You* wait.
4. We like a crisis to keep the blood boiling: budget talks, beach sludge, dogs dying on the six o'clock news—whatever it is, it's everything, it determines everything else. Then a week later, what was it, huh?
5. Riding that roller-coaster of procrastination and crisis, we are naturally too distracted to save and live instead with deficit and on credit. Credit is a state encouraged by continual entertainment by TV and mall, by the intense lightness of watching and shopping.
6. We are too impatient to do things like wait for sanctions to work. We like our gratification immediate—as advertising prefers us to. It's so much easier to wipe out the world than to solve its problems. Anyway, who really believes the apocalypse won't come in lemon-fresh scent?

January 22, 1991

Miles To Go

Advertising always presented the perfect occupational hazard for *thirtysomething*'s Michael Steadman and Elliot Weston. The tension between selling out and buying in would always bounce the boys up against their conscience, their generation, their wives. Their profession made them even truer specimens of the first TV generation. Expert only in the nuances of the media, they were well-suited to straddle the cultural divide of materialism and idealism, as well as the divide's numerical symbols—"the '80s" and "the '90s." It's a change of values that the ad industry, and occasionally an ad-supported TV show, has found useful to publicize.

So last week when Michael quit his agency over a "principle," it cut a deep cultural cleft. But the bite of the episode was in a speech by Miles, Michael's soulless boss, that essentially connected advertising to lies, ignorance, and war.

Michael, whom Miles had previously asked to take over the agency, has finally wrapped up a campaign for Durstin Beer, when the client discovers that the actor starring in it had marched in a demo against the gulf war. The patriotic client says the actor's out, and he'd like a little more flag-waving in the replacement ads to boot. Michael starts off by protesting, "Madonna had to do more than that to get fired from Pepsi." (For what it's worth, Pepsi was not among the show's sponsors.) "We're selling the war," Michael complains. "No," says Miles, "we're using the war to sell." Michael is appalled; for this Miles calls him a hypocrite: "Do you imagine there's anything different between this campaign or any other?"

Michael sucks in his gut, tenses up, and eventually agrees to wave flags. But he has to get in one more idealistic dig. The actor, he says, "was just expressing his opinion." No, retorts Miles, "he expressed an *unpopular* opinion. No one wants to be unpopular. That's why we're here. That's the dance of advertising. We help people become popular. Through popularity comes acceptance. Acceptance leads to assimilation. Assimilation leads to bliss.

"We calm and reassure. We embrace people with the message that we're all in this together. That our leaders are infallible, and that there is nothing, absolutely nothing wrong." Thunder actually claps as the truth shakes Michael into his own personal apocalypse. "I'm sorry you misunderstood the nature of this covenant," Miles says.

The brilliance of the speech was to push the conflict beyond the controversy surrounding the ad and make it about the nature of advertising itself. Ads don't lie only when they wave flags or spout sappy jingles. The cool ads, the edgy ads do it too—the kiss of bliss is puckered all the time.

The only thing is, the same brand of calm and reassurance often laces the show. "I see a bunch of rich white guys sitting around talking about a new world order," Michael moans to Hope. "I mean, am I one of these white guys? Am I selling a new world order?" As she so often does, Hope functions, hardly as comic relief, but almost as ad relief, providing comfort and a semicommercial timing that turns the focus from the political to the individual: "No wonder you can't sleep," she muses.

But did this rending of ad flesh affect how we saw the real ads surrounding the show? Not really. Oh, maybe the program forced some viewers to distance themselves from the ads as they chirped along merrily. But if anything, compared to the Durstin flap, the actual ads seemed like harmless drivel. The only spots that even hinted at the ad world's seething id were those for Saturn and Chrysler Jeep Cherokee. Not because they are vile on their face—they're like most commercials: friendly, whimsical, visually fun, with a dash of humor or irony. But if you burrow beneath the images and recall Chrysler's other patriotic spots—or link the Saturn ad to its creator, Hal Riney, who made Ronald Reagan's "It's morning in America"—Miles's prognosis becomes clear.

Surveying some real admen, *The New York Times* found that "Ad Executives Cheer" the episode. But these execs focused on the antiwar ethical conundrum, not the larger one. Most ad folks see themselves as good people, at worst, a bit calloused by cynicism—but that's just basic survival gear. Their gripes aren't usually over ethics, but over creative frustration and having to ass-lick the client. The sort of gripes that pump the illusion that they are generally valiant underdogs, even victims of commercial culture—an attitude that obscures the real but more subtle covenant of advertising.

Some ad people draw the line at working on cigarette or alcohol accounts, but rarely do they consider that their everyday job is to try to addict their audience, even if just to the feel-good bobbing of television.

Anyway, there are always handy excuses. The man who made the ad for New York's "Operation Welcome Home" ticker-tape parade, for instance, told me his son was very much against the war, and he himself didn't want to make an ad that supported it. The ad—shots of empty bleak streets and the admonition to "fill the canyons of New York with pride"—is no more a *literal* selling of the war than a flag among the beer bottles would be. But the purpose is not to sell the war, but to sell the world that made it probable. Ad people's Steadfastman-like refusal to make connections like that allow them to see their challenge as merely "creative"—a concept that always connotes virtue anyway.

Despite quitting, Michael might go this way yet. At the end of the episode, Miles begs him to come back. Michael, now jobless but newly happy with himself, refuses. He doesn't know what he's going to do, but whatever it is, from now on it will have to be his own thing. "It has to be yours, and nobody else's, and it has to be honest," he says in his best '90s-speak. Which seems to at least leave the door open for him to go the way of Elliot. Elliot's idealistic break from the jaws of the agency a few weeks ago was to freelance as a director of ads.

Integral to the '90s notion of new traditionalism is the sense that the world has overspent itself—and a rejection of advertising is key to this sense. To some extent, ads—and shows about advertising—have to take an antiadvertising stance. Miles would understand.

May 28, 1991

Miles To Go **313**

Modern Times

The *Voice* has moved into a vastly larger, cleaner, more corporate office. Larger, cleaner—great, but more corporate seems like just another chunk of the commercial world ripe for slander. Working in an unadulterated corporate office is like *being* in an ad, with tagline-tight rhythms at every turn. There is, for instance, our new Xerox machine, whose computerized monitor greets you with a warm WELCOME TO YOUR XEROX COPIER; the "occupied/vacant" sign in Helvetica (the typeface, once, of hip officialdom) outside the *executive* conference room; and package deliveries logged in on military time. But, like the corporate sensuality that air-conditions advertising, this crisp cubicular civilization seduces me.

Walking through lanes of fresh cubicle housing—each cell eager to coax the efficiency out of you, its textured cloth stretched taut from plastic border to plastic border, everything neatly tucked in and rising cleanly over shiny blue linoleum floors—makes me feel, it's hard to admit, happy. The straight cubicle lines are rounded ever so quietly at the corners—just like the computer monitor's or the computer keys'. The promise behind each softened square is that it will order chaos and digitalize diversity—but without completely flattening out the "human" element. The corpus of wall-to-wall freeze-dried slabs is usually processed to provide hints of flesh-feel. Each press of a key releases a little oomph of energy, not unlike the moment when you turn on the TV and the air crackles. Pressing buttons, turning gleaming corridors, cubicling off one's own personality unit toward higher productivity—such sensations press *my* buttons.

The television, the telephone, the computer, the cubicle, and combinations thereof are the skin and nervous system of the corporation, and when you come into contact with them you get the goose bumps of corporate sensuality. Corporate (in both the collective-body and big-business senses) sensuality stimulates more ambivalence than even the sexual kind. It's cold, it bulldozes history, it's anonymous—and the windowless areas here can be pretty bleak and depressing. And yet it can be full of promise, it leans toward the future. The new voice mail system here makes one writer "feel large and rich. It makes me feel power." The magnetic card we use to get into the building makes a copy editor feel elite: "Now I can get in and nobody else can."

The lure is containment and control—just the sort of steroids that corporations get hopped up on anyway. It was almost inevitable that Procter & Gamble got caught in the act of using the police to search the telephone records of practically everyone in town—some 803,000 phones in the Cincinnati area—to nab the person who was talking P&G business to the *Wall Street Journal*. P&G is notoriously paranoid: it's been known to instruct writers and secretaries at its ad agencies to lock up the typewriter ribbon at the end of the day if they've used it for a P&G account. Obsessed with making information as leakproof as it wants us to believe its disposable diapers are, P&G is only a more extreme example of a company that spends millions on "everything's swell" advertising (Ivory, Pampers, Tide, etc., etc.) to make its corporate armor seem as squeezably soft as Charmin.

Wherever it pulses, corporate sensuality is hardly new. That's what postmod architecture was all about—lending history and human fillips to the right angles of business. Corporate offices are great for setting off in higher relief things like flowers and personalized doo-dads. But the inducements to cross-dress for success keep on coming—it's what the earnest '90s are supposed to be doing to the greedy '80s.

This tension between machines and the wrenches thrown into them weaves throughout ads as well as offices. In 1981, IBM needed human funk so badly it chose a mascot that today would be taken for a homeless person. The "Little Tramp," the Charlie Chaplin character IBM used for five years to advertise its PCs and brought back last month for the computer's 10th anniversary, was the company's most successful campaign ever, finally thawing out cold Big Blue. In the current spot, the Little Tramp, still disheveled after all these years, watches his old ads on a silent movie screen. In one, his attempts to streamline a hat factory prove fruitless—until an IBM PC organizes his chaos. At the end, the screen tramp reaches out and throws a long-stemmed rose to the viewing tramp—or to you.

Never mind that Chaplin left the U.S. in 1952 after getting fed up with being harassed over his lefty leanings. Or that when IBM replaced the tramp with the actors from the dovish *M*A*S*H,* the company was the 19th largest defense contractor in the U.S. Today, as it brings him back—and he'll be around for the rest of this year—IBM is number 18 with $1.28 billion in military contracts. Just this month it won a contract worth twice that much to provide electronically juiced-up antisubmarine warfare helicopters to the British Royal Navy.

And though IBM's stand-in stands for the little guy, the company still has the largest market share of computers in South Africa (according to the Interfaith Center on Corporate Responsibility)—they just sell them through a shell company called ISM (as in capitalism).

The recent agreement between Apple and IBM, in which they bury the hatchet and cooperate, lends IBM the user-friendly image it sought in Chaplin, while it polishes onto Apple, with its hackers-in-the-garage origins, some of IBM's big business clout.

And so, in the realm of the corporate senses, all of us—Apple, *The Village Voice,* hell, the Soviet republics—are merging with IBM.

That's why the logo is a tramp.

September 24, 1991

Adblisters

If only the people were as fed up with mass commercialism as they supposedly are with politics and the press. That sort of disgust will take generations, if it comes at all—*that* would be true revolution in America. But meantime, many little bulimias are in the works.

They're surfacing in the form of what one practitioner calls "subvertising": an ad is not merely attacked but elements of its own campaign are twisted and used against it. This might take the form of guerrilla ads or political art, social-cause ads that look like art—or art that looks like ads.

For instance, *Adbusters,* a magazine linking the commercial world and ecodisaster, just came out with its second lampoon of Absolut Vodka ads, that campaign so glamo and arty it would seem forever immune from an askance look. Seeing alcoholism where Absolut sees sales, the ad pictures a coffin with the headline "Absolute Silence," and in tiny print adds, "The birthdays, the graduation, the wedding day . . . We were there to toast them all. So from one great spirit to another, here's to the most enduring ritual of all."

The Vancouver-based quarterly often rips advertisers by name, and the companies usually ignore it. (An "American Excess" ad features a sloppy shopping corpulent couple over the legend "Members since birth"—and AmEx is absolutely silent.) But after the first vodka parody—"Absolut Nonsense . . . Any suggestion that our advertising campaign has contributed to alcoholism, drunk driving, or wife and child beating is absolute nonsense. No one pays any attention to advertising"—the upscale-image liquor got low. Absolut Vodka of Canada "threatened legal action unless we surrendered the remaining copies of the magazine, published a retraction, and agreed never again to print similar material," says *Adbusters.* Instead, the magazine sent out press releases, and Absolut backed off. "They just didn't want to take us on in a public debate," says *Adbuster* editor Kalle Lasn. The Canadian distributor for Absolut won't comment, and a spokesperson for the American distributor (different companies but often same advertising) will say only that "no action whatsoever is contemplated."

The anti-ads, which *Adbusters* also sends out to about 100 publications to run as PSAs (fat chance), aren't stunningly brilliant, but wouldn't it be nice to have such commercial-sucking reminders plastered all over the world? *Adbusters* has nothing against Absolut in particular, but targeted the company "because it seems to be the most conspicuous of all alcohol advertisers in the last few years," Lasn says. "They have a right to advertise, but that campaign just needs to be countered. Alcohol companies spend $2 billion a year on advertising in North America."

Absolut's ad success—its share of the imported vodka market rose from 10 percent to 62 percent since the campaign began in 1980, according to Video Storyboard Tests—rests on absolution through art and hipness. The company has techno-teased actual music (via computer chip), jigsaw puzzles, and handkerchiefs into its magazine spreads. And its co-opted dozens of artists by publishing their work as ads with their names writ large—"Absolut Mothersbaugh," "Absolut Caraefe"—as long as they include the Absolut logo and bottle.

So, you might ask (in Yiddish), vod-ka complaining about? Art that sells out is redeemed by its own cheerful corruption, it's, it's . . . ironic, or something like that, we hip people are trained to say. But even if Absolut art is sometimes wonderful enough to take you places, its prime goal is to take you back to the brand and down the buy-hole. The ads lure your attention: The boozy patron of these pleasures is arty, and you can be too.

This spring—and here the "irony" really grates—Absolut commissioned bottle-centered artworks from 16 African Americans and ran the ads in *Black Enterprise* magazine. Like Philip Morris's savvy funding to black arts groups, this campaign bounces grossly off the whitewashing work of the Reverend Calvin Butts in New York and the Reverend Michael Pfleger in Chicago, who've defaced alcohol and cigarette billboards in the inner city. In these areas alcoholism and heart disease rates, as well as the number of smoke- and drink-coaxing billboards, are vastly higher than in white neighborhoods. (The liquor stores of South Central L.A. were targets of arson during the riots for this same reason.)

Art is at the crux of guerrilla advertising or, as the Artfux collective says, "Artfux everything and everything Artfux." Messing with the mass message is a minor art form and was committed long before *Adbusters*. By their clever reassemblage of public space, the graffiti artists of Pompeii—whether etching "Don't go to Lucretia the prostitute" or "Talus, go home to your wife"—were running de-ads of sorts.

Continuing the tradition, artist Ron English has redone more than 100 billboards, either adding crucial touches like explicit penises and testicles for the suggested ones on the face of Camel's "Smooth Character" or putting up a whole new billboard, like the enlarged copy of *Guernica* he plastered under the words "New World Order" during the gulf war. English sometimes works with the New Jersey-based Artfux, which snipes up posters like one of Uncle Sam saying, "I want you to die a horrible meaningless death to sustain a lifestyle that will ultimately destroy the earth."

This leads to those mysterious billboards, 24 of them, across NYC. They're blown-up black-and-white photos of a really inviting bed with satiny sheets rumpled and two pillows indented by now-absent heads. When I first saw it, I assumed it was a teaser campaign and that any day a Calvin Klein logo would be slapped across the bottom.

"It tortures me, because I sleep alone," one young man told me, interpreting it quite differently. But then he also figured it was some kind of AIDS ad—"because two people, gone, death. . . ." Actually, though it's pretty darn obscure, that *is* what the billboard's supposed to "say." It's not an ad at all, but a Museum of Modern Art-sponsored project by artist Felix Gonzalez-Torres, whose lover died of AIDS.

But for me the main effect of the bed in the sky was, how refreshing *not* to have a jaded expectation satisfied, that a logo never did land on what looks like an ad, that an image might float somewhere unanchored by corporate weight.

June 30, 1992

TVTV

Russia's most perfect pop object is that little Lenin doll within a Stalin doll within a Brezhnev doll within a Gorbachev doll within a Yeltsin doll. America's is a TV within a TV within a TV. That this high-tech Matreshka doll is our true flag was brought home by the 56-monitor video wall at the Democratic convention: The home audience could react to the arena audience reacting to the pols reacting to themselves on screen, their images often bursting into infinite multiples, reality layered and refracted and everyone still carrying on. The video wall (is there a more appropriate nemesis for the Berlin Wall?) was the not-

Ask not "TV or not TV?" but "TV *and* TV?"

so-secret weapon that, as ex-Maximum TV host Ross Perot declared, helped "revitalize" the Democratic Party.

This is TV squared, or TVTV, and the Dems have finally learned the algebra—that showing, on screen, people watching screens can validate the home bodies' experience of watching, maybe even validate the person watched.

If the convention was a four-day commercial for the party, it was hardly the first TV ad that tried to revitalize product sales by slapping TVs all over itself. In fact, there's even a company, SMA Visual Effects Corporation in Manhattan, that specializes in shooting TV monitors and video screens for ads and movies, "hundreds and hundreds" of them, says SMA president Mike Morrissey. By my conservative estimate at least 25 advertisers—Excedrin, Revlon, KFC, GE refrigerators, La Quinta motels, Ramada Inn, Mobil 1, to name a few—currently use TV screens as the prop of preference. And that's not counting the dozens of ads for television products, like Magnavox, which puts John Cleese in a TV in a TV in a TV, or for TV stations, which ooze screens, or for computers, whose sleek monitors are TV's high-strung cousin. No, TVTV ads use the TV monitor not as a product but as a basic element of advertising, like voiceovers, taglines, or celebrities.

These ads may ape home videos, with counter displays running in the corner (presumably lending the product authenticity), or they may crackle with some black-and-white TV static (for an EZ postmod wink). Mostly, though, they repeat their own action in on-screen monitors, or they have "live" characters interact with screened characters or screened characters chatting across separate flickering boxes. But regardless of how they're used, the real reason they're used is to show off the screen itself—its slightly frosty shimmer, its cool mint of technology, makes it seem as if someone's thrown open all the windows. The sensory claustrophobia of watching TV two, four, six hours a day is allayed with pictures of windows in the window that is TV.

"It's almost an act of cynicism," says a West Coast copywriter.

TV in TV makes a little Cash.

"Someone figured out that if the TV is on someone will watch it. It's a box within a box—you just keep opening it to try to get at something."

This Sisyphean space is so naturally an ad space that it's odd that multiple monitors appeared in dance clubs, music videos, and department stores long before they saturated TV commercials. Maybe ad people feared that TVs in ads would play like Big Brother. After all, the omnipresent tube represents overarching authority. Monitors in the monitor (do they monitor you?) could make that power *too* clear. But that would have been an old-fashioned reading of the situation. Today, TVTV represents sparky cyberspace—an artificial reality that can be more real than reality. Maybe like in that new John Ritter film, *Stay Tuned*, about a guy who gets sucked into a TV—written by two admen.

And yet within the cyberspace, TV squared allows the expression of some very human needs. Indeed, there are many angles from which to squeeze every last bit out of the tube:

Media Mirror: Although we're all supposed to hate the media, we suspect that maybe life itself emanates from it, and so it's in a commercial's interest to flatter us that in our measly household dramas we, too, are part of the action. This effect can be quickly achieved by tacking up a news show's blinking monitors. (Displaying busy background monitors is one way news shows make sure news *shows*. Lofts expose their beams, stations their monitors: working parts are sexy.) A lady on the fictional "Freezer Talk" insists that since her mother doesn't use Glad-Lock freezer bags, neither does she. "Let's go live to your parents' house," the host suggests, whereupon Mom beams up on a screen and proves her daughter so very wrong. Next up, a guy eating breakfast does a "triple take"—three speeded-up nods of the head—over the great taste of Triples cereal, while the anchorwoman on the TV news he's watching peeks out at him like he's gone mad. But he hasn't—the ad's just suggesting that the boundary between media and "me" has collapsed, forming a third dimension—and that's triple the fun!!!

Here's Lookin' at Me: Olympic long-jumper Mike Powell not only leaps but shoots hoops in a fast-cut spot for Foot Locker. And not only that: Some of his feats are repeated on a small TV that appears from nowhere. He takes a deep breath "live"—then he does it again on the monitor. The slogan asks, "How far can you take it?"

A lash farther, Cover Girl answers. For its new "extension mascara," Christy Brinkley pretends to be doing a fashion shoot in a TV studio. She looks at her face writ large on a huge video screen, her football-size eyes look back, and a voiceover says, "Just when you thought you'd taken your lashes as far as you can go, Cover Girl takes you farther." (Dig: A man extends his jump, a woman her lashes.) Why the towering tube here? "All our ads are a shoot of a shoot," says Dick Huebner, the creative director for Cover Girl at Grey Advertising. "It's a behind-the-scenes kind of thing, it adds another dimension. It also allows a close-up and a faraway at the same time."

But even when celebrities use TVs as narcissistic tools, they're not always really looking at themselves: Christy's video screen, for instance, "was all done in the film processing," says Huebner. "She was reacting against a big blue area, so we could strip in what we wanted to later." (Another Brinkley, David, along with Peter Jennings, performed similar screen tricks during the Democratic convention, says SMA's Morrissey, who handled the job. Whenever they chatted from ABC's "skybox" or "the floor," they were actually in a nearby studio standing in front of a screen upon which convention footage was projected.)

Wired Mascot: At its most assertive, the monitor plays a character, something half android/half pet. Four guys dis a fifth for trying to play basketball in a suit. But as he *flies* to the hoop, a half-dozen TV sets erupt through the asphalt as in an earthquake—each flashing images of him flying. What's it all mean? "He deserves a Bud," the guys deduce. (Miller Lite made the tube/beer link last year with a spot in which a TV screen overflowed with beer foam.)

Let's whack the point home, Nike must have said. We're in a cluttered TV repair shop. A set turns itself on—it's Andre Agassi. Another set follows—hey, it's David Wheaton. And as they slam a tennis ball, their respective TVs bounce and crash in response, burrowing through the shop's clutter, until finally both sets bust through the window. Is Nike saying, "Let them eat image"? Or has it figured that sleek hard boxes are actually the best celebrities to help an ad break out of the proverbial "clutter" of surrounding ads?

Brave New Box: While TV ads would rather die than be perceived as Big Bro, they will occasionally recruit a TV screen to play the heavy, the agent of alienation and repression—but only as long as the product gets to play the liberator. The financial services group GMAC shows bank customers fruitlessly trying to get information from a teller on a monitor. GMAC then swears *it* never acts that way.

In a Southern Bell spot, some *other* company's Tomlinesque telephone operators observe callers on screens—the better to see them squirm under bureaucracy's torture. "You have dialed the wrong number," they say. "You have used the wrong finger. This is a recording." This is funnier than it seems: Florida has announced plans to file a multimillion-dollar suit against Southern Bell for using "boiler room" tactics that misled "hundreds of thousands of customers" into paying for services they never ordered. (Southern Bell says it's taken "corrective action.") Just because an ad has the savvy to inject itself with TVs doesn't mean it's been vaccinated against TV's everyday lies.

Monitor Mondo: The look of the monitor—the cleanest, most well-lit space ever—exerts an allure of its own. It's a thing removed and different from everyday life and yet, contained in a box, it appears almost as something you can acquire, can receive as a present—maybe from your friends at MCI. There appears in the sky an enormous video billboard—98 monitors going, each with a headshot of a different person—as a "live" woman standing on the billboard's scaffolding narrates. Much like the Democratic video wall, the folks in this one testify, this time to the goodness of MCI's Friends and Family program. Then they're replaced by graphics announcing 40 percent savings. The live woman explains that the savings are a gift to customers on F&F's first anniversary. "MCI is doing something big. And think of *this*," she nods toward the video wall, "as the card that comes with the gift."

MCI spent between $1 million and $2 million on this digitally created production "because we wanted something that looked magnificent, we wanted it big, and we wanted to show multitudes," says Barry Vetere, a partner at MCI's ad agency. But multitudes of persons can sometimes look "maudlin," he says. "We didn't want a soggy situation." Technology—multitudes of monitors—could keep it dry: The TV screen as humanity's antiperspirant.

The endless ad on TVTV is this: The TV asks, "What should you be doing?" And it answers, "Watching TV." Because that's where the ads are.

August 18, 1992

New Word Order

After the sponsor-pleasing inaugural celebrations, none of this should be surprising. But suddenly admakers, despite the dangers of demographic mixing, feel free to let "establishment" and "New Age" dance together. Suddenly the much too pretty people we expect in mainstream advertising are backdrops for the metaphysical pitch.

Pointedly debuting on Inaugural Eve was Crystal Pepsi (a name that says "New Age" and "establishment" about as succinctly as possible). Crystal Pepsi is a clear, caffeineless cola that Pepsi hopes will increase its share of the $48 billion soft-drink market—the share of cola itself has dwindled to 59 percent, due in part to the success of quasi-natural, sometimes clear upstarts like Snapple. So all the top pops are trying to burst the hippie sips' carbonated bubble by starting their own "alternatives" (next up is Tab Clear).

Pepsi was lucky—along comes a Snapple-generation president who says "change" a lot, and the copy virtually writes itself. Based on Van Halen's "Right Now" video, Crystal Pepsi's ad floods the viewer with catchy cosmic tips: "Right now change is loose on the planet. Right

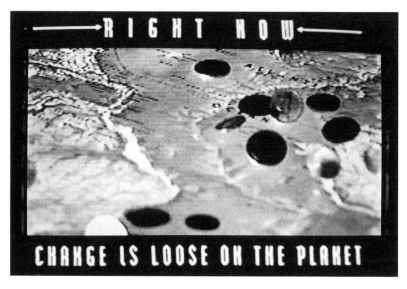

The lies they are a-changin'.

now is different than a moment ago. . . . Right now we're all thirsty for change."

Pepsi may sound all Clinton/Gore about "the planet," but maybe the secret code word here isn't *now*, but *right*. The campaign comes from BBDO, headed by Phil Dusenberry, who's made spots for Reagan, Bush, and the Arthur S. De Moss Foundation, which is running his beautifully produced antiabortion ads on cable. As a Pepsi exec spritzed for a press release, "Change is sweeping the country, and Crystal Pepsi symbolizes that change." That's *exactly* the dread—that another new soft-drink formula in another new bottle will symbolize the extent of the change.

But if you're a commercial in 1993, how do you symbolize "renewal and improved"? The easy solution, which Pepsi also took from the "Right Now" video, is to use the kind of cool graphics in which words are spelled out and scrolled over the visuals, sliding left, right, up, down. The technique was first used in TV ads by Subaru, to show what a maverick car company it was. Arriving hastily from all quarters, words sliced and diced this way become a graphic version of quick cuts. When the linear medium of the written word is made as nonlinear as possible, the real message is, If you're not quick enough to jump with the synaptic short-out, you're not hip.

Does Crystal Pepsi mind that this typeface tango is almost identical to that used by Diet Coke in *its* new ads, introduced just three weeks ago? "Ours is done in a different way," as Pepsi spokesman explains. "And even if there were some confusion, it might have a cumulative effect—one plus one equals three, who knows?"

Diet Coke also uses type to confer hipness, but this time on behalf of a New Age of aging. Its spots feature insanely active people rappelling, diving off cliffs, stopping for no one, with the explanation that "during the Roman era, 28 was considered old"—a woman about that age runs in a grueling race. "In the Middle Ages, 50 was ancient," as an older woman navigates a sailboat. The cross-generational appeal is clearly a sop to all the middle-aged boomers taking over. One spot ends on an inspirational axiom worthy of John Bradshaw: "Live your life like an exclamation, not an explanation." The planet is changing—yessss!—so long as multinational pumpers of syrup and aspartame don't stop thinking about spiritual trends to borrow.

How capable are we of real change anyway when we keep repeating the words of mass marketing?

Recently, in the *Voice*, the wonderful Matt Groening published two lists of "Forbidden Words 1993." Particularly brilliant selections included: *in your face, over the top, new world order, yo, "it's the economy, stupid," empowerment, gangsta, the blame game, toon, affordable, grunge, tree hugger, shock jock.* To which I would only add: *Yessss!* (applied with victorious hiss and sports fan-like fist gesture), *But nooooh!, Right.* (drolly), *the planet, rocket scientist, brain surgeon, just doesn't get it, that's what he does, the [name]-ster, [anything]-driven.*

More than regular chichés, cool-dude clichés share some special qualities: They're usually of recent coinage and TV-distributed. Beyond cynical, they're often about being tough and surviving in the modern jungle of language. They're best delivered with attitude, or at least inflection correctness. *Are we having fun yet?* These verbal tics may be inspired by sitcoms, headlines, movies, talk shows, and ads, or they may originate from the people and get recycled by those media. But it's the sense of "media" coursing through them that gives them their sparkle.

"So my son asks me, what are we doing to save the forests?" a narrator starts right in for Georgia-Pacific. The *so* idea is to sound like you've been caught mid-conversation, real casual-like. Phrases and inflections like these pass through several *filters* (there's one!). If they make it *big-time* (there's another), they might be in for a period of soft ridicule—usually by other *media types* (the last one I'll point out)—for overuse. If they survive that, they win the right to be repeated, but only with irony. If they survive *that,* they get stronger, like Raid-resistant roaches—and they shed the irony, they shed the ridicule, and they begin to seem as indispensable as, say, *Is this fun or what?* They've carved grooves that thoughts expressed otherwise are too fat to fit through; they are, like the Gap ads say, Just What Fits.

So? You gotta problem with that? It's called com-mun-i-*ca*-tion, lady! Lighten up!

My problem with it is that when you hear one person saying "lighten up" or "lady" you hear 10,000 voices saying it. You hear a million voices backing the speaker up. Whatever point the speaker is making, it gains acceptance not on its merits, but on how familiarly it's presented and on how efficiently tongue snaps into groove.

Those moments when we utter mass words are really one- or two-second commercials, one of the hundreds of ads we run daily on our privately owned 500 channels. Ads produced by "the culture," but disseminated, and paid for, by us.

No problemo.

February 9, 1993

Everything Must Go

Do recent developments foretell the end of advertising? What can you make of infomercials for a device that zaps through commercials, ads for cigarettes called "Death" that flaunt cancerous lungs, and brandless and adless products outselling brand names? The smell of burning press releases wafts through the air as the '90s search for authenticity, austerity, whatever, continues.

But because I write this as a victim of fidgetal technology, perhaps sightings of an ad endtimes are merely wish fulfillment. I am confused, overwhelmed, I feel abandoned by traditional media as the "New Edge" culture of 500 channels and a billion boxes—be they computers, TVs, cable boxes—takes over. I'm falling *off* the edge—I want curves and pillows. Wired? Try Tired. And Mired. Five hundred channels means 100,000 advertising maniacs. Not only will Saks deign to home shop with a show on Barry Diller's QVC on May 22, but NBC, according to *Ad Age,* is quietly developing its own direct-marketing shows, too.

With so many cheap channels, advertisers will be able to buy their own—think of the possibilities! The Human Relations Channel by AT&T, the Green Channel by Du Pont. By next year a pay-per-view service called Your Choice TV will allow you to punch up current broadcast fare whenever you want—but though you're paying, in many cases you'll still have to watch the ads. And even Comedy Central is planning a home-shopping show. They'll make fun of the format, probably even the products, but the idea will be to sell the bejesus out of them. "We want to get 1000 people on the phone," CC's Vinnie Favale is quoted as saying, "not 1000 yuks." Ha ha ha ha ha ha ha ha ha ha ha ha ha ha ha ha ha ha ha ha ha ha ha ha.

It's a chintzy world out there, getting more tinny every day. As media and audiences continue to "fragment," so does meaning. With each new element, you must expand until you're stretched thin, so thin you exist only as a receiver. You're kept busy pushing computer/phone/remote buttons as advertisers, promoters, and programmers of every kind push yours. This is a time when, using your channel recall feature, you can switch back and forth between *Bad Girl Dormitory* and an infomercial about how you can earn $35,000 a week or more by buying your *own* 900-number phone lines, complete with instructions on how to exploit other idiots!

It is a time when advertising, sensing the revulsion it has caused, must go against itself. As the Reformation rebelled against High Catholicism and its arrogant displays of wealth, so a few brave advertisers are nailing their dissent to the door of High Advertising. Let's take a look at the three things, perhaps the only things, that can possibly slow down advertising: more technology, the success of going adless, and honesty.

The infomercial for VCR Voice, a new VCR remote control that works by voice rather than buttons, hypes its anti-ad feature: You just say "zap it" and it fast-forwards for 30 seconds. Programming a VCR with voice commands is nice, but the ad zapper is hardly revolutionary: You can already FF through ads with any VCR remote, and some

VCR Voice can be *your* voice!

newer ones have a function that will do it in 30-second increments. But the real media Martin Luthers may be those 'mercial mercenaries in Japan: Mitsubishi has developed a VCR that, relying on signal differences between programming and commercials, will not record most ads in the first place. Fellow advertisers were not pleased.

It can't happen here, where signals don't differ enough. But that makes good pickings for VCR Voice. Its marketing director, former adman Robert Grossman, was asked by *Ad Age* whether he's hurting his old ad-world buddies: "This is a feature that consumers want. . . . And it's a question of loyalties; that was then, this is now." Though he also told me that "Madison Avenue isn't losing any sleep over it," a recent agency study found that when commercials come on, viewership drops an average of 7.9 percent on network TV and 14.3 on cable.

But if Madison Avenue finds a way to outsmart Silicon Valley—and it always will—maybe the demise of brand names will stop the ad implosion. Private labels and/or store brands (which keep down costs by not running ads) now outsell their name-brand counterparts in categories like cookies and ready-to-eat cereals; the phenomenal rise of discounted cigarettes is what led Philip Morris to cut Marlboro's price faster than the product cuts life expectancy.

Which leads to a truly off-brand—Death cigarettes—and the one tack that could smoke advertising—brutal honesty. Death is a small, for-real British brand; its ads show an X-ray of a cancerous lung with the headline "The Shadow of Death." B. J. Cunningham, director of Death, says, "What we're saying is, go ahead and smoke, but if you do it's your funeral." He admits that truth can make a killer ad: "It's a very obvious marketing ploy in a way, but one that's very effective because no one else is doing it." But even if the honest approach isn't stopping advertising, it is killing off some of its own ads: Almost no British billboard company will touch Death's ads.

I suppose I have to admit that even such a go-for-broke strategy is not a sign of advertising endtimes. If technology and radical marketing ideas gently squeeze down the advertising bulge at one end, it just pops up bigger at the other.

Really bigger. In the works is the misleadingly named "Environmental Billboard"—an inflatable billboard the size of 100 football fields that will orbit the Earth carrying the name and logo of any company willing to shell out as much as $30 million. From Earth, the ad will seem the size of the moon. But that hunk of rock is itself logo-ready— nearly every logo devised in the last decade is a planet-shaped sphere striated with telecommunication-like lines—so why not shoot for the moon itself? Space Marketing, the same company that will paint the words *Last Action Hero* on the fuselage of a NASA rocket expected to be launched this spring, figures the billboard is prime for a global marketer. Can you see the Nike swoosh circling the earth, waved to by folks from Somalia to St. Louis, in some places making people feel good about themselves, while in others it's mistaken as a sign of the end of the world?

May 4, 1993

The Ad Mission

Sky and clouds, desert dunes, giant surfs, flying swimmers, Earth, Enya, and Ennio: These are the signs of the spiritual in the commercial. A contradiction? Yes. But with baby boomers (often working in ad agencies) facing their mortality, 12-step programs proliferating, and (as David Koresh could have told you) the millennium looming, more ads more often are invoking a power greater than their product.

Only a few years ago, Planet Earth as seen from space and cerulean sky 'n' clouds as seen from Mt. Haleakala (a popular film site in Hawaii) served as the prime God backdrops. Swatch ran a spot in which a man in trunks swims through the clouds. Today, people not only sky-swim for Crystal Pepsi and (in an ad running in the *Voice*) for Expo '93 NewLife, but they do it breaststroke, arms outstretched Jesus-style. Ad humans have also been flying, in all modes, for Ban for Men, Giorgio's Wings fragrance, Lightning Bolt wear, and Northwest

God is in the retail.

Airlines—not to mention David Robinson for Partnership for a Drug-Free America.

As heaven's surrogate, sky 'n' clouds are still all over the place (and this is amazing, but as I write this, Sonya of *Sonya* is talking about "spirituality and why some people are saying it's the most exciting, most important, most vital thing happening today" before a logo of sky 'n' clouds setting off the segment's title). But these days they're being joined by "Deep Thoughts"–ish shots of sand dunes, ocean waves, and the buttes and mesas of Arizona's Monument Valley. Why figure these for spirit props and not just photogenic background material? Mostly because the music leads you to.

New Age singer Enya or Enya-like sounds accompany many of these ads, most notably for the new Volkswagen Passat spots, which feature her former band, Irish New Agers Clannad (whose lead singer, Maire Brennan, is Enya's sister). Slo-mo shots of road, car, and falling leaves float by to ethereal music with hints that VW can get you in touch with something shinier than a new car: "Volkswagen introduces three new cars, each engineered to recharge the human spirit." Though U.S.

VW sales have been plummeting, the Clannad campaign, says VW, is responsible for a 25 percent increase in Passat sales. Meanwhile, sales of Clannad's album *Anam*—which, in a first of its sort, gets a credit at the end of the ad—have "exploded," says Atlantic Records, shooting from number 39 to number 4 on *Billboard*'s new artists chart.

Enya's music itself was in a Crystal Light spot, and her record publicist claims "she is the most-requested artist for commercials." Some people even hear Enya in Ayer's ads for KitchenAid appliances. One spot aesthetically likens the features of a KitchenAid refrigerator and glacial Alaska—juxtaposing a waterfall and an automatic icemaker; in a second ad, an oven's ancestors are really desert dunes and Monument Valley mesas. Mysterious rock formations have been hot at least since boomer Richard Dreyfuss felt compelled to sculpt a butte in his living room in *Close Encounters of the Third Kind*. Still, something larger than a major appliance is being reached for here—like maybe eternity? "The timeless forms, golden warmth, strength that endures," the voiceover says ovenwise. "The fire of creation. All a little closer to home." The composer of the ooh-ah music, however, is not Enya but Richard Horowitz. "Enya was somebody we wanted to stay away from, because she's so popular with so many advertisers," says the creative director, Susan McFeatters, though she admits "there's a certain kind of musical overlap." She adds, "We weren't deliberately trying to appropriate" anything spiritual, though "I'm sure a lot of people can easily read that into it."

Aware of it or not, admakers often serve as channelers of a specious spiritual spiel. Producers and gofers, art directors and account execs are only a few steps removed from the faithful flocking to Lourdes—except they flock to the world's most hallowed commercial sites, the outdoor temples of image worship. The nature shots they bring back and the music they glorify them with function as a religious respite from the constant chatter of the media mind. Against TV's flashing assaults, commercials that appropriate the sacred seem a broad and soothing canvas. They're would-be holy holes in the television screen, appearing to lead to something more everlasting than what's on the five o'clock news. This is no mere trend—this is the ad mission: As advertising must increase the desire for useless or redundant products, it must keep pumping a concomitant "spirituality." So we won't hate ourselves (or them) too much for being greedy monsters of excess, marketers must sow a higher meaning into the cars and refrigerators they push.

But the problem is that religion should be hard—only images are easy. In Jewish places of worship, images are prohibited because they rival the devotion that God reserves for Himself. Catholicism is of course full of images, but they always progress from suffering to redemption; you can't sell much with a shot of a guy flogged into strips and nailed to a tree.

If Enya-like music is the reassuring, eminently nondenominational melody for commercial transcendence, then Ennio Morricone's score for *The Mission* is the passionate, guilt-wracked Catholic chorus. Like the film's plot about a South American slave trader (Robert De Niro) who kills his brother and finds redemption after a Jesuit priest (Jeremy Irons) forces him to lug a ton of useless junk up a mountain to an Indian mission, the soundtrack expresses a yearning, painful distance from God. Weaving an English choir with Andean instruments, the *Mission* music is, for my money (which is now what it's for), some of the most wrenchingly beautiful ever written. But this transporting sound, originally illustrating the agony of God's absence and the joy of His presence, now serves as His freelance jingle.

And He apparently has an earthly agent. A piece of the soundtrack, "Gabriel's Oboe," first turned up in the mid '80s for Security Pacific Bank on the West Coast, when adman Jim Weller used it to deepen the tagline "We want to be your bank for life." "It's very beautiful and sad," he says. About a year later, other writers at his agency, Hal Riney & Partners, used a different *Mission* piece as the swan song in the last ad for the late Wall Street firm E. F. Hutton. Coming out right after the Crash of '87 but before Hutton's scandal-ridden demise, "New Day" used the divine sounds to imply a resurrection of its brokers' mission (though they were probably the kind of people who bought Quechuan patrimonies and turned them into parking lots). Later, at a different agency, Weller used another swatch of *Mission* for Maxwell House coffee. "We needed something very celebratory and yet something that also captured the torment and the anguish of working in the coffee fields," he says. More recently, Weller used specially written music for upcoming Citizen watch ads—"It sounds like 'Zip a Dee Do Dah' done like *The Mission*."

Curiously, the core *Mission* merchants are Republican admen who are doing God after once doing Reagan. "Hal Riney, Tom Messner, and I all worked on 'Morning in America,' " says Weller. While not all *Mission*-soundalike ads come from this group—a spot for D'Italiano bread springs to mind—many do. Messner's agency had *Mission*-like music composed for a current MCI extravaganza that pulls out all the spirit stops: sun rising over Planet Earth as seen from outer space, Aztec-like drawings in close-up, shots of rapidly moving clouds across a sky, whitecap surfs, a sand dune. From this "cosmic perspective," as the ad's creative director, Jim Scalfone, puts it, the ad homes in on people from all over the world, and then the phrase "One World" is swiftly spelled out in about 40 languages. Were the Cold War not over, those would be fightin' words, commie words. But now "One World" has half a chance of sounding like "One God," and no other long-distance carrier shall go before Me.

The spirituality of the ad is deliberate, says Scalfone. " 'One World' does draw on the sense of Eastern philosophies that in a world of illusion there is separation, and in this ad we seek to connect." But doesn't such big production-value advertising go against the message of *The Mission,* especially the part where a humbled De Niro reads from the Jesuit breviary that "love envieth not . . . is not puffed up"?

Maybe spiritual ads are a telecommunications thing, judging from AT&T's spot "Multiple Suns." To sparse, *Mission*-like strains three, four, many more suns rise and set like bubbles on water (demonstrating "100 Free Days for Business"). As the Great Transmitters, phone companies are particularly eager to use this tack in ads. But come to think of it, the Higher Power pitch would be perfect for corporations of all sorts—that is, wherever their omnipresent, unseen power is the real message.

Advertising has long played many of religion's former roles—it used to be you'd find images of Christ or the Virgin engraved on every utensil and fabric in the home; today, of course, it's logos for Coke and Bud and AT&T. Ads also minister us toward the Promised Land where struggle will cease and peace (a/k/a "satisfaction") will reign. But post-Cold War advertising has a still larger cross to bear. During the '80s, emotional ad moments that couldn't be slotted into family, romance, or greed, could be linked to country and patriotism. But now, without an Evil Empire to kick around anymore, ad emotions must connect with something more enduring. Without an easily identifiable evil other—and yet with a millennial Judgment Day at hand—we might be prone to find some demon droppings in our *own* lifestyle. But spiritual ads can help us to simultaneously see our shallow, materialistic ways *and* exorcise them: We can consume the evil of excess by making every purchase into a prayer.

And yet, don't these ads clang with the contradiction between the abundant material life that commercial culture pushes and the more mystical injunction to shed that abundance in order to focus on what really matters? The contradiction is readily resolved by the ads' *passive* spirituality—be impressed by killer sunsets, feel awe from celestial music—which works right into a consumer kind of spirituality. The very few ads that hint at actually *doing* something in the world, such as Cotton Inc.'s "Fabric of Our Lives" campaign (which shows women protesting, young blacks at a funeral) are, by comparison, liberation theology.

Or as Wayne Dyer said (paraphrasing Pascal) on Sonya's spirituality show, ". . . all man's troubles stem from his inability to sit quietly." He was talking about the need for meditation. But the scary part is that we *do* sit quietly, all the time, in front of the TV, absorbing sermons from corporations on how to get the most out of life. No need for church, no need for Talmudic study, no need for sorrow, no need for meditation—just sit, don't talk, and let heaven wash over you.

June 8, 1993

The Ad Mission **337**

Pop Culture

From a side entrance to St. Vincent's Hospital, he floats toward me gently, a young, well-dressed man asking for a good restaurant "in the heart of the Village." Out of town, eh? Applying for a residency? He chuckles, a little embarrassed. No, he's the PR man for the Pizza Hut blimp, and he's here visiting the pilot with the injured back. No! Impossible! Out of the tens of thousands of New Yorkers he could have crashed into, the PR blimp man lands on me, the girl who'd poke ads with Pepsi syringes if she could. It's a sign!

Though he had to return to Wichita HQ to work on Hut's first crisis-management team, he stopped long enough to say that the fallout wasn't so bad—the heat's on the blimp company, not Pizza Hut. This wasn't big news, but bumping into the blimp man was too perfect—as leads go, I gotta have it! (Pepsi, as we should all know, owns not only Pizza Hut, but KFC, Taco Bell, Frito-Lay, and much of the fast-food fantasia.)

Oh, the humanity! With no one seriously hurt, the blimp bust had been a *good* disaster. "This is the best Fourth of July ever!" a friend kept exclaiming—and he was right, if the Fourth means sparks and the declaration, however brief and accidental, of independence from the (corporate) powers that be. Plus, the deflated dirigible had inversion working for it: Instead of July 4 terrorism as planned, we got evidence of a harmless parallel cartoon universe.

This year, summer product disasters screaming from the local news have become the small-screen corollary to the blockbusters that jam our theaters between June and September—a music video filmed by capitalism and edited by us. Pizza promos plummeting down from the sky, hypodermic needles hiding in Pepsi cans, a salmonella outbreak at a Syracuse Taco Bell—PepsiCo products are the battered foot soldiers in the war for our wallets. The bigger the ploys, the harder they fall: The 75-foot high Times Square blow-up of Arnold Schwarzenegger for *Last Action Hero* had to relinquish its dynamite because the World Trade Center blew; then the rocket that was going to streak *Hero* across the sky couldn't get off the ground. (As a final insult the movie itself bombed.) And now the mile-long inflatable billboard that would orbit Earth flashing moon-sized logos is in jeopardy—it might be shot down by no-fun congresspersons wielding a bill that would ban ads in outer space.

But the blimp—its shape, really—is the star of this year's video: blimp, big limp, semitumescent, soft and hard; blimps are bosoms and phalluses and wombs all blown into one, the ripest of pop (and popable) objects, linked now in history with the Ur male food, pizza.

"We had record sales last week—phenomenal sales," says Pizza Hut spokesman Rob Doughty in Wichita (not my delivery man). He admits it was the blimp—adds, in fact, that "the pizza and the blimp had the same types of images attached to them: big, fun, friendly"—but says that Hut's new Bigfoot pizza has racked up double-digit sales increases since its introduction this spring. Bigfoot's not only bigger than a regular pie—two feet by one foot, 21 slices—but since it's rectangular you can fit more dough into the box. PH created Bigfoot because research divulged that its regular pies weren't big enough "to feed the Little League or fraternities or a bunch of teenagers roaming around without much money." I.e., Bigfoot is "male skewed." Pizza's always been the chow for sweaty good-natured oafishness; pizza makes yuppie men feel working-class and working men feel like they have a seat at the deliverable feast that is the American dream.

Indeed, each TV spot in the $60 million Bigfoot campaign shows guy after guy, some with blimp bellies, stretching their arms wide and crowing, "It was big! It was just *big!*" Out of a dozen dudes only one woman, a quiet hefty one, actually speaks and then only to say, "I can handle it." Handle the calories? The cholesterol? Or the Big Pepperoni? Big feet—we all know what they stand for!

In terms of product catastrophes, maybe the real Fourth of July disaster that was averted was not a latter-day Hindenburg, but a drop in Pepsi sales. As *Ad Age*'s lead story explained, "With July Fourth, the height of the summer selling season, just around the corner, and new Diet Pepsi spots featuring the 'Uh-huh' girls set to break, [the hypodermic needle scare] could have devastated the No. 2 cola marketer. But Pepsi dodged the bullet." The news that the needles were a hoax, the FDA chief's support, and ads in 200 newspapers all helped.

But Pepsi's less heralded tactic was to convert the network TV ad dollars for all its soda brands into just one spot—the Shaq O'Neal ad where a little boy refuses to give him his Pepsi and warns the big guy, "Don't even think about it." A seemingly innocuous spot suddenly functioned as a "make my day" warning to tamperers and naysayers alike. " 'Don't even think about it' really summed up our feelings and all Americans',"says Pepsi spokesman Andrew Giangola.

It's unattractive to see a line from an ad stand for all Americans' opinion, but unfortunately that may be the case, as a potential disaster again turns into a minor windfall. "One week after the scare," Giangola says, "consumers bought more Pepsi than the week before the scare."

Newsweek linked the hypodermic hoax with "America's long fascination with get-rich-quick litigation—and the new vogue for victim chic." But a desire to defile our shiny, perfect objects with threatening or disgusting objects (a crack vial, a bullet, and "mysterious brown goo" were also alleged to have been found in the cans) is inevitable. Disgusting objects, or even rumors of them, are talismans to ward off the totality of "good" objects' power. They are attempts to de-sell, however crudely, to let the air out, to puncture the balloon, a shopping-cart level deconstruction.

Meanwhile, at my own kitchen counter I glimpsed the makings of another product disaster. Squeaking out from the label on the back of a bottle of Dove dish soap were the tiny words "Please Help!" For a moment, I thought a factory worker driven mad by routine might have stuck the message on the bottle. Or maybe, projecting as I tend to do, I imagined it. But no, they were Dove's words, something about recycling the plastic. *Please Help!* It's a sign.

July 27, 1993

Index

ABC network, 183, 285
Abortion, 219–223
Absolut Vodka, 105, 153, 317–318
Action for Corporate Accountability, 123
Acura, 274
Ad Age
  baby boomers/Generation X, 274
  green marketing, 159–160
  patriotism, 264
  Print Campaign of the Decade, 140
  product disasters, 339
  recession, 172
  riot control, 266
  VCR Voice, 331
  war ads, 155
Adbusters, 152
Ad Council, 266
Addiction maintained through commer-
  cialism, 13, 150
Addicts/dealers as others, 251, 252
Adidas, 282, 287
Ad industry, debate within, 227, 311–313
Adolescence, 105
Adoption, 222
Ads Against AIDS (AAA), 259
Adweek, 113, 170, 212
AFL-CIO, 239
African-Americans
  alcohol issue, 318
  Apple computers, 80
  conservative, 215
  Coors, 283
  drug ads, 248–250
  mascots, ad, 82
  models in magazine ads, 63
  used as plot devices, 234–235

stereotypes, abstract/ambiguous,
  252–255
Age politics, 8
Aging, fear of, 206–209
AIDS
  Benetton, 269, 270–271
  big business reaction to, 262
  condom ads, 259–260
  Du Pont, 118
  ghettoizing, 261
  guerrilla advertising, 319
  Ogilvy & Mather, 125–126
Airline industry, 67, 75–76, 144
Aisner, Mike, 288–289
Alcohol, 36–37, 63, 92–93, 152, 251–
  252. *See also* Absolut Vodka; Beer
Allstate, 300, 301
Altschiller Reitzfeld (ad agency), 227
Amaretto Di Sarono, 285
Ambivalence towards consumerism, 28,
  30
American Academy of Pediatrics, 291
American Airlines, 67
American Cyanamid, 120, 121
American Express
  celebrity ads, 140–142
  counterads, 317
  credit cards, 110–111
  logos, 19
  Olympics, 93
  tie-ins, 279
  titles, 41
American Home Products, 124
American National Standards Institute,
  21
American Portrait Films, 220

Amoco, 284
Amurol, 256
Anderson, Laurie, 27–29
Anglo-American Corporation, 237
Anheuser-Busch, 156
Anti-ad ads, 149–152, 289–293,
    316–319
Antidiarrhetic ads, 197–198
Antiviolence ads, 266–268
Antonow, Melissa, 150
Apartheid, 236–237
Apocalyptic fantasies, 310
Apparel industry, 211–212, 225
Apple computers, 79–80, 175, 195, 316
Aramis, 36
Art and guerrilla advertising, 318– 319
Artfux collective, 318–319
Arthur S. De Moss Foundation, 221, 326
Artificiality, 219
ASICS, 55, 56
AT&T
    anxiety highlighted, 96
    communism's fall, 138, 140
    competition with MCI/Sprint, 97–99
    credit cards, 106, 107
    disaster ads, 300
    fear used by, 85–87
    spirituality, 309, 336
Australia, 292
Authentic rebellion, 56–57
Authority and voiceovers, 187
Automobiles
    bigoted ads, 233
    credit cards, 106–111
    Generation X, 274
    go-away-guilt ads, 225
    Japan bashing, 263–264
    lies in advertising, 26, 99–102
    listless is more, 45
    minority actors, 235–236
    nature visuals, 59
    off-road vehicles, 176–179
    patriotism used to sell, 70, 78–79
    penis, alluding to the, 228–230
    recession, 174
    safety measures, 127
    spirituality, 333–334
    transcendental qualities, 52–54
    war ads, 158
Avant-garde selling, 27–29
Avedon, Richard, 23
Avis, 109

Baby boomers, 6, 236, 272–275, 286
Background for ads, 32–35
Bailey, Mike, 219–220
Bankcard Holders of America (consumer
    group), 110
Banning/restricting cigarette/liquor ads,
    151–152
Barber of Seville, The (Rossini), 37
Barbie doll look, 185
Batteries, 302–305
BBDO (ad agency), 56, 167, 326
Beatles, 282
Beer
    homosexuality, 233–234
    mascots, ad, 82
    opposite notions pushed, 94–96
    patriotism, 156
    reputations, bad/stale, 238–239
    sexist ads, 173, 213
    simplistic ads, 43–46
    titles, 42
Bell-Textron, 133
Benetton, 254–255, 269–272
Ben & Jerry's, 120
Berlin Wall, 136–139
Better Business Bureau, 102
Big business
    AIDS, 262
    alcohol, opposite notions about, 94–96
    competition between firms, 96–99,
        111–114, 303–305
    corporate sensuality, 314–316
    credit cards, 106–111
    defense ads, 73–77
    fears played on by, 85–87
    financial psychoservices, 69
    goodness and warmth projected by,
        11–12, 71–72, 87–89
    identity market, 19–22
    image makeover, 83–85
    lies in advertising, 99–102
    mascots, 80–82
    nature visuals, 89–91
    patriotism used by, 70, 78–79
    responsible companies, 120
    rock and roll sponsored by, 281–289,
        294–298
    sexual symbols, 103–106
    socially conscious, 238
    spirituality, 77–78
    tie-ins, 91–93
    touchy-feely ads, 72–73
    war imagery, 67

Bigoted ads, 233
Bikinis, 184–185
Biodegradable products, 203–205
Birth defects, 166
BK Double Sandwich, 299
Black and white ads, 25
Black Enterprise, 318
Black people. *See* African-Americans
Blind Date, 279
Blurring relationship between consumer
    and commercial, 289–290,
    302–305
Bobbitt, Lorena, 228
Bodyslimmers lingerie, 226
Boeing, 156–157, 164–165
Bolla wine, 36
Bon Ami, 189–191
Bookend ads, 49–51
Boorstin, Daniel, 308
Boosler, Elaine, 225
Bossis, Peter, 52, 53
Bounce, 195
Bowie, David, 284
Boxed In (Miller), 6
Boycott, Charles C., 131
Boycotts
    Coors, 238–239, 283
    GE, 107, 155, 167
    Nestlé, 120, 122–126
    rising numbers of, 130–132
    Star Kist, 155
Brand equity, 7–8
British Airways, 36, 76, 144, 309
British business empire, 300
British Knights, 56
British-takeoff ads, 241
Brown, Tina, 269–270
B-2 Stealth, 133–134
Bubble tape, 256–258
Bucci, Jon, 62–63
Budweiser, 173
Bugle Boy, 45, 173
Burger King, 299–300
Burrell, Thomas, 248–249
Bush, George, 38, 39, 199, 200, 203, 246,
    250, 310
Butts, Calvin, 318
Buzz, 297
Buzzworm, 159

Cabaret culture, 81
Calvin Klein, 23–24, 185
Camel, 103, 106, 173

Campbell, 120
Cap Cities/ABC, 250
Cappo, Joe, 159–160
Carnation, 125–126
Carter-Wallace, 259
Casselman, Carl, 198, 199
Catholicism, 296
CBS network, 130, 183, 233–234, 247,
    274
Celebrity ads, 140–142, 216–219, 261,
    294–298
Center for Media and Public Affairs, 241
Center for Science in the Public Interest
    (CSPI), 169
Center for the Study of Commercialism, 4
Century's End (Schwartz), 308
Cereals, 45, 242–243
Chanel, 36, 191–193, 209–211
Channel One, 122, 124–125
Chaplin, Charlie, 315–316
Chemical industry, 68, 77, 117–119,
    129, 159
Chenault, Kenneth, 141, 142
Cher, 216–219
Chermayeff & Geismar (ad agency), 21
Chernobyl, 77, 166
Chess King, 285
Chevrolet, 78–79, 285
Chiat/Day (ad agency), 28, 83, 84, 303
Children, 105, 151, 173, 256–258
Chlorofluorocarbons (CFCs), 118–119,
    127, 129, 153–154
Christian Brothers, 284
Christian Leaders for Responsible Televi-
    sion, 131
Chrysler, 70, 178, 274
Chung Ju Yung, 230
Cigarettes, 5–6, 103–106, 149–152, 173,
    252, 331
Citibank, 71, 142
Citizens for Racial Harmony, 267
Clairol, 184, 224, 226
Clannad, 333, 334
Class aesthetic/attitude, 8, 229–230, 244,
    246
Classical music, 37
Cleaning up images, 18–19
Cleanliness and womanhood, 189–191,
    195
Clichés, 327–328
Clinton, Bill, 108
Clorox, 120
Close Encounters of the Third Kind, 334

CNN, 156, 221
Coalition Against Media/Marketing Prejudice, 242
Coalition for a Smoke-Free City, 150
Coca-Cola
  communism's fall, 149
  competition within soda industry, 111–114
  global advertising, 143
  Hands Across America campaign, 71
  identity-seeking, 19
  mass words, 327
  rock and roll sponsorship, 285, 294, 297
  spirituality, 309
  tie-ins, 279–281
  war ads, 156
Cocaine, 248, 249, 251
Coleman, Jay, 284, 288
College coaches, 55
Cologne, men's, 209–211
Colors, 272
Colquhoun, John, 34
Commercials, television. *See also* Big business; Controversial national/international issues; Otherness; Style, aesthetics, and technique in advertising; Women and advertising
  commercials which aren't commercials, 279–281
  cool, 6–7
  excitement and resolution, 5
  interactive, 2–3
  seduction of the soul, 10–11
  statistics about, 1
Committee To Defend Reproductive Rights, 101
Communism's fall, 136–139, 146–149, 308
Competition between firms, 96–99, 111–114, 303–305
Computers, 67, 79–80, 175, 316
Condom ads, 259–261
Congress, U.S., 133–135, 152, 169, 237, 307
Conoco, 154
Constipation, 197, 268–269
Consumer confidence, 107
Consumer guides, 119–121
Consumer Reports, 189
Contac, 75
Control of ads, 9–10, 48

Controversial ads, 254–255, 269–272
Controversial national/international issues, 12
  boycotts, 130–132
  celebrity ads, 140–142
  cigarettes, 149–152
  communism's fall, 136–139, 146–149
  consumer guides, 119–121
  disability awareness, 117–118
  global advertising, 143–146
  green ads, 152–155, 159–161
  infant formula, 122–126
  integrity within ad business, 311–313
  leftist advertising, 165–168
  misleading ads, 168–171
  off-road vehicles, 176–179
  recession, 171–175
  social realism, 127–129
  war ads, 155–158, 161–165
  weapons systems, 133–136
Converse, 57, 261, 284
Cool advertising, 6–7, 29–31, 327–328
Coolers, 92–93
Coors, 130, 238–239, 281–285
Coors, Jeffrey, 238, 239
Coors, Joe, 238, 239, 282–283
Coors, Peter, 238
Coors, William, 283
Corona, 43–44
Corporate identity market, 19–22. *See also* Big business
Corsets, 186
Cosmetic ads, 206–209
Cotton Inc., 337
Couch potatoes, 291–293
Council on Economic Priorities, 119–121
Counterads, 149–152, 289–293, 316–319
Cover Girl, 323
Crack cocaine, 249
Creative Artists Agency (CAA), 111–114
Credit, nature of, 310
Credit Card News, 106
Credit cards, 106–111, 142
Crisis calls for commercials, 75–77, 266–269, 310
Crotch area and swimsuits, 184–186
Cruise lines, 252
Culture *vs.* product, 7
Cunningham, B. J., 331
Cutting through the clutter, 43–46

D'Arcy Masius Benton & Bowles (ad agency), 72

344 *Index*

Data General, 67
Deadly Deception, 166–168
Death cigarettes, 331
DeBeers, 236–237, 288
Deceptive ads, 168–171
Defense ads, 73–77
Defense contracts, 133–135, 316
Demagoguery, 212–216
Desert Storm, 156, 157, 163–164
Deutsch, Donny, 263
Diamonds, 236–237
Diapers, 197
Diarrhea, 240–241
Dioxins, 205
Dirty Dancing, 193
Disability awareness, 117–118
Disaster ads, 13, 299–302
Disasters, product, 338–340
Discoveries Underwater, 153
Disney, 60, 158
Distancing yourself from ads, 7–11
Diva, 35
Diversity, homogenization of, 145
Divert and launch aspect of defense ads, 75
Dockers, 200–203
Dodge, 158, 235–236
Doig, John, 86–87
Donaldson, Sam, 308
Do the Right Thing, 38
Dow Chemical, 68, 77, 159
Downy, 195
Dress, sponsored, 3
Drexel Burnham, 14, 83–85
Drug wars, 246–252
Dunkin Donuts, 168
Du Pont, 117–119, 127–129, 153–154, 159, 172
Duracell, 304
Dusenberry, Phil, 167, 221, 326

E. F. Hutton, 68, 74, 77, 335
Earth Day, 203
Earthquakes, 301
Eastman Kodak, 120
Ecuador, 154
Education, U.S. Dept. of, 152
Egoiste, 209–211
Elizabeth Arden, 309
El Salvador, 294
Empowerment ads, 223–228
Energizer Bunny, 302–305
Energy, U.S. Depart. of, 166

Energy Awareness, U.S. Committee for, 77
English, Ron, 318
Entertainment Weekly, 272
Environmental Billboard, 331–332
Environmental pitches, 145, 152–155, 159–161, 203–206
Environmental Protection Agency (EPA), 88
Enya, 333–334
Equal, 218–219
Equations, sponsored, 4
Equity between brands, 7–8
Estée Lauder, 207, 208
Ethical/moral choices, 38–40
Ethnic stereotypes, 239–241
Europe, Eastern, 136–139, 146
Eveready, 302–305
Excedrin, 49–50, 75
Excitement and resolution, 5
Ex-Lax, 197, 268–269
Expectations, extravagant, 308–310
Experience sold back to you, 3
Explicitness in personal care products, 196–198

F-14, 133
Facial moisturizers, 206–209
Fairness Doctrine, 151
Faith of Graffiti, The (Mailer), 20
Fallon McElligott (ad agency), 245, 246
Family values, 198–200
Fantastic, 225
Farberware, 309
Fat content in foods, 168–170
Faux walls, 33–34
Fears, playing on, 85–87
Fears & Fantasies of the American Consumer, 72
Federal Trade Commission (FTC), 102, 151, 160, 161, 169, 171
Feel-good ads
  Coca-Cola, 71
  defense contractors, 135
  Dow Chemical, 68
  friendship, 72–73
  GE, 88–89
  global advertising, 143–146
  GM, 109
  goodness and warmth projected by, 11–12
  Merrill Lynch, 87–88
  Nestlé, 122

Feminine hygiene products, 183, 196, 203–206
Fendi, 187–189
Fetuses, use in ads, 101
Fido Dido (ad mascot), 257–258
15-second ads, 50–51
Financial services, 67, 69, 74, 77–78, 138, 324
Firestone, 74
First Amendment rights, 150, 151
First-worlders, identifying with, 243–246
501 campaigns, 46–47, 48, 275
Flattery, 10
Fleischmann, 169
Florida Department of Citrus, 168
Food and Drug Administration (FDA), 170, 207, 208
Food products
  disaster ads, 299–300
  gals concept, 194–195
  guilt-and-fear ads, 225
  infant formula, 122–126
  misleading ads, 168–170
  sky symbology, 59
  tampering troubles, 76
Foot Locker, 323
Ford, 274
Forest Service, U.S., 178
Fox TV, 259, 261, 292–293, 297
Free Congress Foundation, 239
Freedom of Information Act, 166
Friendship, 48, 72–73
Friends of the Earth, 159
Frustration theme in ads, 245
FYI channel, 1

Gals theme, 193–196
Garfield, Bob, 160, 230
Gay baiting, 233–234, 242–243
Gay Men's Health Crisis, 239
Geers Gross (ad agency), 233
Geismar, Thomas, 21
General Electric (GE), 14
  boycotts, 107, 155, 167
  communism's fall, 146–148, 149, 308
  credit cards, 107–111
  green ads, 159
  ignoring past problems, 76, 88–89
  leftist advertising, 165–168
  worldview pushed by, 8
General Foods, 131
General Mills, 120

General Motors (GM), 106–111, 157–158
Generation X, 6, 272–275
Generic individualism, 13, 258
Genesis, 286
Georgia-Pacific, 328
Gerber, 76
Gibbons, Barry, 299–300
Gillmore, Dick, 176, 178
Giorgio Brutini shoes, 273
Give-aways, 92–93, 123, 125
Global advertising, 143–146, 294–298, 332
GMAC (financial services), 324
Go-away-guilt (GAG) ads, 223–225
Gonzalez-Torres, Felix, 319
Good Housekeeping, 143, 198–200
Goodyear, 42
Gorbachev, Mikhail, 140–142
Goude, Jean-Paul, 209
Government use of Helvetica, 21–22
Gravelly voices for voiceovers, 187
Greece, 75–76
Green, Mark, 105, 171
Green ads, 145, 152–155, 159–161, 203–206
Greenpeace, 129, 153–154, 154
Green Seal, 160, 161
Groening, Matt, 327
Grossman, Robert, 331
Gruen, John, 63, 64
Grumman, 133–134
Grunge-art-directed campaigns, 273–275
Guerrilla advertising, 318–319
Guess jeans, 25, 29–31, 36, 131
Guidotti, Bruce, 38–39
Guiliani, Rudolph, 84–85
Guilt-and-fear (GAF) ads, 223–225
Guilt and household cleanliness, 189–191
Gulf War, 156, 157, 163–164, 167

Hair care, 216–219, 224, 226
Hamilton, Bill, 28
Hands Across American campaign, 71
Hanford Nuclear Reservation, 166
Hard Truth, 220
Hatch, Orrin, 39
Hayes, Denis, 159
Heater, Bill, 52
Heaven ads, 57–61, 332–333
Hedrick, Tom, 248, 249, 251
Helvetica typeface, 17–22, 314
Heritage Foundation, 283

Heroism, 128
HHCC (ad agency), 56
Hill, Anita, 213–215
Hilton hotels, 67
Hip exposure in swimsuits, 184–185
Hispanic-take off ads, 239–241
Hocevar, John, 220
Holdsworth, Sam, 298
Hollywood Shuffle, 241
Homogenization of diversity, 145
Homosexuality, 233–234, 239, 242–243
Honda, 178, 274, 285
Honesty in advertising, 77, 331
Hotels, 67, 109
Household Credit Services, 109
Huaorani Indians (Ecuador), 154
Hudson, Hugh, 145
Hugo, Hurricane, 299–301
Humor, 202
Hungary, 308
Hydro compounds, 154
Hyundai, 228–230

Iacocca, Lee, 70
IBM, 175, 315–316
Ichan, Carl, 83
Identity market, corporate, 19–22
Impatience, 310
Improvisational wisdom, 194
Incentive advertising, 76
Individualism
    children, 256–258
    disaster ads, 299
    generic, 13, 258
    hair care, 224
    rugged, 177, 179
    selling, 8–9, 49
Indonesia, 294
INFACT (watchdog group), 88, 89, 107,
    148, 165, 166, 168
Infant formula, 122–126
Infiniti, 52–54
Infomercials, 216–219, 305–307
Injustice/poverty, 266–269
Insurance companies, 300–301
Integrity within ad business, 311–313
Interactive commercials, 2–3, 49–51
Interest rates on credit cards, 110
Interfaith Center on Corporate Responsi-
    bility, 316
International Organization for Standard-
    ization, 21
Interracial mixing, 296

Interview, 153
Irony, 6–7
Isuzu, 26–27, 150, 176–178, 274

Jackson, Jesse, 38
Jackson, Michael, 4, 294
Jackson, Thad, 123, 124
Jackson, Victoria, 305
Jacobson, Michael, 170
Jagger, Mick, 5–6
Jailbait look, 185
Japan bashing, 233, 262–265
Jeans
    age politics, 8
    black and white ads, 25
    cool ads, 29–31
    first-worlders, identifying with,
        243–246
    pride of place, 46–47, 48, 275
    sexist ads, 173
    simplistic ads, 45
Jennings, Peter, 268, 323
Jett, Joan, 285
Jewelry, 236–237, 288
Jobs, Steven, 80
Jockstrap, female, 185
Joe Smooth (ad mascot), 12, 173, 175
John Hancock, 42, 52, 69
Johnny Walker, 131
Johnson, Magic, 259–262
Johnston, Arthur, 242
Jones, James Earl, 142, 261
Jordache, 173–174, 245, 289–290
Jordan, Barbara, 141
Jordan, McGrath, Case & Taylor (ad
    agency), 198
Jovan, 192
Judaism, 335
Junk bonds, 83–85

Kacik, Walter, 18–19, 20, 22
Kaopectate, 239–241
Kasich, John, 135
Kawasaki, 178
Kean, Tom, 38
Kellogg's, 45, 242–243
Kentucky Fried Chicken (KFC), 59,
    148–149
Keough, Donald, 114
Kessler, David, 170
Key, Wilson B., 61
Keye, Paul, 150, 151
Kinney Shoes, 284

Klein, Marty, 281
Knight Commission, 55
Knolls Atomic Power Labeling guidelines, 166
Koop, C. Everett, 94, 259
Kotex, 196

L.A. Gear, 55–56
L.A. riots, 266–268
Labeling issues, 160, 168–171, 207
Lacey, Mary Beth, 194–195
Lasn, Kalle, 317
Last Action Hero, 338–339
Lean Cuisine, 169
Lee, Spike, 38, 259, 268, 271
Lee jeans, 8, 243–246
Leftist advertising, 165–168
L'eggs, 159
Leibovitz, Annie, 142
Leo Burnett (ad agency), 258
Letterman, David, 3
Lever Bros., 161
Levine, Rick, 118
Levi's, 46, 103, 200–203
Lies in advertising, 7, 26–27, 99–102
Life. Be In It. USA, 292
Life of Brian, 8
Lifestyle lifestyle, the, 31–32
LifeStyles, 259
Lighting systems, 146–148
Limbaugh, Rush, 226, 229
Lippincott and Margulies (marketing firm), 19–20
Listless is more, 43–46
Local place, pride in, 46–49
Logos, 17, 19, 71, 269–272
Lori Davis Hair Care, 216–219
Love, Ross, 249
Luvs, 197
Lycra, 227
Lyne, Adrian, 192

Mac Tonight (ad mascot), 81–82
Madonna, 4, 14, 131, 226, 294–298
Madris, Ira, 78
Magnavox, 320
Magritte, René-Francois-Ghislain, 60
Maidenform, 211–212, 225
Malcolm X, 269, 271
Male bonding, 200–203
Malkin, Patricia, 60
Mantell, Janice, 123
March of Dimes, 126

Marciano, Paul, 30
Margaritas, John, 124
Marijuana, 250–251
Marketing Through Music, 14, 282, 284, 288
Market research
    crisis management, 76
    individualism, 9
    pride of place, 47
    technological advances, 2–3
    touchy-feely ads, 72–73
    VALS, 53
Marlboro, 7, 103, 149–150, 331
Marlin, Alice T., 120
Marriage of Figaro, The (Mozart), 37
Married..With Children, 131, 201–202
Marriott Hotels, 109
Martin, Steve, 279–281
Martin Davis & OMON (ad agency), 113
Mascots, ad
    Camel, 103–106, 151, 173, 175
    Fido Dido, 257–258
    IBM, 315–316
    monitors as, 323–324
    unassailable versions of companies, 12, 80–82
Mass words, 325–328
Mastercard, 77, 103
Materialism, 5, 6, 14
Max Factor, 309
Maxwell House, 131, 335
Mazda, 53
McCann-Erickson (ad agency), 111–113
McDonald's
    KFC competing with, 148–149
    Mac Tonight, 81–82
    nostalgia, contemporary, 47–48
    Olympics, 92
    rock and roll sponsorship, 285
    television programming in restaurants, 174
    titles, 41
    war ads, 157–158
McFeatters, Susan, 334
MCI, 87, 98, 109, 324–325
McLuhan, Marshall, 10
Media analysis of advertising, 4, 155, 167–168
Media mirror, 322
Media Watch, 131
Megaconnections, 280
Men protesting penis ads, 228–229
Mercury, 305

Merkley, Parry, 142
Merrill Lynch, 67, 77, 87–88
Merry-Go-Round, 274
Messner Vetere Berger Carey Schmetterer
    (ad agency), 265
Michelob, 42, 235, 285, 286
Middle-American acceptance of urban
    nightlife, 81–82
Middle-management, fears of, 85–87
Milken, Michael, 83–84
Millennium milkers, 308–310
Miller, 82, 94–96, 284
Mingo (ad agency), 266
Minorities. See Race
Misleading ads, 168–171
Mission, The, 335
Mitsubishi, 331
Moakley, Joe, 169, 170
Mobil, 159
Molter, Jeff, 291
Monitors and TVTV ads, 322–325
Moral/ethical choices, 38–40, 198–200
Moral Mission boycotts, 120–131
Morricone, Ennio, 335
Morrissey, Mike, 320, 323
Mothers in sneaker ads, 56
Movies and tie-ins, 1–2, 13, 279–281
Moyers, Bill, 55
MTV, 1, 24, 43, 275
Muratore, Ron, 106, 109
Murdoch, Rupert, 293
Museums, 2
Music videos, 41, 280, 288

Nabisco, 194–195
Nader, Ralph, 292
Nasdaq, 265
National Abortion Rights Action League
    (NARAL), 222–223
National Boycott News, 130, 132, 155
National Food Processors Association,
    160
National Gay and Lesbian Task Force,
    243
National Hispanic Media Coalition, 240
National Institute of Justice, 243
National Institute on Drug Abuse, 259
National Organization of Men, 228
National Right to Life Committee, 131
Natural Resources Defense Council, 119
Nature/nature questions about ads, 9–10
Nature visuals, 57–61, 89–91, 152–154,
    333, 334

Naugles, 241
NBC network, 17, 23, 155, 167–168,
    183, 291–292
Needs created and maintained through
    commercialism, 13
Nelson, Bruce, 78
Nestlé boycott, 14, 120, 122–126
New Balance, 265
New Jersey beer market, 238
Newman, Paul, 120, 140, 297
New paradigm of advertising, 112
Newsweek, 48, 175, 340
New Traditionalism, 43, 148, 313
New York beer market, 238
New Yorker, The, 269
New York's Metropolitan Transportation
    Authority (MTA), 20
New York Times, 250
New York Times Magazine, 33, 202
Nike, 55, 56, 225, 268, 275
Nissan, 45, 52–54, 301
Noonan, Peggy, 214–215
North, Oliver, 39, 282
Northrop, 133–136
Nuclear Power: In France It Works, 168
Nuclear power/weapons
    Chernobyl, 77, 166
    Du Pont, 118, 129
    GE, 88–89, 107, 146, 165–166
Nut & Honey Crunch cereal, 242–243
NutraSweet, 90, 91
Nutrition Labeling and Education Act
    (NLEA), 169–170
N.W.A. (rap music), 266
NYNEX telecommunications, 35, 162–
    165, 267–268
Nyquil, 226

Obsession perfume, 23–24
Off-road vehicles (ORVs), 176–179
Ogilvy & Mather (ad agency), 122, 125–
    126, 142, 172
Oil of Olay, 206–209
Old Milwaukee, 173, 213
Olympic Games, 91–93
On Being Blue (Gass), 60
Opera, 35–37
Orkin pest control, 2
Otherness, 12–13
    drugs, 246–252
    first-worlders, identifying with,
        243–246
    Generation X, 272–275

Otherness (cont.)
  Hispanic-take off ads, 239–241
  homosexuality, 233–234, 242–243
  individualism, 256–258
  injustice/poverty, 266–269
  Japan bashing, 262–265
  logos, 269–272
  minority actors, 234–236
  safe-sex ads, 259–262
  stereotypes, abstract/ambiguous,
    252–255
Outrageous Event boycott, 130
Ovitz, Michael, 111, 112
Ozone depletion, 153–154

Pain relief, 49–50
Pampers, 197
Pan Am, 76
Pants, 200–203
Parody ads, 62–64, 302–305
Partnership for a Drug-Free America,
    246–252, 266, 333
Pastoral pitch, 89–91
Patriotism, 312
  abortion, 222–223
  buying as an act of, 171
  Chevrolet, 78–79
  Chrysler, 70
  Japan bashing, 262–265
  war ads, 155–158
Pay inequalities and gender, 186
Payne, Maura, 103–104
Peeler, Lee, 170
Penis, alluding to the, 228–230
Pepsi
  communism's fall, 136, 137, 140
  Fido Dido, 257–258
  hypodermic needle scare, 339
  Madonna, 14, 131, 294–298
  Magic Johnson, 261–262
  mass words, 325–326
  rock and roll sponsorship, 284
  Shaq O'Neal, 340
  spirituality, 332
PepsiCo, 149
Perelman, Ron, 83
Perfume, 208
  communism's fall, 136–139
  men's, 209–211
  Obsession, 23–24
  opera, 36
  selfishness touted, 187–189
  wild boys, 191–193

Perot, Ross, 107, 320
Perrier, 89–91
Personal care products, 183, 196–198,
    203–206
Pfleger, Michael, 318
Pharmaceuticals, 239–241
Philip Morris, 159, 331
Philippines, 123
Piggyback ads, 51, 140
Pinellas Nuclear Weapons Plant, 167
Pizza Hut, 338, 339
Planned Parenthood, 222, 223
Playtex, 196, 205–206
Poelvoorde, Ray, 20
Poetry, 226–227
Polaroid, 120
Political side of advertising, 8
Polluters' PBS Penance, 153
Pollution, 129, 153, 154, 165, 166, 305
Pontiac, 56, 263
Powerful women, 225–226
Power suits as swimsuits, 185–186
Prejudice maintained through commer-
    cialism, 13
Pride of place, 46–49
Print ads
  background for, 33
  blacks as models, 63
  celebrity ads, 140–142
  empowerment for women, 225
  Helvetica typeface, 17–22
  Rush Limbaugh, 226
  Toyota, 264–265
Private labels/store brands, 331
Procrastination, 310
Procter & Gamble, 119
  consumer guides, 120
  diapers, 197
  environmental issues, 160, 161
  FDA, 170
  gals theme, 195
  secrecy/security measures, 315
  war ads, 157
Product disasters, 338–340
Provocative ads, 254–255, 269–272
PSAs about excessive television watching,
    291–293
Public lands, erosion of, 177–178
Pulham, Elliot, 157
Pulse of the Planet, 153
PUSH, 130
Putnam, Todd, 130, 155

Quaker Oats, 38–39, 120
Quintessence fragrances, 136–139

R. J. Reynolds, 103–106, 173
Raboy, Doug, 267
Race, 130, 239–241, 244
  alcohol issue, 318
  Apple computers, 80
  Carnation, 126
  Coors, 283
  crisis calls for commercials, 266–269
  drug ads, 248–249
  mascots in ads, 82
  narrow definitions of, 215
  as plot device, 234–236
  stereotypes, abstract/ambiguous,
    252–255
  war ads, 158
Radiation, 166
Rakolta, Terry, 131, 201
Ramses condoms, 261
Range Rover, 251–255
Rap music, 249, 266
Rating America's Corporate Conscience,
  119
RC Cola, 139
Reagan, Ronald, 87, 102, 135, 147, 301,
  306
Rebates, 108–110
Rebellion ads, 177–179, 235
Recession, 113, 171–175
Recontextualization of the image,
  270–271
Recycling, 160
Red Cross, 299, 301
Reebok, 225–226, 226
Regan, Donald, 236
Regulating frequency/rhythm of commer-
  cials, 51
Religious images, 335, 336–337
Renteria, Esther, 240, 241
Reputations, bad/stale
  Coors, 238–239, 282–283
  defense ads, 73–77
  Dow Chemical, 68
  Rolling Stone, 282–283
Rescue, The (Millais), 128
Resolution and excitement, 5
Responsible companies, 120
Revlon, 207
Revolution, 297
Rheins, Dave, 284
Right and boycotts, the, 131–132

Riney, Hal, 90, 108, 174, 212–213, 335,
  336
Riots, 266–268
Ritts, Herb, 218
Robinson, David, 333
Rock and roll sponsored by corporations,
  281–289, 294–298
Rockbill, 284
Rolling Stone, 246, 271, 281–285, 296,
  297
Rolling Stones, 6
Roxanne, 279–281
Ru$_4$86 abortion technique, 221
Run-D.M.C., 282, 287
Russia, 139, 148–149, 294, 319

Saatchi & Saatchi (ad agency), 145, 146,
  209
Safe-sex ads, 259–262
Sanitary products, 183, 196, 203–206
Sans serif typeface, 18–19
Sara Lee, 284–285
Saturn, 174, 274, 312
Savannah River Plant, 129
Sawyer/Miller Group (political consul-
  tants), 162, 164
Scalfone, Jim, 336
Scenic America, 159
Schaefer, Leslye, 32
Schafer, Jacqueline, 243
Schmidt's beer, 233
Schroeder, Pat, 133, 134, 135
Schuetz, Gary, 256, 257
Schwarzkopf, Norman, 158
Scorsese, Martin, 259
Scott Paper, 120
Sculley, John, 80
Seagram, 63, 92–93, 105
Sease, Debbie, 178
Secrecy/security measures, 315
Securities and Exchange Commission
  (SEC), 77
Seduction, 3, 10
Seinfeld, Jerry, 110–111
Selfishness touted through perfume,
  187–189
Serifs, 18
7-Up, 258
Sexist ads, 131, 173
Sexual harassment, 213–215
Sexual/nonsexual people, 245
Sexual symbols, 103–106, 201–202
Shame in abortion issue, 221–222

Shearson Lehman, 77–78, 136, 138–139
Shell, 131
Shopping for a Better World, 119–121
Sierra Club, 178
Signs, Helvetica, 17–22
Silent movies, 42
Simmons, Richard, 305, 306
Simplicity in ads, 43–46
Sittin'-around-talkingism, 202
60 Minutes, 130
Sky symbology, 57–61, 332–333
Slater, Ford, 166
Slice soda, 257–258
Slowing down advertising, 329–332
SMA Visual Effects Corporation, 320
Smith, Mandy, 29
Smith/Greenland (ad agency), 267
Smithsonian Museum, 2
Smucker's, 90
Sneakers, 54–57
Snobbery in ads, 243–246
Social censureship, 251
Social change, marketing, 198–200, 271–
    272, 289–290
Social Injustice boycott, 130
Social realism, 127–129
Socolof, Danny, 287
Sodas. *See* Coca-Cola; Pepsi
Sonya, 333, 337
Soul, seducing the, 3, 10
South Africa, 120, 126, 131, 145–146,
    236–237, 316
Southern Bell, 324
Southern Comfort, 273
Space, advertising in, 332, 339
Speakes, Larry, 87
Speech, sponsored, 3
Spence, Roy, 161
Spirituality, 13, 332–337
    big-product wars, 114
    credit cards, 108–109
    financial services, 77–78
    millennium milkers, 309
    nature visuals, 57–61
Spoofs, subliminal, 62–64
Sprint, 97–98
Spuds, 82
Standardization of symbol signs, 21–22
Star Kist, 152–153, 155
Starr, Bob, 261
Statistics on ads, 1
Stay Tuned, 322
Stereotypes, 239–241, 252–255

Stewart, Jimmy, 74
Stimuli, mass-produced, 3
Stock exchange, 265
Stop Teenage Addiction to Tobacco
    (STAT), 105
Stop the Madness campaign, 247
Store brands/private labels, 331
Stouffer, 169
Style, aesthetics, and technique in adver-
    tising
    anti-ads, 289–293, 316–319
    avant-garde selling, 27–29
    background for ads, 32–35
    black and white ads, 25
    Calvin Klein, 23–24
    cool advertising, 29–31
    ethical/moral choices, 38–40
    Helvetica typeface, 17–22
    infomercials, 305–307
    lies in advertising, 26–27
    lifestyle lifestyle, the, 31–32
    nature visuals, 57–61
    opera, 35–37
    pride of place, 46–49
    simplicity, 43–46
    sneakers, 54–57
    subliminal messages, 61–64
    Swatch watches, 24
    technological advances, 329–332
    titles, 40–43
    transcendental qualities, 52–54
    two-piece ads, 49–51
Subaru, 274, 326
Subliminal messages, 61–64, 105, 133
Subliminal Seduction (Key), 61
Subtlety of the sell, 297
Subverting, 316–319
Sugar substitutes, 218–219
Super Bowl, 156, 158
Superliminal ads, 62–64, 105–106
Swatch, 24, 59, 60, 332
Swedish Bikini Team, 173, 213, 225
Sweet, Melinda, 161
Sweet'n Low, 219
Swift sausages, 169–170
Swimsuits, 184–186
Symbol shock, 219–221, 222
Symbol signs, 21–22
Synchronal, 306–307
Systemic lies, 102

Taboo imagery, 196–198
Taco Bell, 273–274, 338

Tampax, 183, 196, 203–205
Tandem ads, 49–51
Taylor, Jordan, 38
Technological advances, 2–3, 329–332
Telecommunications Research and Action Center, 98
Telephone industry, 85–87, 96–99, 138, 324–325
Television. *See* Commercials, television
Television Bureau of Advertising, 50
Tension built into ads, 245
Terrorism, avoiding associations with, 75–76
Texaco, 120, 121, 157
Textured backdrops, 32–34
Thailand, 123
Third World, 120, 122–126, 138
30s and 50s nostalgia, 81, 83
13th-Gen (Howe & Strauss), 273
Thirtysomething, 311–312
This Week With David Brinkley, 308
Thomas, Clarence, 213–215
Tie-ins, 1–2, 13
  Coke/*Roxanne*, 279–281
  disasters, natural, 299–302
  Madonna/Pepsi, 294–298
  Olympic games, 91–93
  product disasters, 338–339
  rock and roll/corporate sponsorship, 281–289
Time, 140–142
Titles in ads, 40–43
Tobacco Education Campaign, 150
Today Show, 155, 167–168
Top Gun, 279
Toscani, Oliviero, 255, 270
Tott's champagne, 36–37
Touchy-feely ads, 72–73
Toyota, 178, 264–265
TransAfrica, 237
Transcendental qualities, 52–54
Transportation, U.S. Dept. of, 21
Trojan, 259–260
Trump, Ivana, 226
Tubehead, 152
Tungsram, 146, 147
Turkey, 294
Turner, Tina, 284
Turner Broadcasting, 174
Tuscany (perfume), 36
TVTV ads, 319–325
TWA, 158
Two-piece ads, 49–51

Tye, Joe, 105
Tylenol, 76
Typeface, Helvetica, 17–22

Ueberroth, Peter, 266
Uniforms portrayed positively, 128–129
Unilever, 120–121
Unimark International (design firm), 20
Union Carbide, 159
United Negro College Fund, 271
United Technologies, 135
US magazine, 246

Value and lifestyle research (VALS), 53
Vanity Fair, 229
Varieties of Religious Experience, The (James), 14
VCR Voice, 330–331
Vetere, Barry, 325
VH-1, 31–32
Videos, music, 41, 280, 288
Viewers as products, 3
Vignelli, Massimo, 20–21
Village Voice, 4, 17, 122, 262–263
  advertising for the, 5
  infant formula, 122
  Japan bashing, 262–263
  logos, 17
  mass words, 327
  modernizing the, 314–315, 316
  reader complaints, 290
Viney, Robert, 160, 161
Visa, 48
Voiceovers, 186–187
Volkswagen, 233, 333–334
Volvo, 36, 99–102, 265
V-22 Osprey, 133

Wagenhauser, David, 98
Wall Street Journal, 315
War ads, 67, 155–158, 161–165
Warding off sponsored images, 7–11
Warner Bros., 1–2, 298
Waste Watch Center, 305
Watches, 24, 59, 60
Wayne, Karen, 292–293
Weapons systems, 88–89, 133–136, 148, 156–157, 316
Weaver, Sigourney, 223–224
Weller, Jim, 335, 336
Wendy's, 139
Wenner, Jann, 283
Whistle blowers, 166–167

White seamless backdrop, 35
Wieden & Kennedy (ad agency), 274
Wild boys, 191–193
Wildmon, Don, 131
Will, George, 308
Winky Dink and You, 49
Woman's Day, 200
Women and advertising, 12, 80, 85
    abortion, 219–223
    American Express, 142
    apparel industry, 211–212
    bubble tape and girls, 256
    celebrity ads, 216–219
    cleanliness, 189–191, 195
    cologne, men's, 209–211
    cosmetic ads, 206–209
    crotch area and swimsuits, 184–186
    demagoguery, 212–216
    empowerment ads, 223–228
    environmental pitches, 203–206
    gals theme, 193–196
    jewelry, 236–237

    Lee jeans, 245
    pants for men, 200–203
    penis, alluding to the, 228–230
    perfume, 187–189
    sanitary products, 183
    taboo imagery, 196–198
    voiceovers, 186–187
    wild boys, 191–193
Women of the War (Moore), 198–200
Women Voiceover Committee of the
    Screen Actor's Guild, 186
Wooden, Ruth, 266
Woolard, Edgar, 154
Words, mass, 325–328
World Health Organization (WHO),
    123, 124
Worldview conveyed through ads, 8
Wrigley, 256

Young, Neil, 294

Zast, Victor, 138–139
Zeifman, Les, 283, 285, 286